THE MAN WHO SHOT THE MAN
WHO SHOT LINCOLN

THE MAN WHO SHOT THE MAN WHO SHOT LINCOLN

and 44 other forgotton figures in history

GRAEME DONALD

OSPREY
PUBLISHING

First published in Great Britain in 2010 by Osprey Publishing,
Midland House, West Way, Botley, Oxford OX2 0PH, United Kingdom.
44-02 23rd St, Suite 219, Long Island City, NY 11101, USA.

Email: info@ospreypublishing.com

A CIP catalog record for this book is available from the British Library.

ISBN: 978 1 84908 170 2
Page layout by Myriam Bell Design, France
Typeset in Adroit Light
Printed in China through Worldprint Ltd

10 11 12 13 14   10 9 8 7 6 5 4 3 2 1

Front Cover: NARA and Library of Congress

For a catalog of all books published by Osprey please contact:

NORTH AMERICA
Osprey Direct c/o Random House Distribution Center
400 Hahn Road, Westminster, MD 21157, USA

E-mail: uscustomerservice@ospreypublishing.com

ALL OTHER REGIONS
Osprey Direct, The Book Service Ltd, Distribution Centre, Colchester Road,
Frating Green, Colchester, Essex, CO7 7DW

E-mail: customerservice@ospreypublishing.com

www.ospreypublishing.com

Osprey Publishing is supporting the Woodland Trust, the UK's leading
woodland conservation charity, by funding the dedication of trees.

CONTENTS

INTRODUCTION

One of the joys of military history, or indeed history in general, is the fact that it literally teems with little-known or unsung characters whose input, although minor and sometimes quite accidental, has far-ranging and pronounced effects on the major events they stumble into. One such character was Wilmer McLean, a chap who had made a comfortable fortune out of the wholesale grocery game and retired to a small estate just outside Manassas Junction. This retirement idyll turned out to be slap-bang in the middle of the site of the first battle of the American Civil War. In fact, the first artillery shot fired by the Union forces came straight down his chimney prompting McLean to move to what he thought might be a quieter life in Appomattox where, of course, the war caught up with him again. His house was commandeered for the surrender signing and, afterwards, it was torn apart by souvenir hunters from both sides.

All major events have their forgotten heroes; take the Nuremberg Trials for example; everyone knows the identities of the high-profile defendants, but who were the Allied judges who refused to sit because there were at the time no laws against genocide so, no matter how horrendous the actions of Germany, no-one could be tried for them. We all know the leading Nazis were found guilty and hanged, but who pulled the lever? That was American Master-Sergeant John C. Woods who, according to some, deliberately bungled the job to deny his charges a quick death. One of the UK's last executioners, Syd Dernley, retired in 1954, is in no doubt that this is the truth of the matter. He concluded that the drop was too short and the trapdoor so small that some had their noses torn off before being left strangling for up to quarter of an hour. Not given to mincing his words when interviewed in 1994, his summing up on Woods' performance was: "He were a bloody twat, that hang-man," a poor epitaph for the man who, setting up an electric chair to dispatch Japanese war criminals on Eniwetok, in the Marshall Islands, was hoist by his own petard through tinkering with the device, unaware it was linked up and live.

And then there are characters such as Otto Skorzeny (1908–1975) who, although hardly low profile, is interesting for his cropping up everywhere. A true adventurer of the old school, Skorzeny was everybody's idea of a German officer, right down to the dueling scar across the side of his face. A commando-supreme, this was the chap who rescued Mussolini in 1943 from his gilded cage in the Campo Imperatore Hotel atop the Gran Sasso mountain. A James Bond-type location, accessible only by cable car, Otto got in and out without firing a shot and whisked Mussolini back to Rome. It was also Skorzeny and his men who, dressed up as American soldiers, were to be found running round sniggering as they changed all the road signs and misdirected complete brigades of American troops before the Battle of the Bulge. Unable to settle to a normal life after the war, he took himself off to the Middle East where he planned the initial strikes by Arab forces into the Gaza Strip in 1953–1954 and trained Palestinian fighters, including Yasser

Arafat. They do not, perhaps mercifully, make them like that anymore.

Others have their exploits "buried" by history simply because of their name. Who today is aware of the activities of Albert Göring and Heinz Heydrich, brothers of the repugnant Herman and Rienhard? Both put their lives on the line for years to help Jews escape the clutches of their siblings, but neither received proper recognition after the war for no other reason than their family names. Readers will also encounter "Madam Kitty" who allowed her top-class Gestapo-bugged brothel in Berlin to be rigged with secondary bugs, installed by MI5 agents, who thus got the low-down on Germany's Operation *Felix* in time to prevent the invasion of Gibraltar. Hitler may not leap to mind as a major innovator in the leisure industry but it was none other than he who invented the pleasure-cruise industry, the concept of the package holiday, and the holiday camp.

While it was tremendous fun researching this book it was in equal parts extremely frustrating; the main problem with hidden players is the fact that they are hidden. Sometimes an unknown name would crop up in a side reference but, after hours of digging, it transpired that there was nothing to say about the character who had no more than a walk-on part in events. Other times, a little preliminary digging opens up a door to a secret garden of intrigue and machinations behind the scenes of well-known events which are not as they first appear. If any reader knows of such hidden hands on the tiller of history then do please contact me through the publisher, all information will be gratefully received.

Graeme Donald, March 2010

KILLER BE KILLED

THE BLIND ASSASSIN

Her real surname a matter of conjecture, but probably Roytblat, the woman who called herself Fanny Kaplan (1890–1918) may have failed to assassinate Lenin but her actions set in train a series of developments that would claim the lives of thousands.

A political activist from an early age, Kaplan first came to prominence in 1906 as a result of her equally abortive attempt to blow up the Tsarist governor of Kiev. A nervous teenager on her first big job and determined to get everything right, she decided to test the circuitry and timer on her home-made bomb one last time before setting off to the official's home. She only just survived the ensuing blast and was still unconscious and smoldering when dug out of the rubble and arrested. Sentenced to life in the Siberian labor camps, she was released by the Revolution of 1917. By this time she was almost totally blind: whether through something that happened to her in the camps or from her own bomb is uncertain but, either way, it does make her an unusual choice of assassin to be assigned a mission to shoot such an important target as Lenin – in the dark!

By the spring of 1918 she was in Moscow and attached to a Japanese-funded anti-Bolshevik terror group, remotely controlled by Grigory Semyonov (1890–1946), who was sworn to kill both Lenin and Trotsky; Kaplan's job was to keep tabs on the latter and update the intelligence files. Semynov had already organized two attempts on Lenin's life but both times his best assassins, Usov and Kozlov, of whom little else is known, failed to get their man. On the night of August 30, 1918 Lenin was attending a meeting at Moscow's

Morozov factory and, when this finally broke up just after 10pm, he was making his way back to his car when a woman standing some way off, supposedly Kaplan, pulled out a pistol and fired three shots. The first hit him in the arm, the second hit him in the jaw and lodged in his neck, and the third hit a female well-wisher who was thanking him for attending the meeting. Still mobile, if a trifle dazed, Lenin was bundled into his car by his driver, a chap called Gil, who whisked him back to the Kremlin as Lenin reckoned, quite rightly, that it was too dangerous to hang around any damned hospital; the doctors would have to come to him. The attending doctors told him two things: first that the bullets had been coated in curare, so he was lucky to have survived the hit in the arm alone, and second that there was no way they could extract the bullet from his neck unless he went to hospital so, unless he relented, it would have to stay in him with all the risks that that would entail. Lenin was not willing to leave the safety of the Kremlin, so that was that.

Reports of what happened at the scene of the shooting are confused and contradictory to say the least. At the time, Gil said he did not have a clue as to the identity of the shooter, other than the fact that he was sure it was a woman. Only after he had been grilled for a while did he "remember" it had been Kaplan, who, according to the initial reports, was arrested red-handed at the scene. Later this was amended to her having been arrested a couple of hours later, with the arresting officers unusually vague as to exactly where this had taken place. A week later, and after Kaplan was safely dead, it was admitted that she had been apprehended in a street in Serpukhov, an old town some 60 miles to the south of Moscow. Others at the scene did claim to have seen a woman matching Kaplan's description, hanging around the factory between 8pm and 9pm, and all these witnesses were united in their statements that she had been carrying the umbrella and small suitcase she had with her at the time of her arrest – hardly the sort of things an assassin is likely to hinder themselves with when out on a job. Add to this the facts that Kaplan had never handled a gun and probably could not even hit the proverbial barn door in well-lit and ideal conditions; she did not have with her the glasses that afforded her periodic bouts of limited sight when not completely blind; and, if it was indeed she who had so accurately hit Lenin in the dark at 10pm, how on earth did she manage to be in Serpukhov at some time around midnight? It just doesn't add up.

Her one statement made it sound as if she was as anxious to take the fall as the authorities were for her to do so: "My name is Fanya Kaplan. Today I shot at Lenin. I did it on my own. I will not say from whom I obtained the revolver. I will give no details. I resolved to kill Lenin long ago. I consider him a traitor to the Revolution." After such a verbose admission, she was shot on September 3, 1918 and buried in an unmarked grave in a Soviet people's communal cemetery. Lenin tried to conceal his concerns over the glaring holes in the case against Kaplan and the speed with which she had been put beyond reach of further interrogation. The man who organized her firing squad was Yakov Sverdlov (1885–1919), who would later arrange, on Lenin's orders, the execution of the Russian royals at Yekaterinburg. Indeed, that city itself had to suffer the ignominy of being renamed Sverdlovsk in his honor in 1924, this shadow not lifted until 1991 when Boris Yeltsin reverted to pre-Revolutionary place names.

Shelving his suspicions over the conviction of Kaplan, Lenin agreed that the assassination attempt, whoever was behind it, was the last straw and ordered the hunting down and killing of anyone who so much as whispered dissent against the Bolsheviks. So began the Red Terror that ran from Kaplan's execution to the end of October. Under Sverdlov's brutal efficiency, thousands met with assorted gruesome ends, including more than 3,000 priests who were variously crucified, burned alive, buried alive, or shoved through holes in the ice. Leaving Sverdlov to do what he did best, Lenin was focused on the most far-reaching fallout of Kaplan's alleged attempt on his life; he had become obsessed with the fact that the bullets fired at him were coated in curare. He read all he could on the nature and characteristics of that fascinating toxin, which, best known for its use in the South American rainforest as the business part of poisoned arrows, is harmful only when injected; like snake venom, curare can be consumed without any ill effects. From his study of curare, Lenin's interest in poisons grew into a broader scheme. He saw poison as a psychologically intimidating way of bumping off his enemies while sending a very loud and clear message to others that none was safe from his silent and deadly reach. By 1921 he had instituted Laboratory Number One, just round the corner from the dreaded Lubyanka, and here it was that the Cheka (the KGB-to-be) started developing their deeply unpleasant and fearsomely effective range of poisons. These could be slipped into food, squirted onto the skin by a passing assassin in a crowd, or, later, fired out of an umbrella gun into Georgi Markov's leg on a London street in 1978. As had proven to be the case in Lenin's and his supposed assassin's brushes with death, guns and bombs were not that reliable, whereas a well-prepared toxin, delivered up close and personal, would never fail and would always bring about a death to make all shudder and remember.

Kaplan's legacy grew to a laboratory of considerable size under the unsavory hand of Dr Grigory Mairanovsky, the first man to carry the epithet of Doctor Death, a nickname bestowed by none other than Stalin himself. Reporting directly to Lavrentiy Beria, Stalin's right-hand man, Mairanovsky produced some highly unpleasant toxins based on curare, thallium, and ricin — all designed to cause agonizing deaths, and others, more clandestine, which were supposed to produce symptoms to suggest heart failure in victims for whom the Kremlin wished to remain blameless. Between 1930 and 1945, these were all routinely tested on prisoners in the Lubyanka but, while the Russians sat in judgment at Nuremberg, such experiments were suspended in case anything leaked out and they were deemed unfit to sit in judgment on the Nazis for similar crimes, albeit on a larger scale. Stalin died in 1953 of a sudden and massive brain hemorrhage after a drinking party, attended by Beria, who was widely suspected of using something from "Kaplan's Lab" to induce the said condition. Either way, Beria immediately made a play for power but ended up with a bullet in his head. Accused of the somewhat euphemistic crime of storing dangerous chemicals in unsafe conditions, Mairanovsky knew enough to keep schtum at his own trial and accept with good grace his ten years in the Vladimir Prison. Upon his early release in 1961 he tried to weasel his way into the new administration under Khrushchev, to whom he wrote a personal letter asking for a suitable position. Perhaps Mairanovsky's spell in the prison had weakened his mind to the point where he had forgotten the nature of the beast with which he dealt but, to plead his case, he reminded Khrushchev of previous "off-the-record" favors he and his preparations had rendered and, two days after his letter had arrived in Moscow, Mairanovsky was found dead of "heart failure."

Lenin decided to have that bullet removed by some German specialists in April 1922, the operation instigating a series of strokes that finally carried him off in January 1924, so perhaps you could say that his assassin, whoever it was, got him in the end. As for Sverdlov's death – it remains something of a mystery as it is still held a state secret by the Kremlin. He is known to have improved the collective gene pool on March 16, 1919 when, according to the official version, he became one of the countless victims of the so-called Spanish flu pandemic that ravaged the globe after World War I. Unofficially, he was himself at the same Morozov factory on the night of March 16 for another rah-rah session with the workers and, at a particularly heated juncture in the debate, one attendee indicated her disagreement with his statements by whacking him over the head with a wrench, killing him on the spot. Kaplan, no doubt, was laughing in her Communist plot.

—⁓—

HIT LE FÜHRER!

The prominence given to Claus von Stauffenberg's abortive attempt to blow Hitler from this mortal coil has left most with the impression that this was perhaps the only concerted attempt on Hitler's life. However many had tried before Operation *Valkyrie*, as it was known, and von Stauffenberg was not the last. Hitler was not a popular chap, even at home – but some, like Colonel Heinz Brandt, would inadvertently save the little man from bomb-plotters, not once but twice.

First was Johann Georg Elser (1903–1945), a carpenter from Hermaringen, in southwest Germany who, although he had flirted with the Communist party, purported to be anti-Nazi on moral grounds. Some time in July 1939 he told friends and family he was going to spend a bit of time in a religious retreat in Switzerland. Instead he boarded a train for Munich, where he intended to blow up Hitler as he made his annual commemorative speech in the Burgerbrau Beer Cellar, scene of the abortive Beer Hall Putsch of November 8, 1923. Making maximum use of his skills as a carpenter, Elser became a regular at the Burgerbrau so he could hide in a cupboard at closing time and then emerge to work through the night, cutting out and shoring up an access through the crawl space in the floor to a point below the pillar behind the speaker's rostrum where his device would be placed. The war he so dreaded began on September 1, and by this time Elser had completed his task of hollowing out the core of that pillar to take his bomb to Hitler's head height.

There is some debate as to the time at which the detonator was set and the exact time that Hitler quit the scene. According to Elser it was set for 9.20pm, at which time Hitler would normally be well into some frothy-mouthed finale to his annual rant but, for reasons variously asserted, on that particular night Hitler cut short his oration and was off the stage at least ten minutes before the explosion. Instead of staying to enjoy the party as usual, he was rushed through the adoring crowd by a chevron of uniformed thugs and out of the building. The established schedule allowed for a much longer speech, and a suitable interval for the obligatory *sieging* and *heiling* before Hitler descended the podium to chat and shake hands with "old comrades" from the 1923

Johann Georg Elser, appearing suspiciously calm, relaxed, unchained, and unbloodied, during his interrogation by the Gestapo after his "Beer Hall Blitz." (Topfoto)

Putsch. The official explanation for the hurriedly truncated event was that fog had grounded all the Berlin flights and that Hitler, with urgent matters to attend, was rushing to catch the last train home. With Hitler more usually having his trains, planes, and automobiles dance attendance until he was good and ready to depart, this explanation raised quite a few eyebrows. There was an equally suspicious reception for the subsequent revelation that Elser had been arrested at the Swiss border, about half an hour before the bomb went off – killing eight and wounding dozens of others, including Eva Braun's father – and that he was already on his way to Gestapo HQ for interrogation hours before news of the incident was made public. William L. Shirer (1904–1993), author of *The Rise and Fall of the Third*

Reich (1960), was still reporting from Berlin at that time and his diary entry for November 9, 1939 reads:

> Twelve minutes after Hitler and all the big party leaders left the Bürgerbräu Keller in Munich last night, at nine minutes after nine o'clock, a bomb explosion wrecked the hall, killed seven, wounded sixty-three. The bomb had been placed in a pillar directly behind the rostrum from which Hitler had been speaking. Had he remained twelve minutes and one second longer he surely would have been killed. The spot on which he stood was covered with six feet of debris.
>
> No one yet knows who did it. The Nazi press screams that it was the English, the British secret service! It even blames Chamberlain for the deed. Most of us think it smells of another Reichstag Fire. In other years Hitler and all the other bigwigs have remained after the speech to talk over old times with the comrades of the Putsch and guzzle beer. Last night they fairly scampered out of the building leaving the rank and file of the comrades to guzzle among themselves.
>
> The attempted "assassination" undoubtedly will buck up public opinion behind Hitler and stir up hatred of England. Curious that the official Nazi newspaper, the *Völkische Beobachter*, was the only morning paper today to carry the story. A friend called me with the news just as I had finished broadcasting at midnight last night, but all the German radio officials and the censors denied it. They said it was a silly rumor.

By November 10, the ever-willing Sturmbannführer Alfred Naujocks (1911–1966) was on his way into then-unoccupied Holland to kidnap a couple of British agents known to be operating near the border. In what became known as the Venlo Incident, Naujocks dragged Captain

Sigismund Payne Best and Major Richard Stevens back into Germany where, accused of being Elser's controllers, they were soon following him to Sachsenhausen concentration camp and thence to Dachau. Shirer was not alone in thinking the whole incident a put-up job with Elser, wittingly or unwittingly, being nothing more than a Nazi stooge whose strings were pulled by Himmler, who in turn was operating with or without Hitler's knowledge and permission. Planned or not, the Burgerbrau bomb and the positioning of the blame on the myrmidons of Westminster united the German people in an open hatred of the British for trying to bump off their beloved Führer, with the added bonus of the Dutch being pilloried as playing willing hosts to anti-German activists and thus deserving of the invasion so soon to come their way. Most curious of all is the fact that Elser, Payne Best, and Stevens were kept alive in the camps instead of swinging from butchers' hooks as was the traditional fate of those who incurred the Führer's wrath. Elser especially, instead of being made to suffer for his actions, seems to have enjoyed special privileges in the camps. He was allowed civilian clothing, spacious quarters, good food, as many cigarettes and bottles of booze as he wanted, along with access to other "pleasures of the flesh." He was also allowed to have a workbench and his carpentry tools to keep him amused.

Stevens is hard to track through the chaos of the close of the war but Payne Best (1885–1978) most certainly survived to write *The Venlo Incident* (1950). This gives an account of Elser's closeted captivity, which endured until April 9, 1945 when, allegedly, he was taken out and shot on Himmler's orders. While it is true that many "loose ends" were indeed "tidied up" by Himmler in the closing weeks of the war, not everyone is so accepting of Elser dying in a such manner.

This is not the place to explore that labyrinth of conspiracy theories so those wishing to do so should conduct an internet search of "Georg Elser – allegedly executed at Dachau during a bombing raid," which will cut through to a fully detailed article within the Dachau Scrap Book archives. This includes recollections from Payne Best and others, such as the Reverend Martin Niemoller, who were convinced that Elser was at best a Nazi stooge or at worst a willing player in a farce.

Most of the 20 or so other attempts to kill Hitler came from his own generals, who seem to have been so keen to be rid of him that it is a wonder he got as far as he did. Various plans were hatched and thwarted by fate but by 1943 the Black Orchestra, as the high-ranking conspirators were known, were heartily sick of their blundering and increasingly erratic leader. When Field Marshal von Kluge learned that Hitler was to visit him at Smolensk on the Eastern Front on March 13, 1943, he and Major-General Henning von Tresckow (1901–1944) resolved that the Führer would never make it back to Berlin. Abandoning any plans of aerating Hitler themselves in the middle of the soup course, they sat smiling through the dinner before wishing all bon voyage, especially to Colonel Heinz Brandt to whom they had given a gift-wrapped bomb, telling him it was a couple of bottles of Cointreau for Major-General Helmuth Stieff in Berlin. Eager-to-please Brandt took the package and, thinking the recipient might want to sample it nicely chilled upon delivery, he decided at the last minute not to carry it with him in the cabin but to stow it in the cargo hold, where not only did the liquor chill nicely but the acid in the timer froze, preventing detonation. When news was received in Smolensk of Hitler's safe arrival in Berlin, Tresckow had to fly in hot pursuit of his package to swap it just in time before it was opened by Stieff.

It was Brandt again who would thwart von Stauffenberg's more celebrated attempt of July 20, 1944, for it was he who, stubbing his foot on the briefcase-bomb, shoved it behind the heavy leg that shielded Hitler when it went off. Peppered with splinters, the Führer's trousers and tunic were apparently blown off to leave him standing startled with smoke coming from his hair and underpants; Brandt was less fortunate, he lost both legs and died a few days later.

It must be said that Tom Cruise's portrayal of von Stauffenberg in *Valkyrie* (2008) only served to reinforce the widely accepted myth that the members of the Black Orchestra represented "The Nazi-but-nice Germany," good men and true, all opposed to the brutal excesses of Hitler and his rabble of psychos. Cruise's von Stauffenberg indulges in much wailing and gnashing of teeth over the fate of the Jews and the wholesale slaughter of the war in general. But in reality the man couldn't have given two "stauffs" for the Jews or the Great Unwashed dying in their millions; after the invasion of Poland he wrote to his wife saying that the Poles were a "rabble of Jews and mongrels" who were best suited to "a life under the knout." He also mused that rounding them up as slave labor would do wonders for the German economy. As a high-handed German aristocrat, von Stauffenberg's main objection to Hitler was that he was a common little man who had made a pig's ear of the war. The appalling death toll of the conflict was simply a matter of figures on sheets of attrition to the members of the Orchestra, a few of whom were themselves enthusiastic war criminals, so any misguided notion of their wishing to rid the world of the evil personified by Hitler is best left on the silver screen. If that was their motive, pure and true, then any one of them could have shot him in the head on any one of a hundred occasions but, as much as they wanted Hitler dead, they wanted themselves alive to take over afterwards. As early as 1943, the Orchestra was in talks with America through the brave offices of another unheard-of hero, Hans Bernd Gisevius (1904–1974), the only main player of the July Plot to survive.

After the Stalingrad debacle of late 1942, the Orchestra was left in no doubt how their war would end so they set up lines of communication to America via the Vatican. Once in direct contact, their main conduit was diplomat/Intelligence Officer Gisevius, who Admiral Canaris, "first violin" of the Orchestra, had managed to set up as vice-consul in Bern, which just happened to be the location of Allen Dulles (1893–1969), leading light of the fledgling OSS, destined to be reborn in 1947 as the CIA. Dulles made it clear that no one was going to sit down and negotiate with Hitler and that as long as he, or anyone like him, was in the driving seat then the war would roll on until Germany was bombed into the Stone Age and brought to unconditional surrender. It was only Dulles' firm stand on that matter that prompted the Orchestra to plan the deaths of Hitler, Himmer, Göring, and a few others; had Dulles expressed an American willingness to sit down with Hitler to talk of peace with honor for Germany then the Orchestra would have thrown such a wall of steel round the horrible little man that no one sharing their previous intentions would have had a cat's chance in hell of harming a hair on his head. Dulles was essentially painting a target on Hitler's head and pulling the Orchestra's strings until they had no choice but to proceed. Dulles and Gisevius were careful to keep face-to-face meetings to a bare minimum, as Bern was crawling with German spies, so the selected intermediary was the "vivacious," shall we say, Mary Bancroft (1903–1997), a bored intellectual who seems to have got her kicks dabbling in espionage. By all accounts much devoted to the pleasures of the bedroom, Bancroft was already sleeping with Dulles when he sent her to monitor Gisevius as a go-between, and she was soon bed-hopping between the two men with letters and updates from Germany.

After the war, Gisevius was a star witness for the prosecution at Nuremberg, particularly at the trial of Göring, before publishing *To the Bitter End* (1946), translation into English by Bancroft, through which he caused uproar at home by branding the Germans at large liars for claiming to have been ignorant of the atrocities committed in their name. Mary continued to attract men in their droves, including Carl Gustav Jung and film director Woody Allen, which must have made for some pretty depressing pillow talk, and Dulles remained head of the CIA until JFK became disenchanted with the CIA in general – and Dulles in particular – after the embarrassment of the Bay of Pigs fiasco in April 1961. Forcing Dulles to resign the following September from the organization he had himself built up, JFK said that he wanted to "splinter the CIA into a thousand pieces and scatter it to the wind." Both Dulles and Mary were firm friends with several members of the rich and politically active Paine family; since the late 1920s Mary in particular had been close friends with Ruth Forbes Paine-Young whose son, Michael, and his wife, Ruth Hyde Paine were in 1963 playing benefactors to a young and troubled couple called Marina and Lee Harvey Oswald who they even had living at their home. It was Ruth who, with help from her contacts, got Lee Harvey Oswald a nice steady job in a book depository in downtown Dallas. Surely no significance there?

THE MAN WHO OFFED THE ROMANOVS

On July 15, 1891, the 13-year-old Yakov Yurovsky joined the crowds in his home town of Tomsk to cheer the young tsarevich, who would become Nicholas II of Russia, as he paraded through the streets in a colored troika. Yurovsky recalled: "I remember how handsome the heir was, with his neat brown beard; as he drew level he nodded and waved back at me." Twenty-seven years later, Yurovsky would lead the squad that assassinated Nicholas and his entire family.

One of ten children, Yakov was deeply resentful when his father removed him from school and apprenticed him off to a local watchmaker to learn a trade and generate some income. This resentment was still very much there in 1897 when, at the age of 19, he led the first workers' strike that Tomsk had ever seen. After the strike was crushed, and the young Yakov marked by Imperialist agents as a dangerous agitator, he found all doors shut to him in Tomsk and, with no chance of returning to his own job, he set out across Siberia, finally deciding where to settle by the age-old method of sticking a pin in a map with his eyes shut; when he opened them, the pin was sticking in Yekaterinburg. With fate having so decided that he should be in the right place when the right time came, Yurovsky traveled to that city, married and settled down to an unsettled existence of Bolshevik agitation, which, come the Revolution, rewarded him with the position of local commissar. He was the obvious choice to take control of "The House of Special Purpose," as the Communists called it, when the deposed Romanovs were held captive there. He had just turned 40 and was by then a hardened anti-Tsarist who had already done his share of killing.

Before the Bolsheviks got their hands on either the reins of power or the Romanovs, the short-lived Provisional Government under Alexander Kerensky (1881–1970) asked both France and Britain to take the deposed Tsar and his family, as he knew it would not be long before the Bolsheviks took over. With World

Yakov Yurovsky, the man who offed the Romanovs , shown here relaxing with a cup of tea. (The Print Collector / Topfoto)

War I still in full swing and Tsarina Alexandra a known German sympathizer, France gave a flat "*Non*" but the British Administration under David Lloyd George, quite open to the idea, gave a provisional yes; after all, the tsar was cousin to George V and his wife a granddaughter of Queen Victoria, so why not? George V had other ideas; for reasons never fully explained he told Lloyd George that his relatives were not to be allowed into the country on any account and when news of their fate reached the UK, George didn't think this reason enough to ruin his day watching the cricket at Lords: every family has its issues, it would seem. As the writing on the wall grew larger, Kerensky fled to Paris, leaving Russia and its royals to the decidedly untender mercies of the Bolsheviks. On April 22, 1918 the Romanovs found themselves in the custody of a brutish Secret Policeman called Vassili Yakolev who was detailed to collect the family from their rural hiding place and return them to Moscow, but White Russian Army activity along the necessary route forced a change of plan. Studying the maps, Yakolev decided it best to make for Yekaterinburg and the Ipatiev House under the commissariat of the equally neanderthal Alexander Avadeyev. Yakolev and the Romanovs arrived there on April 30, he relinquishing responsibility to Avadeyev, who made his charges' lives a misery. When he wasn't stealing their personal possessions he was charging the locals an admission fee to watch them eat a meal, usually hamming it up by dancing drunk round the table and stealing food from their plates to his audience's roars of approval.

There were several reasons why Avadeyev was replaced by Yurovsky; not only was he a drunkard upon whom no reliance could be placed, but his men were all Russian and Lenin had his doubts about their willingness to follow orders when "the time" came; it was still early days and would Russians be ready for such a step or would they turn away? Not only was Yurovsky a 24-carat Bolshevik but he was already nearby with a detachment of Hungarian mercenaries who, Lenin thought, would have no compunction about gunning down the royal family. Also on the plus side was the fact that if the executions caused a massive backlash then the whole affair could be put down to the rogue actions of a bunch of foreigners over whom the Kremlin exercised no control. As for what actually happened that night, who better than the killer himself to give an account; the following is a summary of the report that Yurovsky supposedly submitted to the Kremlin after all was done and dusted, but it does contain one puzzling anachronism, which, if written by him, would indicate forgery but which could equally be a later amendment by others wishing to keep details clear. In the opening sentence he makes reference to Sverdlovsk, this being a name change imposed on Yekaterinburg in 1924 to honor Bolshevik leader Yakov Sverdlov (1885–1919), who passed on Lenin's instructions to Yurovsky to slaughter the prisoners. But, as stated, this *could* be a simple modernization of the text to avoid confusing later readers.

On the morning of the 16th I sent the kitchen-boy, Sednev, away on the pretext that he was to meet his uncle in Sverdlovsk. [The uncle was in fact dead but Yurovsky didn't know this at the time.] Next I prepared twelve revolvers and drew up a list of who was to shoot who and made sure that Comrade Filipp Goloshchyokin had completed his arrangements for a truck to arrive at midnight to take away the bodies for disposal. At 11pm on the night of the 16th I assembled the chosen squad and told them we were under orders to kill the prisoners before sending word to the internal and external guards that they were not to be concerned if they heard shooting and that on no account should they leave their posts to investigate.

The truck arrived late, at about 1.30pm, after which I gave orders for the prisoners to be woken up and moved to the prepared basement room, they being told that nearby unrest made it unsafe for them to remain on the upper-floor. It was about forty minutes before all were dressed and assembled. Each man in the squad had his own designated target so it should have been a quick and easy matter but much went wrong. Alexandra complained there were no chairs so some were brought in for them to sit while the final arrangements were being made and, at this time, they showed no signs that they suspected anything. When I returned, Alexandra was in one chair, with Anna Demidova [lady-in-waiting] and the daughters standing to her left and Alexi was in the other chair with his father in front of him and Dr Botkin, the cook and the others behind. I quickly told Nicholas that the Soviet of Workers' Deputies had demanded their executions and then shot him outright after which the disorganized firing began. The room was smaller than anticipated for the purpose so some of the squad had not taken up designated positions opposite their allotted victim and fired instead erratically through the door from the corridor; someone shot me in the hand at which point, with difficulty, I managed to bring a halt to the shooting. Alexandra and Demidova were still alive but lying on the floor so they were shot through the heart to minimize blood-trace in the cellar. Alexei sat unscathed and terrified in his chair; I shot him. The daughters had been hit but remained unharmed and bayonets failed to do the job either. Finally we had to shoot them all in the head. Only when we got to the forest did I discover the reason it had been so hard to kill the girls...

This is the only point in his account where Yurovsky massages the details. In truth, the execution squad had been drinking for hours before they stumbled down to the basement and Yurovsky had not taken the room's brick walls into account so the wild firing went ricocheting all over the shop; it was a scene of chaotic mayhem with drunken soldiers, some crying, some laughing hysterically, shooting and stabbing away with bayonets and daggers before looting the bodies where they lay.

...After all were confirmed dead and looted items retrieved, everything from the cellar was placed in the care of Comrade Filipp while I oversaw the removal of the bodies to the truck and the cleaning of the execution chamber. It was about 3am on the morning of the 17th when we got moving with Comrade Pyotr Ermakov, the only one of us aware of the disposal site...

Ermakov (1884–1952), also roaring drunk that night, was the one who, after finishing off a couple of the Grand Duchesses, had driven his bayonet twice through the face of Anastasia before repeatedly stamping on her head to make a nonsense of the grasping frauds who would later prey on the Russian émigré communities claiming to be Anastasia, somehow miraculously alive.

...Well into the journey and by now quite tired, I asked Comrade Ermakov if we still had far to go and he told me it was beside the railway tracks, just through the village of Koptyaki. When we arrived at the disposal site the bodies were stripped to burn the clothes and it was at this point I discovered why Alexandra and the daughters had been so hard to kill. Beneath her dress, Alexandra was almost completely wound about with gold wire and the girls' bodices were so completely sewn with precious gems that they were effectively wearing body-armour. The jewels were collected, the clothes burnt and the naked corpses thrown into the mine-shaft.

From this point on the report deals with the problems of disposal after daylight, revealing that the water in the shaft barely covered the bodies, which had to be moved to other locations. Some were burned in conventional fires before being shoved into assorted impromptu graves or disused mines, while others were buried in pits filled with sulfuric acid. It makes for grim reading but those hungry for more detail will find the complete version of Yurovsky's report at www.alexanderpalace.org/palace/yurovmurder.html. This is the 3,000-odd word report he delivered by hand on the 19th to those who had issued the execution orders on Lenin's personal instructions but, as is so often the case with such dirty work, when poor old Yurovsky got to Moscow nobody wanted to know him; everybody wanted the trash taken out but no one wanted to touch the hand that did it. After several years in disgruntled isolation he was "re-acknowledged" and given a job in the Soviet State Treasury where he quickly established a reputation as a seeker-out of theft and corruption until his death in 1938.

—ᢒᢁᢒ—

FLYING INTO LEGEND

Until quite recently the disappearance of American band leader Glenn Miller (1904–missing 1944) had been a mystery, with the lack of facts allowing the lunatic fringe to construct all the usual sort of conspiracy theories – he died of injuries incurred while indulging in bizarre sexual activity in a Paris brothel and it had been hushed up; he had been sent on a sensitive diplomatic mission to Berlin and died there in an Allied bombing raid; or he was successful in that mission and escorted Hitler and Eva Braun to South America before going into hiding in Timbuktu or wherever, no doubt with Elvis Presley and JFK. Actually, the "he was killed by Allied bombs" lobby was spot on, except he was not bombed in Berlin but in mid-air by a flight of RAF Lancasters!

Having completed what would be his last ever recordings at the Abbey Road Studios, made so famous by the Beatles,

Miller drove to the Milton East airbase, near Northampton, to see if he could cadge a lift to Paris, where he intended to put on a Christmas concert for the Allied troops and broadcast it on his weekly show, *I Sustain the Wings*, a rather inappropriate title as things turned out. Having little luck at that airfield Miller drove down to Twinwood Farm RAF Station in Bedfordshire, where there was equally bad news, so he wandered into the officers' mess where, by pure happenstance, he fell into conversation with USAF Lieutenant-Colonel Norman Baessell, who offered him a seat on his own flight the next day. On the morning of December 15 the airfield was socked-in but Baessell assured Miller that the fog would clear in plenty of time for their 1pm take-off. Their pilot, Flight Officer John Morgan, landed to pick them up in a single-engine Noordwyn Norseman C-64 and all three took off, never to be seen again. There was speculation about engine failure forcing them to ditch in the Channel, or perhaps iced-up wings as the temperature was down to about 20°F, but no one knew for sure what had happened – until 1984 when a few hidden players started to remember certain things and put them all together.

As Captain Morgan took off, Miller's nemesis was on its way back from an aborted bombing mission over the railway yards at Siegen in Germany; a flight of 138 Lancasters returning to Methwold as their fighter cover had failed to rendezvous due to prevailing conditions. Aborted missions were not uncommon and in this case it was thought far too dangerous for the planes to land back home with a combined load of 100,000 incendiary bombs, so they were directed to follow the standard jettison procedure and head for Jettison Area South, a 10-mile square patch of the English Channel about 50 miles south of Beachy Head. At least three of the crew of Bomber NF937 would later confirm that as they shed their load from 4,000 feet they saw directly below them a Norseman flying at about 2,500 feet. Also witnessed by the pilot, the bomb-aimer, and the rear gunner, the navigator, Fred Shaw, would later state: "It was obvious to me that the plane below was in trouble, so I watched intently. Just before it disappeared out of sight under the leading edge of the wing I saw it flip over to port in what appeared to have been an incipient spin. Eventually I saw it disappear into the English Channel." As the mission had been aborted there was no debriefing so the incident with the Norseman never got reported by the crew of NF937, who most likely came to a tacit agreement to keep quiet and forget all about it. It should be remembered that this was no hit-and-run in peacetime; the Norseman should not have been on that flight path; the NF937 was following the right ditching procedure; and this was a time when death was all around, the crew of that plane having long come to terms with the fact that their "job" was to kill people with bombs.

Either way, the disappearance of Miller himself was kept under wraps for a short while and no one from the NF937 made the connection until Shaw saw a repeat on the television of the old movie *The Glenn Miller Story* (1954) and realized that the Norseman hit by the hail of bombs discarded from NF937 was most likely Miller's last flight. Shaw had kept all his logbooks from the war and, having checked his facts, ventured to broach the subject but as soon as he opened his mouth he was brought down in a hail of derision from all sides, the most vociferous comments coming from the Glenn Miller Appreciation Society, who would soon have to eat their words. Prior to their public humiliation, the most pointed questions leveled at Shaw by the Appreciation Society concerned an apparent one hour discrepancy between the logged time of the bomb jettison

World famous band leader Glenn Miller before he flew off into legend.
(Corbis)

and the time at which Miller would have been over the Channel; how on earth could Shaw recognize a Canadian Norseman when there were only five such obscure planes in the UK at the time, and all of those on American bases; would a pilot as experienced as Morgan stray into a bomb-dumping zone; and how does anyone know which route

Miller's Norseman took, since Morgan neglected to file a flight plan? Slightly shocked at the spite of the response to his public statement, Shaw tried to duck out of the limelight he had attracted but the subject would not go away.

Eventually, Roy Conyers Nesbit, an aviation historian and RAF Editor of the Public Record Office of the Air Historical Branch of the Ministry of Defence, took up cudgels on Shaw's behalf to announce that the main problem with Shaw's account – that one hour discrepancy – was attributable to the fact that the Americans logged in accordance to local time, which was about one hour ahead of the Greenwich Mean Time used by the RAF. According to Twinwood Farm Control Tower records, by then released into the public domain, Flight Officer Morgan landed at 1.30pm, apologizing for being late and blaming the weather. They took off again at 1.55pm after Morgan had been briefed to follow the Supreme Headquarters Allied Expeditionary Force (SHAEF) shuttle route to Paris, which is why there was no flight plan filed by Morgan; he did not need one. This route would take him south from the airfield and along the edge of the London no-fly zone, down to Beachy Head from where he would have to turn slightly southeast for Dieppe. From Twinwood, this was the only sensible route to take that avoided all the antiaircraft batteries on the lookout for VIs and with a reputation for shooting at anything they did not immediately recognize – and, as the Glenn Miller Appreciation Society so vehemently pointed out, few in the UK had ever seen a Norseman. It was also a route that would take the plane within 5 miles of the bomb-dumping zone.

Conversely, Shaw and his colleagues had taken off at 11.30am with instructions to bomb the marshaling yards at Seigen, about 40 miles to the northeast of Bonn, but 90 minutes into their flight they were ordered to abort as fighter cover could not be arranged given the prevailing conditions; they were further ordered that, on the return leg, they were to pay a visit to the Jettison Area South before attempting to land back at base. According to the logs of that flight from 149 Squadron, bomb dumping began at 1.43pm, which, given the different times on which the respective flights were operating, puts it spot on for them all being in the right place at the wrong time. Nesbit further revealed that Shaw had completed his flight training in Canada, where Norsemen were as common as muck and that the other four Norsemen in the UK at the time were all accounted for and nowhere near the Channel. On top of that Morgan, with some justification, distrusted the flight instruments of the day, and in the conditions that prevailed on December 15 preferred to rely on his compass, accepting the inaccuracy of such instruments, especially flying in reduced visibility and over water, which would eliminate any use of landmarks as fixed reference. Under such circumstances, Morgan would need to be a fraction of a degree out of kilter to end up flying straight through the middle of Jettison Area South. But why blame him? Perhaps the returning Lancasters were themselves slightly off with the bearings and started shedding their loads outside the designated area; who knows? Navigation was not then a precise art and all instruments were prone to malfunction.

Anyway, Nesbit's findings divided the Glenn Miller Appreciation Society into two rival camps, one humming loudly with hands over ears and the other, led by a chap called Alan Ross, who wanted to dig further. Ross placed a notice in *Air Mail*, the RAF Association journal, asking if there were any other surviving members of the crew of NF937 who would care to say their piece. Forward stepped

Vincent Gregory, captain of that plane, to confirm all that Shaw had said and explain his reluctance to speak up before. "When we got back from that raid, it was an aborted raid, so there was no debriefing. Don't think me unsympathetic or callous, but when I heard [through the in-board RT] of the plane going down I would have said that he shouldn't have been there – just forget about him. My concern was getting my own aeroplane and crew home safely. We were fighting a war and lost thousands of planes. We had some pretty grim raids to conduct after that and they didn't announce Miller's death until later, by which time it had gone completely from my mind." After E. A. Munday of the Ministry of Defence Historical Branch had gone over everything from top to bottom he wrote to Shaw in 1985 stating:

> Until your story appeared in the South African press in 1984, the RAF had always considered Miller's death as a strictly USAF matter, as the result of some sort of flying accident, probably as a result of poor weather conditions. We have received letters at various times asking about it, some of which put forward theories, some feasible and some not so feasible. Up until 1984, the only RAF connection was that Miller's plane had taken off from the RAF airfield at Twinwood Farm, Bedfordshire, in weather conditions that could be described as marginal, or at least marginal for that particular kind of aircraft. Your story, to a greater extent, changed this, and we carried out an investigation earlier this year into the aborted bomber operation of 15th December, 1944. Because the mission was aborted there was no raid report on Bomber Command records, as would have been customary, but we did find reference to the intended course and the use of Jettison Area South on the return.

Shaw did not long survive the vindication of his story, leaving his widow and daughter, Mrs Cheryl Fillmore of Southampton, to put all his logbooks and correspondence up for sale at Sotheby's on April 13, 1999, where the lot fetched just over £22,000. The next year, the logbook of the NF937's flight engineer, Derek Thurman, came to light. On the relevant day's page Thurman had written that when the bombs were dumped, "three crew members on board the plane spotted a light aircraft below which seemed to have been downed in the hail of bombs. The bomb-aimer saw it first from the nose and commented on it whereupon the navigator shot out of his seat to the side-blister to have a look. Hew saw the plane whip by and, seconds later, the rear-gunner called up to say, 'It's gone in; flipped over and gone in.'"

—⟨∞⟩—

KITCHENER'S SINK

Although some maintain Lord Kitchener (1850–1916) made a better poster than he did a general, it seems that even that is untrue. The famous pointing-finger poster began life as the cover design of *London Opinion*, September 5, 1914, and when it was trialed in poster form public opinion hailed it too "in your face" to be effective. As the initial rush of enthusiasm for the slaughter was forced into retreat by the steady advance of first-hand accounts of what the Great War was *really* like, conscription was tabled as early as September 1915, with the necessary legislation passed the following January; it was only after the war that the Kitchener poster attained its iconic status. Either way, the seeds of the assassination of Kitchener, aboard the HMS

Hampshire, just off the Orkneys, were sown 15 years before, far away in South Africa and largely by himself.

Kitchener's conduct of the Boer War still provokes animated debate, as he instituted what can only be called a scorched earth policy and tacit approval of the wholesale execution of prisoners. To deprive the Boer Commando squads of their support and provisions, Kitchener ordered the burning of all the homesteads in the Transvaal and Orange River territories, the slaughter of all livestock, and the internment of all women, children, and old men in concentration camps, where they died of starvation and disease in their tens of thousands. To discourage the repeated mining of the railways Kitchener ordered that a couple of cattle trucks, filled with Boers, should always be shunted ahead of the locomotive. So it is not hard to believe that he gave the nod to a take-no-prisoners policy, which was dragged into the public arena by the trial and execution of Harry "Breaker" Morant (1864–1902). His death is still a cause célèbre in Australia, where, when it comes to injustice, they have memories that would shame an elephant.

Morant was a lieutenant in the predominantly Australian Bushvelt Carbineers operating out of Fort Edward under the overall command of Colonel F. H. Hall. Morant's unit commander, Captain Frederick Percy Hunt, explained to Morant upon his joining the unit that one of Kitchener's aides, Lieutenant-Colonel Hamilton, had recently made it clear that the take no-prisoners policy should be followed in all but the most exceptional cases; Colonel Hall was obviously aware of the policy and routinely congratulated Hunt and his men on their actions. After Hunt was himself killed in captivity by Boers on August 5, 1901, Morant set out on a reprisal raid during which he presided over the killing of a dozen Boer prisoners and a German missionary called Hesse who was suspected of partisan activity. The timing could not have been worse; the German government demanded an investigation and the Boers, close to agreeing the terms for the Treaty of Vereeniging (signed May 1902), climbed on the bandwagon to make political capital, despite the fact that they themselves routinely shot prisoners in similar numbers to those executed by the British and their allies. Also, the dust had not yet settled from Kitchener having been attacked in the world press for the brutality of his concentration camps so, even on a personal level, he could ill afford the negative exposure.

Kitchener publicly denied having ever issued any such orders; Colonel Hall was whisked off to India before Morant's trial began; Hunt was dead; and Lieutenant-Colonel Hamilton clammed up tight. Morant never made any bones about his routinely shooting prisoners, claiming it was universally understood to be the express wishes of Lord Kitchener and widely practiced with the full knowledge of the Officer Corps. But the defense was not allowed to summon Kitchener, nor any of his aides, nor put before the court martial any of the documented proof of hundreds of other incidents of prisoners being shot out of hand, and of such executions being regarded as routine and acceptable by officers present at the time. Of the eight defendants, only lieutenants Morant and Peter Joseph Handcock (1868–1902) were found guilty and condemned to death with a third Australian, Lieutenant George Witton (1874–1942), being granted a last-minute reprieve by Kitchener and shipped to England to begin a term of life. All the others walked free, including the British Captain Alfred Taylor (1862–1941), for whom Colonel Hall had actually thrown a party to congratulate him on his "tally" of executed prisoners, which had been racked up before Morant even arrived at Fort Edward. Morant faced his firing squad with typical Australian verve, refusing a blindfold and his last words – "Shoot straight, yer bastards; don't make a mess of it!" – are still a rallying cry Down Under. The constant pressure from an enraged Australian press and public secured the release of Witton in August 1904 and, as World War I loomed inevitable, the Australian government first secured from the British the written promise that no Australian soldier would ever be subject to British military courts, no matter the charge, before Prime Minister Andrew Fisher made his famous declaration that Australia would stand beside the mother country "to the last man and to the last shilling."

Although Kitchener did all he could to distance himself from his conduct in South Africa, one man, Fritz Joubert Duquesne (1877–1956), could neither forgive nor forget the horrors he had seen and resolved to make it his life's ambition to kill Kitchener for what he had done. A truly remarkable character, Duquesne joined the Boer Commandos at the commencement of the war in 1899 and rapidly gained a reputation on both sides for his daring panache and, only known to the British as the Black Panther, there was soon a price on his head. Luckily for him, when he was finally captured it was by the Portuguese, who shipped him off to prison in Lisbon. Ever the lady's man, he began an affair with the daughter of one of his guards, she helped him to escape and make his way to Paris where he pondered his next move. Finally deciding that the best place to hide from the British was right under their noses, he made his way to Aldershot in Britain to enlist in the British Army as a lieutenant and, applying for a posting to South Africa, he managed to get back home at his enemy's expense. Once there, he tried to organize a troupe of saboteurs but was betrayed and sentenced to life imprisonment in exchange for what he professed to be the keys to the codes used by the Boer Commando. His circle of 20 cohorts were all executed and by the time the British found out that the codes were useless Duquesne had escaped and made his way to New York, where he talked his way into a job as a roving correspondent for the *New York Herald*, reporting on big-game hunting and other outdoor adventures.

His rather overblown tales of intrepid safaris across the African Velt attracted the attention of President Theodore Roosevelt, who hired Duquesne as his personal shooting instructor and took him along on many of his own fabled hunting trips as correspondent/consultant. And it was through his association with Roosevelt that Duquesne finally met up with the other man he was sworn to kill, Frederick Russell Burnham (1861–1947). Something of a proto-Rambo, this was the American who trained and deployed the Scouts for the British, who used them as the spies and saboteurs who so plagued the Boers. Raised on an Indian reservation by his missionary parents, Burnham was always out hunting and tracking with the Indians and learned from those mentors how to survive in the wilderness with nothing but a knife and his wits. By the time he was seconded to the British Army in South Africa his skills were almost legendary, with the native Africans calling him He-who-sees-in-the-dark. It was Burnham, with his woodland and wilderness skills, who inspired Baden-Powell, then serving in South Africa himself, to set up the Boy Scouts, initially designed to give feckless youths a sense of worth and prepare them for military life. It was also Burnham who raised the Lovat Scouts, a regiment that would soon produce the British Army's very first sniper unit and troops that can only be described as the forerunners of the SAS. Anyway, neither

Burnham nor Duquesne knew that each had been after the other during the Boer War until they met and got chatting in Washington in 1910. With all thus revealed, the two became quite close friends, although Duquesne did not know at the time that his old adversary was still very active in counter-intelligence for America and Britain – nor did he then know that the pair of them were again destined to play cat-and-mouse, this time throughout World War I.

When not attending society parties or advising Roosevelt on how to lengthen the list of endangered species, Duquesne spent all his spare time in Washington establishing links to German intelligence and, working on the principle that his enemy's enemy must be his friend, at the outbreak of World War I took himself off to Brazil where, masquerading as a mining engineer called Frederick Fredericks, he managed to sink several British ships by consigning to their cargo massive bombs, crated up as mineral samples. This ruse was likely modified to play a part in his plan to kill Kitchener on June 5, 1916. Tipped off by German intelligence that this was the date that HMS *Hampshire* would sail out of Scapa Flow to take Kitchener and David Lloyd George, then Minister for Munitions, on a diplomatic mission to Russia, Duquesne slipped back into Britain to make preparations. Masquerading this time as Duke Boris Zekrevsky of the Russian Imperial Court, he had no trouble gaining passage on the ship and had soon loaded his belongings, including several large crates. It is not clear what happened as the *Hampshire* passed within half a mile of Orkney; if there was a U-boat involved in the sinking then this was likely the U-75, with Kapitänleutnant Kurt Beitzen at the periscope; he is known to have been in the area at the time and laying mines. But whether a bomb was on board, a mine, a torpedo, or any mix-and-match of those three possibilities, Duquesne made signals to some sort of craft in the nearby waters and abandoned the *Hampshire* a few minutes before she was sent to the bottom by a massive explosion that left but 12 survivors out of the 662 on board. Luckily for Lloyd George, he had been detained in London by a last-minute problem that prevented him making the journey.

In the meantime, Duquesne was lauded by Berlin and given the Iron Cross for the sinking of the *Hampshire* and, fearing the British would be out for his blood with renewed determination, he placed newspaper announcements of his death in Brazil at the hands of drunken natives before scuttling back to America where he thought he would be safe, as he had taken citizenship in 1913. Unfortunately, with his packing-crate exploits in Brazil having been revealed to the authorities by Burnham, he was arrested in New York on November 17, 1917 for making fraudulent insurance claims against his lost consignments. This was in the main a "holding" tactic by Burnham, who knew damned well that while his British friends wanted to get their hands on Duquesne, the road to extradition would be a long and winding one. Naturally, the same thought had passed through Duquesne's mind so, while in detention, he feigned stroke-induced paralysis to get himself transferred to the New York Bellevue Hospital from where he subsequently escaped, dressed up as a nurse.

Next assuming the identity of retired British major Frederick Craven, he cropped up in 1919 working as a journalist and publicity agent for the Nazi-loving-bootlegger Joseph Kennedy (1888–1969), a man with whom he had much in common. The rest of the interwar years passed uneventfully for Duquesne but in 1939 he was again in Berlin's pocket, setting up what is reckoned to be one of the largest spy rings ever detected. Under the ever-watchful eye of the FBI, the 33-strong Duquesne spy network blossomed in America by placing its members in sensitive work environments, including the Norden bomb-sight factory. After a two-year investigation, the entire ring was arrested on the night of June 28, 1941 and sentenced to a total of 300 years between them. Duquesne stood firm at his trial and remained adamant that he had never intended harm to befall the United States of America and that all his efforts were intended to do harm to the British in retaliation for Kitchener's conduct of the Second Boer War. Sentenced to 18 years without remission, Duquesne was by then 64 and well beyond any theatrical escapes. His health deteriorated in prison and, on compassionate grounds, he was released to die in hospital in 1956 at the age of 78.

IL DUCE VITA

1926 was not a good year for Benito Mussolini; assassins of all ages and nationalities were, quite literally, falling over themselves to take a pop at him.

First up to the plate was the decidedly batty the Honourable Violet Albina Gibson (1876–1956), a minor member of the Anglo-Irish aristocracy with an obsessive interest in the kind of hard-line socialism that would have her and her kind swinging from lamp posts, since she was the daughter of Edward Gibson, 1st Baron Ashbourne (1837–1913), one-time Lord Chancellor of Ireland. It is claimed by those who defend her that, although at first a great admirer of Mussolini, she felt he had strayed too far from his initially avowed principles and objectives and so resolved to kill

Mussolini showing the rhino-result of Violet Gibson's Pinocchio shot. (Topfoto)

him for the "best" of political motives. A few even venture to suggest that she was not mad but a misunderstood activist who was only branded mad to lock her away. But the lady cannot be defended in such a manner, for weeks before she mounted her farcical attack on Mussolini, she had been stamping round the city either talking to herself or haranguing anyone daft enough to listen, saying that she was going to shoot everyone from the Pope down. The vast majority, her family, and Mussolini himself were in no doubt as to the state of her mind and treated her accordingly.

Either way, she came closer to success than any of Mussolini's other would-be assassins but how she managed to miss him from a distance of perhaps two feet is itself a mystery. On April 7 Mussolini had just finished giving a speech on the great advances in medicine being made by Italian doctors and was leaving the International Congress of Surgeons in Rome when he was mobbed by fans who stood about simpering as he puffed up and gave them a photo shoot Fascist salute from the running board of his car. As soon as he lifted his arm, Gibson cut loose with an old .22 from less than a yard away and, despite Mussolini standing proud of the crowd and nicely profiled against the sky, she managed to hit him only once – straight through that famous nose of his.

Nearly lynched by the mob, she was dragged away for questioning by the police while Mussolini nipped back into the conference to see if anyone present had been making major advances in the patching-up of unwanted third nostrils. With his nose in a "Pinocchio" bandage and his booming voice now sounding more like that of an adenoidal Porky Pig, Mussolini went to the detention center where Gibson was being held to see for himself the measure of his would-be assassin. By the time he arrived it had been established beyond any reasonable doubt that Gibson was a few sandwiches short of a picnic, and had been driven by nothing more sinister than her own insanity. Although she was detained for several months in an asylum, Mussolini knew a publicity coup when he saw one, so, instead of having her shot or locked away for life, he resolved to harvest brownie points by playing the magnanimous clement, ordering that Gibson be treated gently and released into the care of a medical unit which would accompany her to England. And thus it was that Violet came home; her plane was met by British doctors who took her straight to St Andrew's Hospital in Northampton, the asylum where she would spend the rest of her days.

Mussolini's nose recovered its poise, albeit still a little squint, just in time for that year's second attempt on September 11. This was a more "formal" and politically motivated affair, which had been some time in the planning by Gino Lucetti (1900–1943), a disaffected Italian in exile in the south of France whence he had fled after being shot in the ear by rival anarchists. Nose, ears; what is it with these Italians and extremity wounds? Anyway, Lucetti's main contact in the home country was the infamous Italian anarchist Errico Malatesta (1853–1932) who, with a surname translating as "crazy," turned out to be the perfect overlord for what unfolded. Borrowing money from anyone stupid enough to lend it, Lucetti managed to get himself set up in Rome and establish contact with the two names given him by "Crazy Eric." Of the two, Stefano Vatteroni and Leandro Sorio, the former was the more important in that he had an unnamed contact in Mussolini's secretarial department who would have access to itinerary plans. While in Rome, Lucetti had to keep changing addresses on account of his blowing up of flats and bedsits as he struggled to produce a viable bomb for the job. When it finally dawned on him that he was not the bombsmith he thought himself to be, and that one more try might be his last, he reluctantly sent out for a couple of "pret-a-bombas" from Sorio and told Vatteroni to find his contact to get some idea of Mussolini's movements in the forthcoming week. News came back that Mussolini had a trip planned for September 11 when, traveling in his famous open Lancia, his route would take him down the Via Nomentana to the Porta Pia. After Lucetti had reconnoitered the Nomentana–Pia junction, he decided to go for it.

Hiding in his chosen doorway, Lucetti waited for the motorcade to hove into view but, as he leaped from hiding to throw his bomb, he startled a nearby cat, tripping over it in mid-stride. As he engaged in a bout of impromptu disco dancing to retain his balance, Lucetti let fly the bomb as the Lancia drew level but it hit the windshield, bounced off onto the running board and exploded on the pavement several yards away. As Mussolini's driver took off like a startled gazelle, the bodyguards fanned out and soon spotted Lucetti hiding in the doorway of number 13 Via Nomentana; they stopped kicking him around the pavement only when they realized he had yet another bomb under his coat. Relieving the unconscious Lucetti of his second bomb, three pistols, a pocketful of dum-dums, and two daggers – no one could say he didn't go prepared – the bodyguards carted him away for the inevitable brutal interrogation. Before long, both Vatteroni and Sorio were in custody and all three were sentenced to 20 years on the prison isle of Santo Stefano, just outside the Bay of Naples. On September 15, 1943 Lucetti managed to escape and, stealing a small boat, made his way to the island of Ischia, on the other side of the bay. Thanking his lucky stars for his safe deliverance from the sea, he landed on Ischia on the 17th and made his way to the address of an anarchist contact. He had just stepped inside the house when it took a direct hit from an Allied bomber.

The final attempt of 1926 was a short and sorry affair played out on October 31 during a sham parade in which Mussolini "re-enacted" his fabled March on Rome. According to the Mussolini publicity machine, on October 28, 1922 he, astride a white stallion, had led a column of 30,000 Fascists in a march on the city to seize power. In fact, Victor Emanuel III had sent him a letter asking him to come to Rome and form a government. Ensconced in Milan at the time, Mussolini and his small entourage chose to make the journey by train, which, in accordance with the time-honored tradition of the Italian railways, arrived nearly two hours late. There was no March on Rome, Mussolini did not have to seize power, as it was handed him on a plate, and there was certainly no white stallion. All that aside there he was, posturing astride such a steed at the head of the 1926 parade when the 15-year-old Anteo Zamboni tried to shoot him off his white lie. The lad was immediately grabbed by a nearby cavalry officer called Carlo Alberto Pasolini, who was given little choice but to relinquish his charge to the lynch mob. The Piedmont branch of Zamboni's family had previously immigrated to America where they were busy perfecting their now-famous ice-rink machine as Anteo swung from his lamp post. As for the officer who first grabbed the lad and disarmed him, his son, Paolo, would grow up to be the flamboyant Italian film director.

With Zamboni's death things calmed down a bit for Mussolini who, like Hitler, chose to perceive the failure of all assassination attempts as a sign from above that all was destiny. The only other attempt on his life – apart from the final one, which left him and his mistress, Clara Pettrelli, swinging from lamp posts of their own – was a foiled plot by the American anarchist Michael Schirru, who was arrested in his Rome hotel on February 3, 1931. Taken down to the Trevi police station for questioning, he suddenly whipped out a pistol and shot all three interrogators before putting the gun to his own head and pulling the trigger. Unfortunately for Schirru, he was the most seriously wounded of the lot and it took all the "great advances of Italian doctors" to keep him alive to face trial and execution, a conclusion that is still debated in certain circles. While he recuperated from his wounds, the police discovered that he had rented a second room in the same hotel and in that they found his bombs and plans to kill Mussolini. Questioned in his hospital bed, Schirru made no attempt to deny anything, stupidly thinking his American citizenship would prove adequate defense against Mussolini's thugs and besides, he reasoned, he had only injured a couple of policemen so it was hardly a hanging matter. Back in America, Schirru's wife did all she could to get the State Department to pitch in behind her husband but they were not, it seems, inclined to be galvanized into overexertions on behalf of any anarchist assassin caught red-handed in a foreign land. At the time, only the murder of the king or Mussolini attracted the death penalty, but Schirru was condemned on May 28, 1931 by a bench that disallowed both jury and defense council. In fact not even Schirru was allowed to speak so, needless to say, he was found guilty in a matter of minutes and shot the next morning.

Even though Schirru was an anarchist and a would-be assassin, there were international murmurings that shooting him for simply *planning* to kill Mussolini was not quite cricket. These criticisms were countered by a vehement tirade from none other than Guglielmo Marconi (1874–1937), who told the world in no uncertain terms to mind its own business and let Italy run its own affairs. The overriding memory of Marconi as an innovator in the field of communications tends to obscure the fact that he was a most ardent Fascist and a close friend of Mussolini, who had been best man at Marconi's 1927 marriage.

HARPER'S BIZARRE

Where one stands on John Brown largely depends on where one stands on people who are convinced that it is their God-given right and duty to kill those who disagree with them. It is perhaps enough to say that a man who felt quite at ease ranting passages from the Bible while hacking up or shooting those who displeased him is bound to stir up strong emotion on either side of any contemporary debate. His damp-squib raid at Harpers Ferry is a well-known story but the incident is worth delving into round the edges as it roped in many bit-players who would later become famous for other reasons.

Denouncing all who would not take up arms and follow his lead as "cowards or worse," Brown already had several murders under his belt by the time he led a force of 19 others in his doomed attack on the US Army armory in Harpers Ferry. The purpose of the raid was to steal as many guns as possible and arm slaves in open revolt. He was already in possession of 200 Sharps rifles, sent to him in crates declaring the shipment to be Bibles from the Church of Henry Ward Beecher (1813–1887), brother of Harriet Beecher Stowe (1811–1896), author of Uncle Tom's Cabin (1852). In fact Beecher's congregation raised the money for so many such rifles that a Sharps is still known as a Beecher's Bible in some states. No matter; Brown was after guns and ammunition in abundance to form an army of vigilante-slaves to march right through the South, swelling its own numbers with those it freed en route. As Brown and his raiders moved into the town, first to be taken prisoner was retired colonel Lewis Washington, great-grand-nephew of George, from whom Brown stole a rather valuable sword that had been presented to the president by Frederick the Great; this was the sword Brown would wield during the rest of the raid.

All was going according to plan until a train rolled into town at about 1.30am and a chap called Hayward Shepherd, a black night porter employed by the Baltimore and Ohio Railway, ambled up to the crossing, intending to join the train bound for Washington. Few of the men with Brown, his sons included, could have been described as the sharpest knives in the box and, instead of just letting Shepherd board the train and get about his business, the trigger-happy Dangerfield Newby (1815–1859), gunned down the hapless and unarmed Shepherd when he refused to move away from the boarding step. The noise of the shooting woke, among others, local physician Dr John Starry who hurried out to find Shepherd beyond help. Instead of detaining the doctor and the train, Brown simply wandered off, causing some today to conjecture that he was perhaps already by then a trifle unbalanced – there was a history of mental problems in his family – or that he actually wanted to get caught. Either way, he got his wish; the train continued to Washington where the conductor made a report of the incident and Starry rode straight for the military post at Charlestown to report matters to Lieutenant Israel Greene (1824–1909), who immediately rallied about 80 men and then searched about for an office to lead them. Told that there was a lieutenant-colonel in town on leave, some chap called Robert E. Lee, Greene went to hunt him down. He found Lee chatting to another officer who was trying to elicit his support for his bid to get the army to adopt a new saber-sling he had designed and this man, J. E. B. Stuart, readily agreed to serve as Lee's aide in the venture.

As the alerted military rallied and headed for Harpers Ferry things had unraveled completely with the locals, who, come dawn, were aware that their town had been invaded. Not knowing the identity or intent of the raiders, the locals sporadically engaged the interlopers, with another of their number, Thomas Boerly, being shot by Newby. Standing well over six feet, Newby was easy to pick out and someone got him with a spike-gun, all but severing his head, after which the infuriated locals descended on the body and mutilated it before flinging it into the local wallow where it was partly consumed by hogs. By the time Lee and his command arrived, three other locals had been killed and Brown, with his remaining men and hostages, was ensconced in a small brick engine house. Brimming over with the kind of arrogance displayed by all self-appointed "messiahs," Brown grossly underestimated the level of ill-feeling he had engendered with the depleted locals, who, unaware of his identity or his motives, simply resented his violent and murderous intrusion into the community. Too wrapped up in himself to rightly judge the tension of the situation he had created, Brown rather foolishly sent out his son, Walter, under a flag of truce, to suggest to the townsfolk that they simply let bygones be bygones and let the raiding party ride away. Naturally, Brown was shocked when the townsfolk thought about it for a second or two – and then gunned young Walter down where he stood.

The locals kept Brown and his party pinned down until Lee and Stuart arrived on the morning of the 18th and, having stood down the locals and positioned his men, Stuart approached the engine house to call on those within to surrender. The only response he got was from Lewis Washington, who shouted out that the troops should open fire regardless of the hostages. A few minutes later, and a clear indication that the reason for the fate of Walter had failed to register with the old man, Brown said he would come out if he and his men were given a head start to escape. At this, Stuart lost patience and gave the signal to batter down the doors. This final assault was led by Greene, who cut down Brown but failed in his intention to kill him. According to Greene's own account, once inside there was considerable confusion and gunfire, during which Washington pointed out Brown, who "turned his head to see who it was to whom Colonel Washington was speaking. Quicker than thought I brought my saber down with all my strength upon his head. He was moving as the blow fell, and I suppose I did not strike him where I intended, for he received a deep saber cut in the back of the neck. He fell senseless on his side and then rolled over on his back... Instinctively as Brown fell I gave him a saber thrust in the left breast. The sword I carried was a light uniform weapon, and, either not having a point or striking something hard in Brown's accoutrements, did not penetrate. The blade bent double." It is perhaps no exaggeration to say that, had Greene been carrying his heavier combat saber and killed Brown as planned, then the Civil War might have been averted; it was only the trial and execution of Brown that pushed America into civil war. Most agree that if Brown had been killed in the fracas it would have been no more than a storm in the teacup of the local and state press.

Legally speaking, the trial was a farce; Judge Richard Parker leaned so far in favor of the prosecution that it was a miracle he managed to stay in the seat. He expressed far more indignation that the descendant of George Washington should have been abducted and held hostage than he did over the thuggish shooting of the black baggage handler and the other "lesser mortals" of Harpers Ferry who had been likewise gunned down in the street. If there was any one, single, *éminence grise* present to ensure Parker came to the "right" verdict, that would have been Congressman Clement Vallandigham (1820–1871) of Ohio. But his presence was superfluous; all involved in Brown's passage from Harpers Ferry to the gallows were Southern sympathizers who would soon don the Gray in the conflict they were rapidly making inevitable. Only Brown's defense lawyer, George H. Hoyt (1837–1877), would fight for the Union, teaming up with a young James Butler Hickok (1837–1876) to hunt down the Confederate raiders operating in Kansas. Brown was hanged on December 2, 1859, after which he proved to be far more dangerous dead than alive. The local military was decidedly twitchy as that date dawned; there were constant rumors of an Abolitionists' plot to free Brown under arms at the last minute. To increase the show of strength at the event, the Richmond Grays were ordered to Charlestown and, as it happened, a certain young actor was in town at the time, rehearsing to open at the city's Marshall Theater. He infuriated the management by walking out of the production to join the Grays so he could be sure of witnessing the death of the man he believed to be the devil incarnate. He got his wish, but John Wilkes Booth (1838–1865) nearly fainted and had to be steadied by Philip Whitlock of the Grays and a tutor from the nearby Virginia Military Institute, a chap called Professor Jackson who would later pick up the nickname of "Stonewall."

Between the trial and the execution things had been bad enough; everyone picked their side and, as one might expect, countless left-wing figures chose to climb onto Brown's bandwagon. Longfellow's quill was smoking, as was that of Henry David Thoreau; even old Victor Hugo got in on the act. After the execution, such people kicked into overdrive, presenting Brown as a messianic Moses-in-buckskins, one hand holding aloft a Beecher's Bible with the more dangerous version brandished by the other. To be fair, by the time of his execution he did look very much like a wild-eyed version of Charlton Heston's Moses. Thoreau drew an analogy between the crucifixion of Christ and Brown's execution, those subscribing to that fantasy doing so while blithely ignored his catalogue of sanctimonious slaughter; meanwhile, in the Abolitionist camp, there were more than one or two who let go a sigh of relief that Brown was safely out of the picture. But, unfortunately for all, whichever way you sliced it, Brown's death was the key that locked the country into war.

Vallandigham went on to become the leading light of the Copperhead Movement, a not insignificant lobby within the Union that did everything it could to subvert the Northern war effort, including sending aid to the South and encouraging Union troops to desert. Vallandigham overplayed his hand by publicly renouncing his country so Lincoln responded by having him thrown out of the yet-to-be United States, an action that prompted Edward Everett Hale to write the classic yarn *The Man Without a Country* (1863). (Edward was the descendant of Nathan Hale [1755-1766], America's first spy, shot by the British, of whom there is a prominent statue in the CIA HQ at Langley, also in Virginia.) After Lincoln's assassination, Vallandigham returned to the re-United States and resumed his legal career, which was to prove his undoing. 1871 saw him in Lebanon, Ohio, where he was defending one Thomas McGehan, who was charged with shooting some chap in a barroom dispute. Vallandigham believed his client's version of events, which had the victim actually shooting himself with his own gun, pulled from a pocket while rising from a kneeling position. Demonstrating this for the jury with what he mistakenly believed to be an unloaded pistol, Vallandigham's re-enactment was indeed realistic, right down to his shooting himself in exactly the same place as the other chap and dying as a result. McGehan was acquitted and left the state.

And the last hidden player in the story was another John Brown, whose name got confused through song to produce the Union's favorite marching song of *John Brown's Body*, as morphed into *The Battle Hymn of the Republic* in 1862 by Julia Ward Howe (1819–1910). Irwin Silber, a well-known American musical historian, has traced the true origins of the song, which celebrate Sergeant John Brown, a Scotsman of the 2nd Battalion, Boston Light Infantry, not the above. Sergeant Brown was second tenor in the regimental choir, which was a popular turn at the Fort Warren concerts and other venues in the city where their rousing rendition of *Say, Brothers, Will You Meet Us*, sung to an old Scottish marching tune introduced by Brown himself, was the all-time favorite. It was troops from the Boston regiments who sang ditties about this John Brown, and in the summer of 1861 the Boston 12th Regiment marched into New York singing some version or other and the crowds went wild. Much the same happened during the French Revolution when a column of volunteers from Marseilles marched into Paris singing their pet song, also destined for national honor. Anyway, as soon as the song gained national acceptance, most presumed, quite naturally, that the John Brown of the title just had to be the one from Harpers Ferry and came up with suitable lyrics of their own.

THE MAN WHO SHOT THE MAN WHO SHOT LINCOLN

Before looking at Boston Corbett, for it was he, it is worth looking at the other bit players in Booth's box-office hit, for there were quite a few and some with surprising descendants. To work through the events as chronologically as possible, it is perhaps best to start off with the Booth who actually saved a Lincoln. Before the famous night at the theatre in question, actor Edwin Booth (1833–1893) was waiting with John T. Ford for a train out of New Jersey in August 1864, bound for Washington for the anniversary celebrations of the opening of the latter's theater, which would become infamous the following April. There was something of a kerfuffle, resulting in a young chap being jostled off the platform and onto the rails. Swift to act, Booth dragged Richard Todd Lincoln (1843–1926), Abe's first son, clear of danger by the scruff of his coat. Although it definitely sounds like the sort of thing that is made up afterwards to enrich the already overflowing coffers of apocrypha, the incident is true and acknowledged as such by Richard Lincoln in a letter he presented in 1909 to *The Century Magazine*:

> The incident occurred while a group of passengers were late at night purchasing their sleeping car places from the conductor who stood on the station platform at the entrance of the car. The platform was about the height of the car floor, and there was of course a narrow space between the platform and the car body. There was some crowding, and I happened

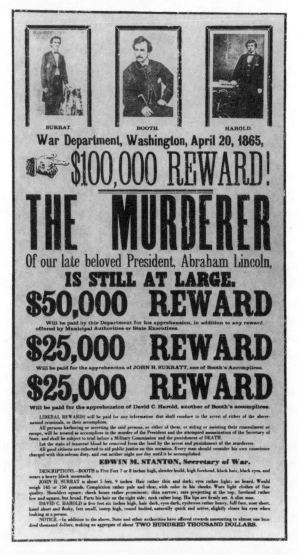

"Wanted" broadside issued by the War Department on April 20, 1865, offering rewards for the apprehension of John Wilkes Booth and his co-conspirators. (Topfoto)

to be pressed by it against the car body while waiting my turn. In this situation the train began to move, and by the motion I was twisted off my feet, and had dropped somewhat, with feet downward, into the open space, and was personally helpless, when my coat collar was vigorously seized and I was quickly pulled up and out to a secure footing on the platform. Upon turning to thank my rescuer I saw it was Edwin Booth, whose face was of course well known to me, and I expressed my gratitude to him, and in doing so, called him by name.

Richard Lincoln also seems to have been something of a jinx when it came to presidential assassinations, he being personally involved in three. He was expected to be in the box on the night of his father's death but cried off at the last minute, leaving some to conjecture that had he been present, in his allotted extra chair, then he would have blocked Booth's shot. Secretary of War to the administration of President James Garfield, Lincoln Jr. was present at the Sixth Street Station in July 2, 1881 when his boss was gunned down by religious nut Charles J. Guiteau, whose subsequent trial was the first in America to consider insanity as a defense. In Guiteau's case, however, the consideration was rejected and he was executed. Richard Lincoln was next present, by personal invitation of President William McKinley, at the Pan-American Exposition in New York when his host was shot by Leon F. Czolgosz on September 6, 1901, and after that he refused to attend any more presidential functions, saying: "No, I am not going, and they'd better not ask me because there is a certain fatality about presidential functions when I am present." And so to John Wilkes Booth (1838–1865).

Born into an English-American acting family, he made his stage debut in a series of walk-on parts in Baltimore's

Holliday Street Theater, owned by close family friend John T. Ford (1829–1894). He moved to join Philadelphia's Arch Street Theater where he made a hash of his first main speaking part in a production of *Lucrezia Borgia*. At his first entrance he was supposed to introduce himself, the eponymous lead: "Madame, I am Petrucio Pandolfo!" but instead thrashed about, spoonerizing, "I am Pondolfio Put... no; Pedolfio ... no; Pantucio; damn it, who am I?" None of this mattered; the public and most critics loved him so he was soon taking in a leading part in *The Marble Heart*, the opening production of Ford's Theater in Washington. A sort of proto-Pygmalion, Booth played a sculptor whose statues came to life and on the opening night, with the American Civil War by now in full swing, many noted that when he had cause to deliver aggressive or admonishing lines, he frequently did so staring right at Lincoln, sitting in the very box where he would die. Lincoln was that night in the company of his sister-in-law, who would later recall that on one particular occasion when Booth had gone as far as actually pointing his finger at the president, she remarked something along the lines of, "Mr Lincoln, he looks as if he meant that for you," to which Lincoln observed, "He does seem to be looking pretty sharp at me, doesn't he?"

As the war dragged on, Booth became increasingly vocal in his condemnation of Lincoln, this leading to his arrest in 1863 in St. Louis for making treasonous threats. By 1865 Booth had become so vehemently anti-Union that he had fallen out with Edwin, his brother, and alienated himself from most sane and balanced people on both sides of the divide. He had also gathered about him a small team of like-minded loonies, including David Herold, Lewis Powell, George Atzerodt, John Surratt and his mother, Mary, who ran a boarding house at 604 H Street, Washington, where the group routinely met to discuss various plans of kidnap and murder. Booth secretly became engaged to Lucy Hale, daughter of John P. Hale, Senator for New Hampshire and she, somehow ignorant of his well-known antipathy to Lincoln, invited him to escort her to the president's second inaugural party on March 4, 1865 where, for reasons unknown, he failed to act, despite having numerous opportunities. Some say that at this stage Booth intended only kidnap, but this seems unlikely. No matter, it was at this party that he learned of the president's intention to visit one of the main soldiers' homes outside the city on the 17th and hurriedly made plans for an attack on the road leading to that destination. He and his cohorts lay in wait to no avail; there had been a last-minute change of plan and the president was instead attending a function back at Washington's National Hotel, where Booth himself was staying.

On the morning of April 12 Booth called as normal to Ford's Theater to pick up his mail and was told by an excited John T. Ford that the president would be attending the opening night (April 14) of *Our American Cousin*; Booth hurried back to his hotel to contact his co-conspirators and make plans. Although many still think of Booth acting as a lone-wolf assassin, he had in fact planned for more than the death of just the president. In a meeting held on April 13, Booth assigned George Atzerodt (1835–1865) to kill Vice President Andrew Johnson at the same time as he, Booth, was killing the president, and Lewis Powell (1844–1865) was bumping off Secretary of State William Seward, he of Alaska Purchase fame. Thus it is clear that Booth was not embarked on some personal vendetta against Lincoln; he wanted to cut off the head of the administration in one clean sweep. And Booth knew the exact time they should all strike; in Act III, scene 2, there occurs one of the play's "funniest" lines, with a woman being branded a "sockdologizing old man-trap" and, with his intimate knowledge of the play, Booth thought that to be the best time to rush into the presidential box and fire, when the usual roars of laughter would muffle the shot.

As things turned out, only Booth would succeed and, pushing past his fallen victim, Booth also stabbed Lincoln's friend, Major Henry Rathbone, forebear of actor Basil Rathbone. Leaving Lincoln dying and Rathbone seriously injured, Booth now realized he was the center of attention and, ever the ham, couldn't bring himself to leave the scene without a theatrical gesture. Mounting the edge of the box he proclaimed "*Sic semper tyrannis*!" or "Ever thus to tyrants" (the state motto of Virginia and allegedly what Brutus cried as he stabbed Caesar) to the shocked audience before leaping down to the stage to make his escape. Unfortunately he caught a foot in the ceremonial bunting and landed in a heap, breaking his leg, before exiting stage left with an undignified hobble.

Unbeknown to Booth at the time, Atzerodt had lost his nerve and hit the bottle. He had booked himself into the Kirkwood House Hotel where Johnson was staying but, come the allotted time, he was unconscious in the hotel bar. He later reeled off into the night and stumbled back the next morning demanding to know where Johnson was; in light of the previous night's events, he was arrested on the spot. Powell was made of sterner stuff; he broke into Seward's house at precisely the time that Booth was shooting Lincoln, making his way to Seward's bedroom where he lay recovering from injuries sustained in a carriage accident. When his pistol misfired, Powell stabbed Seward several times in the face and neck with a Bowie knife before hacking and slashing his way out, seriously injuring several members of the household en route. Had Seward not been so seriously injured in the carriage incident he would surely have died that night; it was only the surgical braces to his lower face and neck that saved him. Powell went into hiding until the 18th when he ventured to Mary Surratt's boarding house, just as she was being arrested, giving the Washington police a bonus.

David Herold (1842–1865), who had accompanied Powell but not ventured inside the Seward house, had quit that scene and joined up with the fleeing Booth, who planned to ride through to anti-Union Virginia. But by dawn of April 15 he had barely made 20 miles on account of his leg, and stopped at the home of Dr Samuel Mudd to seek attention for what Mudd would later claim he believed to be a riding accident. Unfortunately for him, he kept quiet about a series of encounters he had had with Booth across the previous 12 months so he too would be arrested.

Booth and Herold were long gone before Mudd was arrested and had made their way into Caroline County, Virginia, where they sought lodgings at a farm run by the Garrett family, who, although decidedly Southern-sympathizers, knew nothing of Booth or the assassination. Presenting themselves under false names, the two men languished there unaware that a posse led by Lieutenant Edward P. Doherty was hot on their trail, and in its midst rode Thomas "Boston" Corbett (1832–?).

Like the Booth family, the Corbetts shipped out of England for America in search of a better fortune, arriving in New York in 1839 where young Thomas first found work in a hat factory.

Corbett married and moved to Boston where he hooked up with a sect of Evangelical and flagellant individuals and, when his wife died in childbirth in 1864, Corbett knew just what to do. Inspired by Matthew 19:12, which, rambling on about eunuchs being jolly fine chaps, observes: "and there be eunuchs which have made themselves eunuchs for the kingdom of heaven's sake," Corbett picked up a pair of scissors and castrated himself to better resist the temptations offered by the Bostonian brothels to which he had resorted after the death of his wife. Wrapping the offending member in some old newspaper and popping it into his pocket for safekeeping, Corbett toddled off to one of his sect's prayer meetings where even the self-flagellant members of the flock blanched as Corbett proffered for viewing the soggy proof of his inspired self-modification. Only then did Corbett take himself off to the nearest hospital to get patched up.

Once all had healed, Corbett joined the army, deserting and re-enlisting as the mood took him but in June 1864 he was captured by Confederate forces and confined to the hell-hole prison at Andersonville in Georgia. One of the few to survive the camp, Corbett would later testify at the first ever war crimes trial, that of Andersonville's camp commander, Henry Wirz (1823–1865), who was executed on the highly suspect and contradictory testimony of Corbett and others. He was still in uniform when "volunteered" into Doherty's posse on April 24, 1865 and was one of six ordered to surround the barn at the Garrett farm on the 26th. Herold came out at the first demand to surrender but Booth would have none of it, shouting defiance from within. All the groups scouring the countryside were under direct orders from Secretary of War Edward McMasters Stanton to bring Booth back alive, no matter what, so, reminding his men of that prime directive, Doherty set fire to the barn to drive out its occupant. Booth was apparently standing close to and facing the barricaded doors, gasping for air, when there was a shot. The barn was a fairly rickety affair and, as the light from the flames intensified, Corbett had a clear view of

Booth through a crack and took it into his head to fire, hitting Booth in the neck, virtually severing his spine. Booth was dragged out to die on the porch of the Garrett home and Corbett was arrested.

When interrogated, Corbett claimed that he could see Booth getting ready to fire through the doors but he would later change that statement to a claim of his acting on a direct order from God; neither is very likely. That aside, Stanton ordered Corbett's release, with a share in the reward posted for Booth's capture, after which Corbett secured a discharge from the army and drifted back into hatting and other jobs. He also turned a dollar by giving lectures on his part in the capture of Booth but these invariably degenerated into a religious rant, the highlight of which was the stunned audience being treated to a peek at what was no longer there. By August 1875 his mental condition had deteriorated to such an extent that when he attended a regimental reunion in Caldwell, Ohio, he ended up threatening with loaded pistols anyone who spoke to him. By 1878 he had drifted into Kansas and dug himself a hole in the ground outside Concordia, where he lived like a hobbit for seven years. Enjoying a temporary respite from lunacy in 1887, he secured a job as the doorman for the Kansas House of Representatives in Topeka but was soon back to his old ways, threatening politicians with pistols until he was locked up in the Kansas State Asylum for the Insane. Not a chap to tarry long in any one place, Corbett escaped in the May of 1888 and went back to his troglodytic existence, scaring the living daylights out of any who inadvertently stumbled across his various des reses. His last hobbit-hole was in the woods around Hinckley in Minnesota and the last sighting of him was a few days before the famous fire of September 1894 laid waste to that entire area. It is presumed by most and accepted by many that he died in the conflagration as he was never heard of again and the death toll mentions a Thomas Corbett.

Edwin and other members of the acting family thought a tactful retreat to Europe and England might be for the best. This not only proved right and profitable but it also "rekindled" the UK branch of the family to eventually produce Cherie Booth, daughter of actor Tony Booth and wife of retired prime minister Tony Blair. Mary Surratt, George Atzerodt, Lewis Powell, and David Herold were hanged at Washington's Fort McNair on July 7, 1865 on the piece of ground that now serves as a recreational tennis court. Dr Mudd was convicted of complicity in the assassination and sentenced to life in Fort Jefferson in Florida's Dry Tortugas, as were Michael O'Laughlen, Edmund Spangler, and Samuel Arnold, Booth's conspirators in various abortive plots to kidnap Lincoln. After fighting off an epidemic of yellow fever in the prison, Mudd was pardoned by President Johnson on February 8, 1869 and returned to Maryland to quiet retirement. As for Major Rathbone, it was all downhill for him. In the July of 1867 he married his stepsister, Clara Harris, and took up the position of United States Consul to Hanover in Germany, where, like Corbett, he started to show signs of increasing madness. On December 23 this had reached such a peak that he murdered his wife and tried to kill his own children with an axe before trying to hack himself to death. He spent the rest of his life in various German asylums before his death in 1911. The one player in the whole affair to escape justice and outlive the rest was John Surratt (1844–1916).

After the assassination Surratt fled first to Liverpool and then to the Vatican, where, under the name of John Watson, he enlisted in the Papal Zouaves only to be recognized and arrested on November 7, 1866. He escaped prison but was quickly recaptured and shipped home to stand trial on June 10, 1867. Although Surratt admitted he was party to plans to kidnap Lincoln he steadfastly denied any prior knowledge of the fatal shooting and, after hearing from nearly 200 witnesses, the trial collapsed with a hung jury on August 10. The government withdrew all charges and Surratt remained in America to become something of a model citizen. In 1872 he married Mary Hunter, a descendant of Francis Scott Key, author of the words to "The Star Spangled Banner," and one of his later-born cousins would grow up to be writer F. Scott Fitzgerald. Between various jobs, commercial and in teaching, he annoyed a lot of people by earning a tidy sum with his lectures and books on his involvement in the Lincoln Conspiracy and his subsequent flight, capture, and trial. It was this unseemly profiting from the death of Lincoln that brought the first demands for the outlawing of miscreants profiting from their misdeeds by whatever means.

WOODY'S LAST HUNTING TRIP

On the morning of December 9, 1945, Private Horace "Woody" Woodring (1926–2003) was driving generals George Patton and Hobart "Hap" Gay into the countryside near Mannheim, Germany, where the two planned to spend the day hunting pheasants. At about 11.45am, as their Cadillac 75 cleared the appositely named Neckarstadt, they were involved in a minor low-speed collision with an American Army truck driven by Technical Sergeant Robert L. Thompson. Executing a left turn, the truck was doing no more than 10mph while the Cadillac itself, with its path blocked by the turning truck, had already slowed to perhaps 20mph. It was in such unusual circumstances that Patton received impact injuries sufficient to break his neck, while the other occupants of the car walked away without a scratch. First on the scene, officially, was Military Policeman Lieutenant Peter Babalas, who would subsequently file a report stating that the nature and extent of the impact was in no way conducive to such an outcome. Paralyzed from the neck down, Patton was taken to the military hospital in Heidelberg where he died on December 21, supposedly of a pulmonary embolism exacerbated by heart problems. In the meanwhile, Babalas's report went missing and Thompson was shipped out to London.

Although Patton was a superb self-publicist, his carefully crafted public image had started to unravel on August 3, 1941 when he visited an evacuation hospital outside Nicosia and began slapping and kicking an enlisted man he mistook for a malingerer in that he had no visible wounds. After slapping Private Charles Herman Kuhl around his bunk, Patton dragged him to his feet and butt-kicked him out of the admissions tent, screaming at the medical staff that Kuhl was a "yellow-bellied son-of-a-bitch coward" who should be sent back and that he, Patton, would shoot anyone who invalided him out. As it turned out, Kuhl was there for advanced and chronic dysentery and malaria. A week later, on August 10 and at the 93rd Evacuation Hospital, Patton again went loopy, this time with Private Paul G. Bennett, who had been sent there, against his wishes, as his nerves were so shot that his commanding officer felt him to be unreliable to the point of endangering his comrades. Unaware that Bennett was pleading with the medics *not* to send him home, Patton, with many more colorful expletives, began to knock Bennett about, telling him that if he did not go back to the front then he would be put up against a wall and shot. Then, and this was likely the last straw that prompted the medics to submit a formal demand for Patton to face disciplinary charges, he put his hand on his famous pearl-handled Colt 45 and, lifting it almost free of the holster, said, "In fact, I ought to shoot you myself, you whimpering coward." Naturally the press had a field day and from then on Patton was a lame duck with, if more recent revelations are to be believed, worse to come.

On September 25, 1979 Douglas DeWitt Bazata (1911–1999) stunned the 460 assembled and former elite of the OSS, forerunner of the CIA, who were gathered at the Hilton in Washington, with a speech informing them: "For diverse political reasons, many extremely high-placed persons hated Patton. I know who killed him because I was the one hired to do it. Ten thousand dollars. General William Donovan himself, Director of the OSS, entrusted me with the mission. I set up the accident. Since he did not die in the accident, he was kept in isolation in the hospital where he was killed with an injection." Had this statement come from a "nobody" or someone lower down the ranks, perhaps it could have been dismissed out of hand, but Bazata was no ordinary player. During World War II he conducted countless operations in Occupied Europe and, just prior to the D-Day Landings, was one of a team of three dropped into France to organize and coordinate the activities of the French Resistance to the maximum distraction of the Germans. After the war he became something of a celebrity artist, with sponsors such as Princess Grace of Monaco and the Windsors, and no less a person than Dali running up a canvas entitled *Homage to Bazata*. In short he was no side-act seeking his 15 minutes of fame and he never wavered in his account of what he claimed to have happened on December 9, 1945.

During the push for Berlin, Bazata claimed that he and his team had been given the task of doing all they could to slow Patton's advance on that city. An under-the-counter deal had been struck by Roosevelt, Churchill, and Stalin to ensure that the Russians got to Berlin first so they could establish a presence and mark off what would become their East European Bloc. All manner of supplies and fuel were allegedly diverted as Patton became increasingly frustrated and annoyed, but his opinion of Stalin was well known and no one could afford for him to get to Berlin first, or even at the same time, and start the fight with the Russian of which he so frequently spoke. Patton was all in favor of siding up with what was left of the German Army and pushing straight on for Moscow. The man was definitely a loose cannon. Bazata claimed that, after the war was over, Patton found out about the "little arrangement" with Uncle Joe and the subterfuge employed to delay his own advance, and that he intended to make all this public, along with his estimate that the delay had cost an unnecessary 20,000 American deaths and injuries. According to Bazata, the truck driven by Thompson was an irksome coincidence; Bazata and his team had a heavy vehicle parked further up the route, which was meant to crash into Patton's car at a much higher speed. Forced to take advantage of the situation, as the other occupants of the car were ushered away, Bazata shot Patton in the neck with a Czech device that fired low-velocity but extremely heavy rubber projectiles to try and finish him off. He had this with him, he said, in case the "real" crash did not prove fatal.

With Patton proving to be uncooperative, to say the least, when he started to show signs of improvement in the hospital, NKVD agents dressed up as doctors and administered one of their infamous poisons designed to induce what looked like natural causes. Suspiciously, there was no autopsy, so no one can say for sure exactly what killed Patton in the end.

───◦◦───

MERCADER'S PROJECTION

In early June 2005 one of the most famous of all assassins' weapons surfaced in Mexico City, it being offered to the highest bidder by a housewife in a quiet suburb, not far from where it had been used in 1940 to kill its equally famous victim, Leon Trotsky. The vendor, Anna Alicia Salas, was the granddaughter of the deceased Commander Alfredo Salas, late of the Mexican Secret Police, who had apparently stolen it from the evidence locker some time after the trial of the otherwise unknown Ramon Mercader, who, on Stalin's orders, had used it to pick Trotsky's brains, so to speak. Actually, although "everybody knows" that Trotsky was killed with an ice pick, most, quite understandably, presume this to have been the stiletto-like spike one finds behind most American bars and which was the weapon of choice for Sharon Stone's character in *Basic Instinct*, but it was instead a short-handled ice axe of the kind employed by those scaling escarpments of impacted snow. This is hardly the kind of weapon that would immediately spring to the mind of an assassin faced with the problem of smuggling a weapon into a fortified and heavily guarded household in which the justified paranoid fear of assassination causes visitors to be searched on their way in and out. In fact with Mexico hardly famed for its winter sports, ice axes are hardly the sort of thing one might then have picked up at the local supermarket; the very choice of such an unwieldy weapon raises a couple of questions; but first a bit of background.

About the only things Stalin and Trotsky had in common was that neither was Russian and both enjoy lasting fame under their pseudonyms. The former, Iosif Dzhugashvili (1878–1953), was raised in a non-Russian-speaking household in Georgia and, in the secrecy of pre-Revolution Russia, had used the codename Stalin, or Man of Steel. Although remembered as someone of imposing stature he was in fact just under five foot four and slightly deformed from a carriage accident in his youth; the present recollection of his physical presence is due to his habit of shooting painters and sculptors who failed to exercise artistic license. As with Hitler's intimates, many of those close to Stalin, wives and offspring alike, chose suicide as an attractive alternative to prolonging their association with the crass and sadistic little bully.

Lev Bronstein (1879–1940) was Ukrainian, this and Yiddish being his native tongues, and after he broke out of jail in Odessa in 1902 he went on the run with false papers made out in the name of Leon Trotsky, one of his previous jailers. Constantly at loggerheads with Stalin, the question is not why Trotsky was finally bumped off but why did it take Stalin so long to get round to it; perhaps the answer to that lies in the man's sadism. Prior to sanctioning the "hit" on Trotsky, Stalin had systematically wiped out virtually all of Trotsky's family: ex-wife; children; brothers; in-laws; anyone whose death might cause Trotsky emotional pain and remind him of what was eventually coming his way too.

Having been banished from the Soviet Union by Stalin in 1929, Trotsky himself had traipsed through several countries before finally settling in 1937 in Coyoacan, or Coyote-town, an arty-Bohemian enclave of Mexico City. He had been invited there by Diego Rivera and Frida Kahlo, both artists, the former celebrated for his enormous murals showing rose-tinted views of Mexican peasant life and the latter a decidedly weird narcissist who painted nothing but self-portraits. More to the point, both were dyed-in-the-wool Stalinists smarting from their expulsion from the party for having voiced objections to the Stalinist backlash against Trotsky and his followers. Ignoring such a minor detail, Leon and his wife moved in with this volcanic couple, Trotsky soon bedding Kahlo, who was probably seeking such revenge on her equally wacky husband who was then sleeping with Cristina, Kahlo's younger sister. Accustomed to, but not tolerant of, her own husband's proclivities in the bedroom, Mrs Trotsky eventually put a stop to such shenanigans, pointing out to her errant spouse that no matter how promiscuous Rivera was, he was an insanely jealous man who extended no such license to his own wife. The Trotskys moved to a nearby house they turned into a veritable fortress with solid steel doors. But the scene was by now set and various players were circling.

Although on the surface a straightforward result of internal Communist party strife, it must be said that the Germans too had their part in the killing of Trotsky and perhaps Rivera and Kahlo too, but more of them later. Mexico City – focal point of the infamous Zimmerman Affair of World War I – was positively awash with Gestapo agents and on August 23, 1939 Ribbentrop and Molotov, he of cocktail fame, had signed the German-Soviet Non-Aggression Pact. Trotsky meant nothing at all to Berlin, where the thinking was all in favor of buttering up Stalin by lending a helping hand in his mindless vendetta against his one-time comrade. In the Kremlin, Alexander Orlov (1895–1973) was appointed overseer of Operation *Duck*, so named from the Russian expression "the ducks are flying," meaning the game is afoot. He was not only Trotsky's nemesis but also the puppet-master who embroiled the likes of Philby, Burgess, and McLean. Orlov handed the planning of the actual "hit" to Pavel Sudoplatov (1907–1996), a colonel in the OGPU (later the KGB) who in turn selected Leonid Eitingon to handle the "wet" end of the business, as it was called. (It was the Stalinist assassins who first used "liquidate" as a euphemism for "kill" as a play on their Capitalist enemies' use of the term in reference to the closing down of a company and the liquidation of all assets.) Probably Stalin's most reliable and enthusiastic hatchet man, Eitingon soon announced he had lined up the perfect chap for the job – his girlfriend's not-too-bright son, Ramon Mercader (1914–1978).

Eitingon, Caridad Mercader – a somewhat unstable Spanish Communist activist – and her son, Ramon, traveled to New York in 1939 where they set up a cover operation in the form of an import–export business, with Ramon rekindling a romance with Silvia Ageloff, one of Trotsky's American secretaries. Ramon had entered America on forged papers he had knocked up for himself in the name of Franck Jacson [*sic*] (the poor chap really wasn't the sharpest knife in the box) but because he had previously known Silvia in Paris in 1938, where he was known as Jaques Mormand, son of a Belgian diplomat, he managed to convince her that his new identity was a ruse to dodge military service. Silvia returned to Mexico in the October of 1938, with Ramon close behind, but before the trio had any thought of using Ramon as an infiltrator or lone assassin through his connection with Silvia, they tried a brute-force-and-ignorance play in the May of 1940. On the night of the 24th a 20-strong squad, including Ramon, broke into the compound and cut loose on the house with machine guns in the hope of striking lucky; they did not. Some say the squad was let in through the gates by one of Trotsky's own bodyguards, American Communist Robert Sheldon Harte (1915–1940), but his defenders refute this as preposterous. Maybe, but he was the only person taken away from the compound after the failure of the mission and, according to later statements from Sudoplatov, this was because Eitingon had already decided that if the blunt approach failed then Ramon was to be the stalking horse and he did not want to risk Harte's later recognition of him. Either way, Harte was taken away by the squad and shot.

Now resigned to the longer haul of subtlety, Ramon was told to up the ante with Silvia – talk of marriage and so forth – while Eitingon and Caridad went to Mexico to set up contacts with Gestapo men Christian Zinsser and Hermann Erben. (It was Erben's sustained contact and close friendship with pro-Nazi movie star Errol Flynn that gave some the concern that Flynn too might be an agent; this was never proved one way or the other.) The Gestapo began detailed surveillance, photographing every movement in and out of the target compound; Silvia was now working for Trotsky in Coyoacan and Ramon, now regarded as her common-law husband, became such a frequent visitor to the household that he ceased to be searched. Finally ready for the kill on August 20, 1940, Ramon drove to the compound with Eitingon and his mother following in the getaway car. Ramon had a dagger, a pistol, and *supposedly* the ice axe hidden in his raincoat; if this is true it must have been an

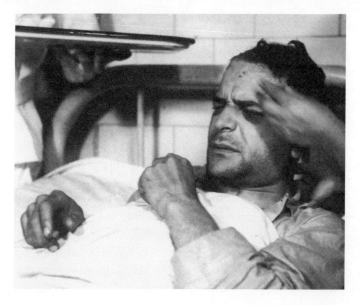

Mercader recovering in hospital after Trotsky's bodyguards and the Mexican Police had expressed their disapproval of his actions. (Topfoto)

awfully large raincoat to disguise the profile of such an implement with a foot-long haft and a similar blade span. It is the very use of such a weapon that raises the possibility of another "Harte" on the inside placing the axe somewhere handy for Ramon in case he failed to get his other weapons inside. Either way, Ramon got Trotsky into his office alone on some pretext and struck him right through the head with the pointy end of the blade as he looked down at some papers. Ever a game old bird, Trotsky turned and attacked Ramon, still wrestling with him when the guards burst in and still rational enough to demand he should not be shot but be made to talk. After that, Trotsky collapsed, dying the next day of irreparable damage to that fearsome brain, which even his enemies had to admire. Eitingon and Caridad, seeing a bloodstained Ramon being bundled away, thought all had gone pear-shaped and fled to Cuba, only returning to Russia when Trotsky's death was made public.

Throughout his arrest, interrogation, trial, and subsequent 20 years in jail, Ramon never once acknowledged the truth of his mission and never once implicated Russia, claiming instead that he had killed Trotsky for personal reasons. In fact, he never even admitted to being Ramon Mercader, constantly inventing fresh identities and motives until everyone gave up questioning him. There were two attempts to break him out of jail but both were foiled by Ramon himself blowing the whistle; not knowing that he was a hero in Moscow, he thought Stalinist assassins had come to break him out to silence him, whereas it was in fact his mum come to his aid. Finally released on May 6, 1960, Ramon was given a hero's welcome in Cuba before a similar reception in Moscow; for the next 18 years of his life he flitted between the two countries, lapping up the adulation. Caridad drifted into obscurity; Eitingon continued his career under Sudoplatov, infiltrating the American Manhattan Project and garnering high-grade intelligence from several on the project, including Oppenheimer himself, before doing something to upset Stalin and ending up in jail. After Stalin's death in 1953 he was released by Beria (1899–1953) but Khrushchev soon had Beria executed and Eitingon put back in jail for the rest of his life. Erben was executed by the Gestapo, who wrongly suspected him of double-dealing and Orlov, rightly judging himself to be top of the bill in Stalin's next paranoid purge, defected to the United States in 1938. Here he kept up a steady drip of information that was just enough to keep the Americans happy and confident that there was more to come. In fact one of his first revelations was designed to scupper the Trotsky assassination that he himself had set in motion.

Now determined to goad Stalin from the cloistered safety of American protection, Orlov sent a letter to Trotsky cautioning him to beware all newcomers and to double-check those already close; he knew there was an assassin coming to Mexico but did not know the identity as all had been delegated, and he could hardly phone home for an update. As a gesture of good faith, Orlov tipped off Trotsky that the man known as Etienne to the Paris Group, run by Trotsky's son, Lev Sedov (1906–1938), was in fact Mark Zborowski (1908–1990), an agent of the dreaded NKVD. Trotsky chose to dismiss the letter as a cynical ploy designed to destroy his faith and working relationships with those close to him and his son, which, as things turned out for both, was a big mistake. On February 8, 1938 Lev was admitted to a private clinic for a simple appendectomy and was making a normal recovery when he began to manifest a whole gamut of strange symptoms before dying in agony a day or two later. "Etienne" had tipped off the NKVD where Lev was being treated and they had sent in a couple of "wet-boys" to finish him off with one of their unpleasant toxins.

With Lev dead "Etienne" took over the Paris group and it was he who "fed" Silvia to Ramon Mercader to set in train the murder of Trotsky himself. The Nazi invasion of France forced Zborowski to flee to the United States, where he began an academic career with the help of Margaret *Coming of Age in Samoa* Mead (1901–1978), who got him established in Harvard as a research assistant. From here he co-published with Elizabeth Herzog *Life is with People* (1952), an internationally acclaimed study of Jewish life in pre-World War II Eastern Europe, still in print. Now an established medical anthropologist, Zborowski's life seemed sweet and stable but his past was about to catch up with him. By 1955 Orlov was scraping the bottom of his intelligence barrel so he exposed Zborowski, who, after courtroom machinations in front of a Senate Subcommittee trying to find out if his NKVD activities had continued in America, was found guilty and given four years for perjury. Upon release he returned to the academic life, publishing *People in Pain* (1969), a study of how pain is handled and endured in different cultures, before taking the post of Director of the Pain Institute at San Francisco's Mount Zion Hospital.

But what of Rivera and Kahlo; were they also involved? Both would later boast of having lured Trotsky to Mexico for the express purpose of having him killed but both were so awash with drink and drugs that anything they said must be taken with a very large pinch of salt. That said, Kahlo was most certainly in Paris at the same time as Mercader and not only closely involved with Lev's coterie but also on intimate terms with "Etienne" and co-instrumental in the introduction of Mercader to Silvia. Guilt by association is rarely helpful and frequently confusing, but it has to be said that the man who led the abortive machine-gun attack on the Trotsky compound on May 24, 1940 was none other than David Alfaro Siquerios (1896-1974), another prominent Mexican artist, a rabid Stalinist, and close friend of Rivera and Kahlo. It was immediately after that attack that Rivera's chauffeur was arrested while Rivera himself fled across the border into America to spend time with another of his conquests, screen star Paulette Goddard (1910–1990). Apart from their individual and old-fashioned motives – Rivera's revenge, and Kahlo perhaps miffed at being thrown over – both were clamorous for readmission to the Stalinist camp, which they duly were after Kahlo publicly denounced her now-dead former lover as a coward and a traitor to Communism who routinely stole things from the house while a guest. Both were taken in for questioning after the killing, but released.

Although eclipsed by her husband while alive, Kahlo was "discovered" in the late 1950s, her overpriced self-portraits now a must-have for the likes of Madonna, Tracey Emin, and other devotees of the present Kahlo-cult. But she makes an odd feminist icon. She was drink-sodden and drugged up to the eyeballs for most of the time; she was promiscuous, bisexual, hirsute, and mustached; completely besotted with her dominating tormentor, Rivera; narcissistic; hypochondriac-Munchausen, and seems to have had a great deal of difficulty separating fact from her own fantasies. On the other hand, she was by all accounts great fun at parties; always ready with a witty quip or a smutty pun. All her self-portraits dwell mawkishly on her own plight and, to be fair, she did harvest more than her share of ill fortune. Afflicted with polio in her youth, which left her with a withered leg, she was also at the age of 18 involved in a rather bad bus accident, during which a shard of metal pierced her vagina. That said, close friend Dr Leo Elosser, who also treated her for a number of years, was of the firm opinion that the inordinate trial of operations she underwent − 36 in all − were largely unnecessary and nothing more than ploys to seek attention from Rivera.

As for the ice axe, the last word at time of writing is that it still lies unsold and unloved in a box in Anna Salas's bedroom cupboard. The Trotsky Museum, in the house of the murder, say they want nothing to do with it and Trotsky's grandson, Esteban Volkov, refuses to give validating DNA material to prove the blood on the axe to be that of his forebear; without that, no one is willing to part with any serious money. Esteban's daughter, Dr Nora D. Volkow [sic], who looks scarily like her great-grandfather, is another leading American academic and Director of the National Institute of Drug Abuse where her work on the "mechanics" of addiction that take place in the brain has earned her international acclaim. So perhaps Stalin, Orlov, Sudoplatov, Zborowski, and Mercader all failed in the end; that famous Trotsky brain power seems to be marching on in her.

HIDDEN PLAYERS
IN MAJOR EVENTS

BLUEBIRD'S ROVER, THE WHITE CLIFFS OF DOVER

By the close of 1943, D-Day was barely six months away. The Allies had picked their landing beaches in northern France and gathered as much intelligence as they could regarding the defenses and troop-placements; the only thing they did not have and could get neither from the French Resistance nor from observation and aerial photography alone was soil samples. All the planning in the world would be useless if the physical formation of those beaches would not take heavy traffic. After a lot of digging, of the metaphorical kind, in some unbelievable ancient sources, it was finally decided that someone had to go across the Channel and take those samples.

Prior to this mission being sanctioned, Operation *Overlord* turned to some surprisingly non-military sources as assorted academics began rooting away in obscure archives held by the British Museum and others in private collections in Oxford. It was known that the sub-strata of the Normandy beaches consisted of peat and clay, and, as both these had been regarded as valuable resources by the Romans, Professor J. D. Bernal (1901–1971) was detailed to scan through the old Roman surveys of northern Gaul. Other sources examined included the 12th-century *Roman de Rou*, which detailed the flight of William the Conqueror, before he held such title, from Cherbourg through to sanctuary in Ries. The writer obviously had good knowledge of the Baie des Ryes, and where it was safe to ride at low tide, and there was also valuable information to be gleaned from the

14th-century documentary records of the protracted legal dispute between Le Sieur de Courselles and the French Crown over taxes raised against the harbor and beach facilities, as well as the peat-gathering rights. Moving forward, the 19th-century records of the Linnaean Society of Caen also gave good indications as to which reaches of the coastline were waterlogged marsh and which were stable. All such highbrow research was fine as far as it went but all it could do was pinpoint locations requiring hands-on investigation. This boiled down to Major Logan Scott-Bowden of the Royal Engineers and his sergeant, Bruce Ogden-Smith, swimming ashore under the German guns to dig holes in the beaches.

After dummy runs at Norfolk's Branchester Beach, during which the two volunteers proved their ability to get ashore with all their equipment and conduct surveys right under the noses of posted sentries, it was back to COHQ to meet Bernal for a briefing on the lay of the land before meeting another unlikely savior of D-Day – playboy and speed freak Sir Malcolm Campbell (1885–1948). He had been brought into the fold by Mountbatten, who was aware that, although a bit of a flash Harry, when it came to taking and "reading" samples from beaches and salt flats, few men alive knew more than Campbell, since he spent so much of his time driving up and down them at lunatic speed in his Bluebird dragster. In short, Campbell's "hobby" marked him out as the best consultant for the team, in that had he ever made so much as one mistaken reading of one core sample, then he would not then have been alive and talking to the two Royal Engineers about his home-made tool for the job. Nicknamed "Rover," because it could dig a hole as neatly and quickly as his favorite dog, Campbell showed the men how the powerfully spring-loaded contraption could punch a

14-inch core-plug out of any beach and then, at the push of another lever, piston it out into a suitable container for safe-keeping. Campbell said he found condoms to be best suited to the job but he also had with him some screw-topped metal tubes. Being "British," Ogden-Smith and Scott-Bowden opted for the metal containers, such coyness almost costing their lives.

On the night of December 31, 1943 they set out from under the shadow of the Dover cliffs in a small fishing boat, which they took to within a couple of miles of the enemy shore. From their anchorage it was an arduous swim to the beaches at Vierville-sur-Mer, Moulins St. Laurent, and Colleville-sur-Mer in the Omaha Beach zone before moving on to the Orne Estuary, which would play host to Sword Beach. Having made full use of Campbell's "Rover," by then fitted with solid rubber "bump-stops" for silent operation, it was back to the boat and it was on this swim that the weight of the now fully loaded metal pipes nearly proved their downfall. Seriously exhausted, both made it back to the boat to bring home the bacon for examination. Campbell knew that it took at least 14 inches of good sand to take wheeled vehicles and few of the cores showed anything like that. Worse still, some of the clay proved thixotropic, which meant it would turn to mush at the passage of the first heavy vehicle. And then there were the tanks to consider, so attentions turned to Major-General Sir Percy Hobart (1885–1957), a bit of a wild card but a genius when it came to solving problems with mobile armor.

Brother-in-law to Montgomery, it was Hobart who had set up and trained the Mobile Force (Egypt), better known as the Desert Rats, and he was also the chap responsible for modification to tanks such as the flailing chains to clear minefields and the double "coating" of bedsprings to stop bazooka projectiles striking square-on. In next to no time at all, Hobart unveiled his "bobbin" tank, which, carrying a massive roll of heavy-duty canvas, could lay before it a load-dispersing "road" up the beach for others to follow. On January 16, 1944 Ogden-Smith and Scott-Bowden returned to the French coast to take samples from other beaches but this time they went in the mini-sub the X20, which stayed on station as they made trips to and from the relevant beaches. This time the engineers took with them a large box of condoms.

⧉

CUSTER, BY THE SHORT AND CURLYS

The basic details of Custer's cock-up at the battle of the Little Bighorn have been debated to a standstill and it is now broadly accepted that, having refused a battery of Gatling Guns (which would have evened things up no end) and told the men to leave behind their sabers as there was not going to be any close-quarter fighting, Custer ignored all intelligence from his scouts regarding the size of the Native American encampment and, launching a doomed attack on a vastly superior force, he got a serious spanking. Pro-Custer websites and publications insist on emotive terms such as "massacre" and "slaughter," whereas it was simply an overwhelming victory for the home team. There was no great "Last Stand," rather a disorganized rout with some shooting themselves or their comrades to avoid capture, others trying to make a run for it leaving behind a few trapped pockets of men who were left with no choice but to fight to the death. Many of Custer's men were raw recruits in their late teens and early 20s who, far from battle-hardened, had not even learned to ride properly so it is fair to say that the Native Americans had little problem in wiping them out. Or did they? – wipe them out, that is. One of Custer's Crow scouts, Curly, certainly escaped and there were also six unaccounted for after the battle: three lieutenants, two enlisted men, and one doctor. Screeds were written about this disaster at the time but few of those authors bothered to read the accounts put down by persons peripheral to the event and it is on these we will concentrate. First there is the statement of the diminutive Bighead Kate, a Cheyenne woman who saw all from her vantage point above the conflict. Next the complementary statements made by the two Curlys, and the guarded comments from Frank Huston, one of the whites fighting with the Native Americans. Then there is the account of Custer's widow – not Elizabeth, but his Native American wife, Monahsetah –and those of the two female warriors credited with killing old Baldilocks himself (Custer's much-vaunted "Yellow-Hair" had deserted him long before June 25, 1876.) So, first the Short and then the Curlys.

Otherwise known as Antelope Woman or Short Kate, Bighead Kate was small but feisty and frequently observed battles at the request of her nephew, Noisy Walking, so she could write songs of his deeds. According to her, it was two small boys who, returning from their hunt, first brought word of soldiers in the area and all in the camp prepared for the attack. "I found a pony and followed the warriors, [riding] round the fringes of the fighting, staying out of range of the bullets as I searched for Noisy Walking. In this way I could see all of what was happening. More and more soldiers were getting off their horses, preferring to hide or crawl along the ground. The river became a focal point as bands of warriors moved toward the soldiers [crawling] toward them along crevices and gullies." As is known, other troopers made for the ridge, which also came under heavy attack: "As hundreds of Indians surrounded this ridge I saw one soldier point his pistol at his head and pull the trigger. Others followed his example, sometimes shooting themselves, sometimes each other." It was common practice to keep the last round for such purpose or have prearranged suicide pacts between friends, as a quick death was infinitely preferable to being taken alive by the Native Americans, who handed captives over to the women and children to "play" with. This group on the ridge was quickly overwhelmed and their guns and ammunition gathered up by the warriors who:

> walked among the white men, cutting off the legs or feet or arms of the bodies. Some of the soldiers were still alive ... but they were quickly killed and parts of their bodies also severed.
>
> When the shooting stopped the Indians thought all the soldiers had been killed but seven soldiers were still alive and rushed out from behind their [dead] horses and started running. I could not see what happened to these seven because of all the dust raised by the Indian ponies.

It was at this point that she again went in search of her nephew but, as things turned out, there would be no songs for Kate to sing as Noisy Walking was one of the 30 or so Native American fatalities. But the point is that her broad account not only matches the archaeological evidence from the site, but it jibes with almost every other Native American account of the encounter. It was a very short and brutal affair from which many soldiers, possibly Custer too, opted for a quick exit.

The more important of the two Curlys was the man erroneously known to whites as Crazy Horse (1840–1877). To his mother, Rattling Blanket Woman, he was always Curly, although his first given name, at the age of seven or eight, was Among The Trees, as he was always wandering off in a daydream. It was his father who was called Tashunca Uitco, or His Horse Is Crazy, on account of his psycho war pony. At some point in Curly's teens the pony died so, for reasons unfathomable, the father reinvented himself as Worm and handed down his old name to Curly, who thus became His Horse Is Crazy – but never Crazy Horse. It is worth pointing out here that many Native Americans had half a dozen names that ran concurrently and it is a myth of white invention that the Mother Nature-orientated naming structure for which the American Indians are famed derives from the father walking out of the birthing lodge and naming the child after the first thing he sees. So unfortunately for the wags who tell tales of a war chief called Two Dogs Humping, there never was any such person. In fact the Sioux, like many other tribes, deliberately *avoided* the giving of names at birth, preferring to wait until the child grew and developed characteristics or habits that suggested something apposite. And as that person grew and altered, so too would their name. His Horse Is Crazy Jr., for example, was also known by the respectful title of Slow One, because he always thought before he spoke and took his time over important decisions.

Anyway, slow or crazy, this was the man who planned the reception for Custer who, foolishly splitting his command into three, placed himself at the head of a column of 210 men to lead them to their doom at the hands of more than 7,000 Native Americans. Optimistic or what! There is little in

His Horse Is Crazy's account that differs from that of Bighead Kate, who was coincidentally his first cousin, but he does explain that, as the women and children fled north from the village prior to the attack, Custer set out in charge after them. His Horse Is Crazy split his command of perhaps 2,000 braves, half of whom placed themselves as a defensive wall between Custer and his fleeing quarry, while the balance subdivided into other columns, one to cut off any chance of Custer's retreat as others rode to outflank him. Apart from outnumbering the enemy ten to one, the Native Americans had about 300 of the new Winchesters, which outranged and out-everythinged the old-fashioned Springfield carbines carried by the soldiers. Also, His Horse Is Crazy seems to have had help and advice from a surprising quarter.

Apart from the unfortunates led by Custer, the rest of the soldiers at the Little Bighorn were under the sub-commands of captains Frederick Benteen (1834–1898) and Marcus Reno (1834–1889). It was Reno who led his column in a simultaneous attack at the opposite end of the village to that approached by Custer but, quicker than Custer to get to the meeting point, he pulled a sharp U-turn for what is now called Reno Hill. Here he dug in, soon to be joined by Benteen and his men, who, like Reno and co., saw little point in going to Custer's aid. Whether these men were possessed of a stronger sense of self-preservation than befits a military man or they were just plain realistic is now largely academic but the most interesting thing to come out of their collective statements is the repeated and consistent mention of bugle calls that seemed to be directing the brigades of Sioux and Cheyenne warriors in their various attacks. It seemed for all the world to the men on Reno Hill that there were cavalry-trained buglers, familiar with standard tactics, orchestrating the action from vantage points above the Little Bighorn.

This is far from impossible; countless Confederates refused to swear allegiance to the Union after the close of the American Civil War, with some heading south into Mexico and others, like Captain Frank Huston, heading west to join the Native Americans in *their* struggle against the dreaded Blue-bellies. Huston and several other non-natives were very much a part of that massive camp but he later denied having been there when Custer came a-calling. He always claimed to have been on the way back from a hunting trip at the time of the battle but would say, "But oh, how I wish I had been there to join the fun." And whenever questioned as to the presence and number of any other whites in the camp, he would always wryly ask the questioner to state who in their right mind would admit to having been there fighting on the side of the Native Americans in light of the incredible backlash of public opinion after the event. The only action to which he did admit was his having been part of the raiding party that broke Rain In The Face (1835–1905) out of jail in 1873 after he had been arrested and seriously beaten by Captain Thomas Custer (brother) in Fort Abraham Lincoln. This Lakota war chief freely admitted to being the one who had so seriously mutilated the body of Thomas Custer after the fighting at the Little Bighorn. American historian and editor Arthur Sullivant Hoffman (1876–1966) examined all Huston's statements and came to the conclusion that Huston had in fact been there for the battle, as in unguarded moments he let slip the odd snippet that would have been known only to someone who was there during the fighting. Hoffman also acknowledged that Huston was correct in his assertion that it would have been suicide for any white who publicly admitted involvement, so it is unlikely in the extreme that the truth on whites' involvement in the battle will ever emerge, unless, of course, hitherto unseen papers are unearthed.

The other Curly (1859–1923) was one of the four Native American scouts telling Custer that attacking the village would be sheer folly. (The other three were called Hairy Moccasin, Goes Ahead, and Whiteman Runs Him.) No matter what is seen in westerns, scouts were never required to engage in any action unless under attack but themselves, realizing the seriousness of their situation, all four had abandoned their uniforms in favor of their native garb, thinking this might best prepare them for the afterlife they felt sure was their imminent destiny if Custer had his way. Wrongly perceiving their actions as defeatist, Custer got quite shirty with them, saying he no longer needed them as he had found his village so they might as well toddle off. Needing no second bidding, Hairy, Goes, and Whiteman rode off while Curly remained at some little distance to see what would happen. His account of the ensuing engagement is pretty consistent with that of "Curly-Sioux" and Kate Bighead but, as his field of vision was restricted by the ravine in which he hid, his account has its blind spots. That said, the following is part of his debriefing as released to *The Helena Herald* in Montana and published on July 15, 1876:

Custer, with his five companies, after separating from Reno and his seven companies, moved to the right and around the base of a hill overlooking the valley of the Little Bighorn, and on through a ravine just wide enough to admit his column of fours. There was no sign of the presence of the Indians in the hills on the other side of the Little Horn [river] and the column moved steadily on until it rounded the hill and came in sight of the village lying in the valley below them. Custer appeared very much elated and ordered the bugle to sound a charge, and moved on at the head of his column, waving his hat to encourage his men. When they neared the river the Indians concealed in the underbrush on the other side opened fire on the troops which checked the advance. Here a portion of the command were dismounted and thrown forward into the river, and returned the fire to the Indians. During this time the warriors were seen riding out of the village by hundreds, deploying across his front to his left, as if with the intention of crossing the stream to his right, while the women and children were seen hastening out of the village in large numbers in the opposite direction.

As suggested by all other accounts, Custer thought he was going to have an easy day of it, riding down a whole village of women and children as he had done at Washita in 1868, except this time he charged in unaware that more than 2,000 of their menfolk were tooled up and sniggering in the bushes. With the fighting spreading out in a radial pattern as a result of the soldiers' running or riding in all directions in desperate bids for escape, Curly realized that his hiding place would soon be engulfed but also that riding out on his army mount might not be his best move. Breaking cover casually and on foot, he simply took a blanket from a dead Native American, wrapped it around himself, and strolled through the Native American lines, pausing here and there as if interested in what was going on, before making his way to safety. The other three scouts would also survive, having run into Benteen and Reno, and remained with those troops throughout their successful defensive action on Reno Hill. That said, Curly is generally accepted as being the only true survivor of the battle of the Little Bighorn – but there was one other, the romantically named Giovanni Martini.

Born in 1853 in Sala Consilina, Martini was always vague about his birth detail as he was a foundling whose baptism had been organized by the local mayor. His first taste of army life was as a drummer boy for old Garibaldi himself, and by 1874 Martini was in America, enlisting in the 7th Cavalry as a bugler. When Custer first spotted the village and its fleeing women and children, he summoned Martini and told him to ride for Benteen with fresh orders, bidding him come with all speed and to bring all the ammunition packs he had. A nearby Lieutenant W. W. Cooke, reminding Custer of Martini's somewhat broken English, scribbled down the order on a piece of paper, which, still extant, read: "Come on. Big village. Bring packs. W.W. Cooke. P.S. Bring pacs [sic]." And he thought Martini's English was bad! Anyway, it is known that Martini got through to Benteen, in whose effects that original note was found after his death, but by the time they made it the 3 or 4 miles back to the Little Bighorn Benteen thought it best to hunker down with Reno's men and leave Custer to his lot. Martini survived that stand on Reno Hill and retired from the army as a sergeant in 1904. He returned to New York and when not recalling old times in countless bars, he worked as the ticket collector at the 103rd Street subway station. Eventually the drink killed him; on Christmas Eve 1922 he was run over by a beer truck while making his way home unsteadily from protracted celebrations.

As to who actually killed Custer himself, this too is clouded because in the final rush on his ever-dwindling entourage the attackers killed anything that moved. But according to the bulk of Native American accounts and oral tradition, tales of his having committed suicide are groundless, as it was one of two women who finished him off. Most white sources (and how would they know?) say it was the Miniconjou warrior White Bull (1849–1947) who did the deed, but nowhere can be found any such assertion from White Bull himself; he only ever made a guarded statement to the effect that he did recollect a hand-to-hand struggle with a soldier who *might* have been Custer but he was in no way sure. Custer, a lieutenant-colonel at his death, not a general, is always imagined to have been standing proud to the end in a pristine buckskin jacket, white shirt, red necktie, and with his flaxen locks cascading from beneath his nice white hat, so who could fail to remember taking down such a figure? But he was riding in his shirtsleeves, he no longer had a cascading mane of yellow hair, and would be known only to Native Americans who had seen him before – or who knew him intimately. As stated, the ones who were there at the time have their opinion divided between two of the many female warriors fighting on the day – Native American society was nothing like its misogynistic and patriarchal white counterpart. The first, and it must be said the least-favored, candidate is Moving Robe Woman, whose version presents a problem in that her claim includes an Oglala brave called Fast Eagle holding Custer's arms while she stabbed him in the back. Unfortunately for her, the burial party sent days later to the area mentioned nothing about a knife wound in Custer, who was found in a sitting position, naked save one boot, with a bullet hole in his chest, another in the left temple (unbloodied and likely post mortem), and, intriguingly, his penis staked to the ground by an arrow – which may be more significant than someone's idea of a prank. On the other hand, blackened and swollen after a couple of days in the harsh Montana sun, any wound inflicted by a thin blade would by then pass unnoticed to members of the burial detail, who, understandably, just wanted to get clear of the site as soon as possible in case the Native Americans returned.

Custer, photographed here as a West Point cadet, and already showing the arrogance for which so many others would have to pay for with their lives. (Topfoto)

By far the more serious contender – and the one favored by the overwhelming majority of Native American accounts – is the more famous Buffalo Calf Road Woman (1853–1878), who just the week before had distinguished herself in the battle of the Rosebud on June 17. This had been a minor Native American victory, which halted the advance of General Crook and sufficiently delayed his joining up with Custer as to leave that detachment of 7th Cavalry out on their own at the Little Bighorn. At some point in the battle her brother, Chief Comes In Sight, was unhorsed right under the guns of the enemy and saved only by Buffalo Calf Road Woman taking her own war pony under those same guns to effect the rescue. On June 28, 2005 in Helena, Montana, a representative committee of the northern Cheyenne made a public statement that they were now happy to break inherited vows of silence over that last intriguing detail of the battle and state categorically their conviction that it was Buffalo Calf Road Woman who had killed Custer at the Little Bighorn. And so to the most intriguing of the hidden female players – the other Mrs Custer, Monahsetah.

On November 27, 1868 Custer attacked a non-hostile camp of Cheyenne under Black Kettle (1803–1868) on the banks of the Washita river in Oklahoma. Black Kettle and his wife were shot in the back as they tried to ford the river to safety and in all some 150 Cheyenne were killed, most of them women and children. After the carnage, Custer ordered the slaughter of more than 600 ponies, rounded up those who could still walk, and headed back to Fort Dodge. After the initial jubilation at yet another "great victory" for Custer, the truth leaked out and there was a tremendous backlash in the press as an increasing number of people started to suspect that Custer was not the golden boy all had previously thought. But the important thing as far as we are concerned here is that this is when he met Monahsetah, who, like Kate Bighead, was a close relative of His Horse Is Crazy. It is well established that many of the officers at the fort enjoyed intimate relationships with some of the Cheyenne captives and Custer grew increasingly close to the by all accounts rather beautiful, although heavily pregnant, Monahsetah. After she gave birth the following January it seems she became his "plains wife," as it was quaintly known, they going through a Cheyenne ceremony that, although it doubtless meant little to Custer, was regarded as a binding honor by Monahsetah. She went on to have a further child, almost certainly by Custer, but he soon tired of the "marriage" and gave Monahsetah her marching orders, blaming his other wife's jealousy as the cause. Elizabeth was certainly aware of Monahsetah's presence in the fort and must at some time have met her, as she wrote of her looks that were "not pretty in repose, except with the beauty of youth, whose dimples and curves and rounded outlines are always charming" and that when she smiled "the expression transfigured her, and made us forget her features." There is nothing to suggest that Elizabeth knew of their intimacy, but then it is hardly the sort of thing she would mention in her later writings, all of which were crafted to bolster up the false reputation of Custer the hero. On the other hand, most men are cowards when it comes to telling a woman that their relationship is over and maybe Custer invented Elizabeth's ire as a more palatable excuse than "I am just fed up with you." After all, this was a proud lady who had already kneecapped a Native American at the fort for his pressing his unwanted attentions a little too aggressively.

The fact that Custer alone was unscalped and unmutilated has caused all sorts of conjecture and speculation down the years; that he had perhaps shot himself and no Native American would touch a suicide – but half the troopers there likely shot themselves and were later hacked ~~them~~ up good and proper. It was out of respect for a noble adversary held in high regard – but the Native Americans hated the vainglorious and swaggering popinjay; after Washita, the Cheyenne certainly called him Squaw Killer. No, the arrow-through-the-penis suggests the gentle hand of a wronged woman and, according to surviving sources, that was the hand of Monahsetah. The mutilation and amputations inflicted on the dead by the Native Americans were not imposed out of mindless brutality, the thinking was to restrict that person's enjoyment in the next life; whatever "shortcomings" you took from this life you carried into the next, so it is pretty clear in which department Monahsetah wished her hubby-dear to be restricted. Apart from that one imposed "condition," she was most likely the one who asked others that, apart from her rather pointed comment, he be left untouched.

Naturally there are Custerphiles who pooh-pooh out of hand the very idea of his having a plains wife but many of Custer's contemporaries, Captain Benteen included, mention the liaison. In 1938 the aforementioned Sioux war chief White Bull returned to the Little Bighorn with David Humphreys Miller, the well-known historian and artist who sketched and took statements from all the participants who survived into the 20th century. Apart from discussing various parts of the battle in relationship to the landscape before them, White Bull recalled:

> While we were together in this village I spent most of my time with the Cheyenne since I knew their tongue and ways as well as I did my own. In all those years I had never taken a wife although I had been with many women. One woman I wanted was a young Cheyenne called Monahsetah, or Meotxi, as I called her. She was in her mid-twenties but had never married any man of her tribe. Some of my Cheyenne friends said she was from the southern branch of the tribe, just visiting, and they said that no Cheyenne could marry her because she had a seven-year-old son born out of wedlock. They said the boy's father had been a white soldier chief named Long Hair; he had killed her father, Chief Black Kettle in a battle in the south eight winters ago, they said, and

captured her. [The old warrior was a bit confused here; she was in fact the daughter of Chief Little Rock, also killed at Washita.] He had told her he wanted to make her his second wife, and so he had her. But after a while his first wife, a white woman, found out about her and made him let her go.

When asked by Miller if the child was still with her at the time of the battle he said: "Yes, I saw him often around the Cheyenne camp. His name was Yellow Bird and he had light streaks in his hair. He was always with her in the daytime so I used to have to wait until night to talk to her alone. She knew I wanted to walk with her under a courting blanket and make her my wife, but she would only ever talk to me through the tepee-cover and never came outside." In 2005 Gail Kelly-Custer published *Monahsetah: The Concealed Wife of General Custer* and, claiming to be Custer's granddaughter from that illicit union, is still trying to organize DNA verification of that claim. The more mainstream historian Mari Sandoz (1896–1966) certainly believed the story true, and as Nebraska's foremost writer specializing in the everyday lives of the pioneers and plains Indians, she refers to the relationship in what is perhaps her best-known work, *Cheyenne Autumn* (1953).

After Monahseta had bid her wayward ex *bon voyage* in her own inimitable style, the Native Americans broke camp, most heading for Canada to avoid the inevitable retaliations, which brings us to the burial details. The first and temporary graves were the hurried shallows dug by men from the column of General Terry, who arrived on the scene two days later – after 48 hours in the open, with the local fauna treating the site as a veritable smorgasbord, it would have been a hard job to know who was who. Unaware that the hostiles had in fact quit the area, the burial detail left at the scene completed their task with irreverent haste and left asap, ever fearful that another war party might come along. The butchered remains of the enlisted men were lucky to get a shovelful of dirt thrown over them, while the officers got shallow graves. The conjectured names of the men buried – many had their heads crushed under rocks or had been, quite literally, defaced with knives – were scribbled on bits of paper and stuffed inside spent cartridge casings, which were then hammered into the uprights of the impromptu grave markers. But who was *actually* in which grave would have been anybody's guess.

In the following July, and mainly as a result of relentless pressure from Elizabeth Custer, a detail under Captain Michael V. Sheridan (1840–1918) was ordered by his more famous brother, General Phil Sheridan, to go back to the Little Bighorn and bring Custer and his fellow officers home for proper burial. Captain Sheridan took with him the 1st Company of the 7th Cavalry under one Captain Henry J. Nowlan, who had overseen the original and hurried interments. Emigrating to America and taking a commission in the 7th Cavalry in 1866, Nowlan was a Sandhurst man who had fought in the Crimea and, it is said, survived the infamous Charge of the Light Brigade. There are also intriguing hints that he was actually related to Captain Louis Edward Nolan, the man whose garbled delivery of certain orders set the Light Brigade on the road to legend in the first place but, so far, this author has not been able to find any link between the two. Anyway, by the time Sheridan arrived at the Little Bighorn things were even more confused; all the shallow graves had been dug up by scavenging animals and the bones strewn among those of the skeletons left unburied. At a loss for anything else to do, Sheridan and his party simply filled up the Custer-coffin with one skull and approximately the right number of bones before nailing it shut, with Sheridan himself opining that it did not really matter if the bones therein were those of Custer or not, the only thing that mattered was that people *believed* they were. With the other coffins likewise loaded and nailed shut, Sheridan and his party came home to stand suitably stern-faced on October 10, 1877 as their box of bits and pieces was given an elaborate military funeral at West Point, the academy where, 34th out of the 34 in the class of 1861, Custer had come so close to expulsion that he could have saved everyone the trouble in the first place.

CAMELOT'S HEAVENLY MIST

At JFK's inauguration in January 1961, few paid attention to the unassuming little Japanese chap who sat quietly throughout but it can be argued that he – more than anyone – was responsible for the image of Kennedy as a war hero which won him the election, because he was the man who tried to kill him in 1943.

Late on August 1, 1943 a flotilla of 15 American torpedo boats was sent out to see if they could intercept what was known as the Tokyo Express, the group of Japanese destroyers that kept running supplies throughout the Solomon Islands to sustain the Japanese troops fighting there. Having had no luck, the bulk of the flotilla returned to base leaving three PTs on station in the Blackett Straits to see if they could catch the Express on its return leg. These were the PT 162, the PT 169, and the PT 109 under the command of the young and very inexperienced John F. Kennedy. No one really knows what happened in the early hours of August 2 as the three PTs sat in the water, engines idling and the props in neutral, because the 162 and the 169 fled the scene after the 109 was cut in two by a Japanese destroyer and the surviving members of the 109 were, naturally, never keen to discuss who or how many of them had been asleep at the time.

The intersecting vessel was the *Amigiri*, or the "Heavenly Mist," and according to Lieutenant-Commander Kohei Hanami who was on the bridge at the time:

We lacked fast transport vessels so five destroyers were assigned to deliver supplies to our men on Kolombangara. Although we knew we might encounter Americans at any moment, we reached the island without incident and the supplies were quickly unloaded. Now all we had to do was get back to Rabaul, through the Blackett Straits. *Amigiri* was the last ship to leave. The night was extremely dark with frequent rain squalls. I was on the bridge and at about 2am a dark object was sighted dead ahead but slightly to the right. By its size and profile I had to assume it was an American motor-torpedo boat. Our speed was 30 knots so I estimated we were not more than 20 or 30 seconds from collision. To veer away would have meant exposing our flank to torpedo attack from point-blank range so I gave the order to ram. Our lookouts scanned the waters for survivors but all they saw was bits of wreckage. The *Amigiri* began to vibrate almost immediately and I ordered engines stopped to investigate the damage. I suspected that one of the screws had been bent. The ship finally lost headway some 4,000 yards past the point of impact but there was little sign of damage to either the prow or the screws so we returned to Rabaul at 24 knots.

Two crew members died in the collision and another, Leonard Thom, was badly burned; although seriously bruised and dazed, the rest were OK, considering the circumstances. Having sustained the back injury that would plague him the rest of his life, Kennedy gathered his men together in the water, waiting in vain for the other two PTs to come to the rescue. The 162 had spotted the *Amigiri* as it loomed out of the dark and tried to fire two torpedoes but both presumably failed. After the collision the 169 did loose two more at the *Amigiri* but missed and then also departed. Since we know from Hanami's postwar statement that the *Amigiri* simply carried on after the impact, perhaps the kindest interpretation we can place on the actions of those two crews is that the devastating nature of the impact and subsequent petrol fire made them presume that no one could possibly have survived. Either way, both boats simply sped away, leaving Kennedy and ten others bobbing about in the water.

What happened next is fairly well known; with Kennedy towing the injured Thom, they all swam to Plum Pudding Island, which, only a few hundred yards in length and breadth, was no more than a resting station before they carried on to the larger Olasana Island. Here the crew remained while Kennedy swam on through the shark-infested waters, island-hopping until he managed to secure his men's rescue through eventual contact with an Australian observation post. Although this was without doubt a heroic effort, there were – and still are – those who interpret his actions as those of a man under an obsessive drive to assuage the guilt of having caused the predicament in the first place. No one has ever come right out and said that Kennedy himself was asleep at the switch, so to speak, but he is the only man of any navy in the world to have ever lost an MTB in such a way. His boat, for example, was powered by three

1,500hp Packard engines and with one twitch of the throttles the 109 would have been away like a scalded cat. Add this to the facts that the 162 certainly saw the *Amigiri* in time to attempt to fire on her prior to the collision; the *Amigiri* certainly saw the 109 some quarter of a mile off, and, finally, even if the crew of the 109 were awake and somehow miraculously failed to notice the *Amigiri* heading straight for them they certainly would have heard her – destroyers rampaging through the waves at about 30mph are not the quietest of things in the dead of night. Everything points to all or most of them, Kennedy included, being asleep at the time. Behind all the hullabaloo organized by the Kennedy clan to promote Jack the Zipper, as he was already known, to the people as a hero and savior of his men there were other more measured voices, such as those of General MacArthur and Admiral Nimitz, who were of the opinion that, instead of being awarded the Navy and Marine Corps Medal, Kennedy ought to face an inquiry to determine how all his men ended up in the drink in the first place. How could he, at the controls of one of the fastest, most responsive, and maneuverable crafts in the world, just sit there in the water while a lumbering destroyer ran him over?

But all such sanity was brushed aside by the power of the Kennedys, who made sure that the media as a whole went with the "right" slant to concentrate on the post-incident heroics, this paying dividends when JFK ran against Nixon in 1960. Although Nixon too had served in the navy throughout the American involvement in the war, he never saw action so the Kennedy publicity machine resurrected the wartime heroics and beat that drum until they won the day. What Hanami thought of the whole affair is unknown, as he only ever stated the bare facts as above, steadfastly refusing to be drawn into conjecture as to why the 109 just lay in the water like a sitting duck. The last surviving member of the crew of the 109, George Zinser, died in 2001 and, according to him, Kennedy still owed him five bucks.

—ᙇᔆᔆᙆ—

DON'T WORRY ABOUT IT! IT'S BREAKFAST TIME

By 3.30am on December 7, 1941, US Army Air Force Lieutenant Kermit Tyler was already on the road to his new duties at the information center at Fort Shafter on Honolulu. He was surprised that the car radio was picking up KGMB, a local radio station that played Hawaiian music, as that did not normally start broadcasting until 7am – but then he remembered a pilot had once told him that when flights were expected from the mainland, that station stayed on round the clock so the incoming pilots could use the signal as a homing beacon. Trouble was, the Japanese were also aware of this fact and were about to use it to terrible advantage.

As Tyler began his shift at 4am, privates Joe Lockard and George Elliot were already settling down to their shift in the radar observation station up on Opana, a small mountain on Kauku Point, they being last-minute substitutes for privates Lawrence and Hodges who had managed to fix themselves up with 24-hour passes. Of the two, Lockard was the more experienced radar operator so he kept an eye on the oscilloscope while Elliot maintained the log and generally pottered about. The American radar program was still in its infancy and yet, bizarrely, on most days, Sundays included, the lookout stations were manned only from 4am to 7am, and at 6.45am Lockard received a phone call telling him to shut down and "go get some breakfast." As the station was about 9 miles from their barracks and their return transport had not yet arrived, Lockard agreed to Elliot's demands for him to keep the system running so he could get in some training time on the screen.

Still familiarizing himself with the equipment at 7.02am, Elliot called Lockard over to look at an enormous blip moving toward them. "It was the largest group I had ever seen on any oscilloscope," Lockard would later report. "It looked like a main pulse [malfunction] and that is why I was confused at the time as to whether it was a flight or not." Elliot started to panic and say they should get on to "Little Robert," codename for the information center at Shafter but, according to Elliot's later statements, Lockard told him not to get so het up as: "Our problems ended at seven o'clock." With the blip now almost filling the screen, Elliot tried to phone on the tactical line but got no answer. When he tried the admin line he got a Private Joseph McDonald, who told him that everyone in the information center had gone for breakfast together, leaving the room unattended. Elliot told McDonald to get hold of someone – anyone – and make damned sure that person phoned him back at Opana. At 7.20am Lieutenant Tyler rang Elliot and, laboring under the misapprehension that what Elliot was looking at was an incoming flight of B-17s that was expected to land at just after 8am, told him to calm down, switch off, and go to breakfast. Elliot kept insisting that the blip, far too big for a small group of incoming "friendlies," was already 132 miles off Kauku Point and advancing steadily at 3 miles a minute, so it was too fast for a flock of geese, which was Tyler's other helpful suggestion.

Eventually Elliot realized that no one was going to take his concerns seriously and the call ended with Tyler uttering his immortal line: "Don't worry about it; go get some breakfast." And unfortunately that was that; Lockard and Elliot powered off and quit the station as Tyler went back to join his colleagues at their ill-advisedly collective breakfast, which would be rudely interrupted at 7.48am.

Hindsight is an easy weapon to wield and it is perhaps unfair to point the finger at Tyler alone as his mistake was but one command failure in a fatal chain of such errors and overall complacency. On top of all that, there was significant interservice rivalry on the island, resulting in the navy and the army hogging their own intelligence, each refusing to share with the other. Tyler's defenders maintain that by the time he was busy pooh-poohing Elliot's radar alert so he could get back to his breakfast, it was already too late for the fleet. Without doubt this is true, but that 30-minute warning would have been enough for the ships to be standing ready to make the Japanese pay heavily for waking their sleeping giant; it would also have dramatically reduced the nigh-on 3,000 ground casualties. But, as stated, Tyler was not the only complacent player in the pack. An hour before his conversation with Elliot, the USS *Ward*, a destroyer on routine patrol outside the harbor, had spotted and sunk one of the Japanese mini-subs and, despite the fact that the very presence of such a craft in the vicinity should have set off all the alarm bells, the report of the encounter did not filter up the chain until the attack was long over. Five days before the attack, on December 3, Admiral Kimmel, overall navy commander of the base, had actually received a warning from Washington telling him that all Japanese embassies and consulates were busily destroying their code machines and burning documents, so something serious was imminent.

For reasons best known to himself, Kimmel did not see fit to inform General Short, his opposite number in the army; had he done so perhaps those army-run radar stations would have been heeded no matter what they called in.

Going back even further, on January 27, 1941, Ricardo Rivera Schreiber, the Peruvian Ambassador to Tokyo, paid an urgent visit to American Ambassador Joseph Grew to tell him that he, Schreiber, had heard from several sources, Japanese and non-Japanese alike, that war was now being planned and that it would begin with a pre-emptive and surprise attack on Pearl Harbor. (This would coincide with the time it is now known that Yamamoto was putting the finishing touches to his plan for the strike.) In the summer of 1941, double agent Dusko Popov was ordered to Pearl by Berlin and, when he reported his mission to American intelligence in the August, he stressed that the very nature of the information he was ordered to gather made it obvious, even to a blind man, that Pearl was in the frame for a massive aerial assault. As the weight of such intelligence built up, on November 3 Grew again wrote to Secretary of State, Cordell Hull, to warn that: "War with the United States may come with dramatic and dangerous suddenness." In short, there were so many ignored warnings from so many high-level sources that it is little wonder that, within days of the attack, rumors (all false) were flying about that Roosevelt knew of the impending attack yet sat back and let it happen. And then there was the little-known British involvement.

Not only had the British Foreign Office been running a clandestine program through which they sent undercover experts, such as Colonel William Forbes-Sempill, to Japan to advise and oversee the building of the Imperial Navy's fleet of carriers but there was also rogue ex-Squadron Leader Frederick Rutland, who, long in the pay of Tokyo, had been funded by his Japanese paymasters to set up a dummy business near Pearl from which he could keep an eye on movements in and out of the harbor. As to how the Japanese overcame the problems of using torpedoes in shallow waters, the British had solved that problem for them too. On November 11, 1940 the British launched Operation *Judgement*, which was the first all-aircraft-on-navy attack in the history of modern warfare. The target was the Italian fleet riding at anchor in Taranto Bay Naval Base, which, like Pearl, drew only some 13 or 14 feet. Normally 100 feet of draft would have been needed for such an operation as torpedoes dropped from planes go pretty deep before coming up to their running depth. But British ingenuity had sorted out that problem by fitting plywood box-sections to the tails of the torpedoes and nose vanes so the torpedoes were arrested at their running depth as soon as they hit the water. Doubtless unaware that Yamamoto had already secured navy staff blessing for his Pearl plan in the preceding February, the British invited a handful of Japanese naval observers along for the ride and it was recalled how diligent they were in their observational duties; how attentive they were during the lectures on the modifications to the torpedoes, asking all manner of questions as others sat about looking bored. The Japanese were already conducting low-level practice attacks in Kagoshima Bay – which bore a striking resemblance to Pearl in many ways – and with the British modifications to their torpedo runs, they were ready for the real thing.

As for that incoming flight of B-17s that got Tyler off the hook; well, they made it in on time, many to be shot down by American ground-fire, which by then was being aimed in panic at anything in the sky. When the smoke cleared, everybody was left standing in a circle, pointing the finger at everybody else. The transcript of Tyler's inquiry can be seen in full at www.ibiblio.org/pha/myths/radar/tyler_4.html. Joe Lockard was hailed the Hero of Pearl by an excited press, and in March 1942 he was invited to Washington DC for a White House reception and presented with the Distinguished Service Medal. In August 1946 a rather miffed George Elliot refused the Legion of Merit on the grounds that it was an insult to present him with a lesser medal than Lockard's, especially in view of the fact that it was he, Elliot, who had badgered for the warning call to be made while Lockard was all for ignoring the whole shebang and following Tyler's lead to breakfast.

HIS MASTER'S VOICE?

Setting aside flights of fancy such as *The Eagle has Landed* (1976), Winston Churchill never used a double in any real sense of the word; there is apocryphal evidence that men of similar size and stature were employed to give any remote viewer the impression that he, Churchill, was within some secure building or at some airfield or other, but at no time did anyone, as was the case with Field Marshal Montgomery, parade themselves in public pretending to be Churchill. That said, it does seem that on one occasion the Germans mistook someone for Churchill and took the appropriate steps. On June 1, 1943 the tall and slim English actor Leslie Howard, best remembered for his role as Ashley Wilkes in *Gone with the Wind* (1939), flew out of Lisbon for Bristol in the company of his manager, the decidedly portly Alfred Chenhalls, and, to be fair, the pair did bear an uncanny likeness to Churchill

Norman Shelley, rumored to be the man behind some Churchill broadcasts during World War II. (Getty Images)

and his bodyguard, Walter Thompson. Churchill, accompanied by Thompson, was at the time on his way back from North Africa and the pair were occasionally known to blend in with the herd on regular civil flights to "hide" in the open, so to speak. Spanish and Portuguese airports, as part of an obvious route home, would most certainly be under special watch by the Germans but, either way, a flight of eight fighters was scrambled from Staffel 14 at Bordeaux with orders to bring that plane down. Eight fighters to go after one unarmed DC-3 would certainly indicate an unusual level of determination and Churchill himself was of the opinion that Howard, Chenhalls, and the others on that flight died for that reason, he expressing his regrets for such in his postwar memoirs. Nevertheless, while Churchill never used a body double it does seem he used a voice double.

BBC actor and voiceover artist Norman Shelley (1903–1980) claimed until his death that he had on several occasions during the war stood in for Churchill on broadcasts when the PM either was too busy to make it to the studios or when it suited the intelligence services for the Germans to think he was still in Britain when he was in fact elsewhere. Others have since embellished these claims by stating that Shelley also had to stand in on occasions when Churchill was too drunk, but this is nonsense sitting uneasily on the widely believed myth that the man was a soak; he was not. The myth of Churchill having run the war in an alcoholic haze is largely based on a habit he acquired in South Africa and India, where it would have been folly to drink the water. He and many others on such military service would add a shot of whisky per half pint of water to render it safe, and this would be used for anything from quenching the thirst to brushing the teeth; Churchill simply never got out of the habit. The tales of his constant drinking are based on the fact that he always liked to sip water and kept to hand a tumbler of whisky- or brandy-tinctured water that can have only registered a fraction of one percent alcohol per volume. On the other hand, he is widely recorded as having admonished those drinking neat spirits that they would not live long with such a habit and in 1936 won a bet with Viscount Rothermere about his abstaining from drink for a year, all of which makes it clear the man was no toper. But what of those broadcasts and extant recordings of famous speeches such as the "finest hour" and "fight them on the beaches"? Whether Shelley made live broadcasts from the BBC, pretending to be Churchill, to fool the Germans into thinking him safe in London, we shall never know, but the quality of his Churchill impersonation and the fact that in war deception is a valuable stratagem make it far from impossible, especially given the fact that actual BBC recordings of Shelley as Churchill have come to light.

Any suggestion that Churchill was "doubled" on broadcasts and recordings still draws heavy fire from certain quarters, not least from The Churchill Centre, which, as one might expect, flatly rules out any such possibility. In the BBC written archives, there is a recording/broadcast agreement signed by Churchill on the majority of occasions, but not for all his alleged appearances. Historian and journalist Christopher Hitchens has raised questions about the apparent contradictions between BBC recording times and dates, and Churchill's diaries placing him elsewhere at the time. Robert Parker, the sound expert working on the Churchill recordings that were to be used in the television series *Britain at War*, started to notice niggling little incongruities that only became apparent to a trained ear when the recordings were played one after the other for comparison: "Two in particular stick out. 'We shall fight them on the beaches' and 'Never was so much owed by so many to so few.' The voice seems different on both and so does the speech impediment."

More recently, Sally Hine of the BBC sound archives wrote to the *Guardian* newspaper to confirm that Shelley had indeed been sent to the Regent's Park Transcription Studio to record the "fight them on the beaches" speech and in 1990 this was one of 20 "authentic" Churchill recordings sent over to the Sensimetrics sound laboratories in Massachusetts for rigorous comparison against known recordings of Churchill's voice. Their results were quite clear: the three most famous recordings, "fight them on the beaches," "finest hour," and "blood, toil, tears, and sweat" ("blood, sweat, and tears" is a more recent corruption) were undoubtedly made by someone other than Churchill. Finally, in 2000 Shelley's son, Anthony, uncovered some forgotten storage box in the attic of his father's house in Chepstow, South Wales, and in it found an old BBC 78rpm recording labeled "BBC. Churchill Speech: Artist Norman Shelley: 7th September 1942." This was Shelley doing a recording of the "fight them on the beaches" speech, speaking as if Churchill, and speaking to the technical staff as himself afterwards.

ICE-CREAM TERRORISTS

The importation of camels into Australia was something of a double-edged sword as things turned out. The first stock arrived in October 1840 and these animals, ideally suited to the outback, were pivotal in the opening up of the Australian interior, right through to Alice Springs. The Ghan, the famous 3,000 kilometer-long train that traverses the continent, takes it name from its following the transcontinental route opened up by the Afghan "camel-wranglers" who ran the caravans, and it was two such men who instituted the first Jihad-inspired terrorist attack against non-Muslims in modern Western culture.

The so-called battle of Broken Hill in New South Wales was instigated by a frothy-mouthed rant by Turkish supremo Enver Pasha (1881–1922), the erstwhile leader of the Young Turks' rebellion that put him in power in 1908. Pasha could not understand why the Allies of World War I regarded him as hostile and a legitimate target just because he had thrown in his lot with Germany, so he called upon all good Muslims, wherever they be, to rise up and smite the infidel. Most let his words wash by but this call to Jihad was not ignored in Camel Camp, just outside Broken Hill, where neighbors Badsha Mohammed Gool and the Mullah Abdullah sat sulking over the latter's recently imposed fine for continuing to slaughter animals in the Halal manner in non-authorized buildings, in contravention of New South Wales legislation. Spurred on by significant intake of the strong marijuana that Gool kept in abundance, the two malcontents decided to attack the new year's picnic train that was scheduled to take revelers from Broken Hill to their annual junket at nearby Silverton. Comprising 40 open trucks, each accommodating 30 people, this was picked on as an easy and soft target.

Armed with a Snider rifle, a Martini-Henry, two pistols, and as much ammunition as they could find, these first modern Islamic jihadists set out on their mission on January 1, 1915 in Gool's camel-drawn ice-cream cart, by then sporting a home-made Turkish flag. They lay in wait for the train, and when the cart was in plain view, opened up on the unarmed men, women and children, who, at first misunderstanding the terrorists' intentions, unfortunately stood up and cheered what they mistook for celebratory gunfire to welcome in the new year. As people began to fall, the full horror of what was happening dawned on the remaining passengers, who took belated cover. Fortunately the guard on that particular run was a local sharpshooter called Eric "Tiger-Eye" Nyholm, who, from his van at the rear, returned fire of such accuracy that Gool and Abdullah rushed back to their ice-cream cart and took off. The incident was immediately reported to a nearby army base at Cootamundra, which sent out a detachment under the command of Lieutenant Richard Resch. Joined by countless locals brandishing personal arms, the ever-increasing posse set out after Gool and Abdullah, who, having shot at any who crossed their path, were now holed up in a formation known as White Rocks and settled in for a siege.

In the ensuing three-hour gunfight the only injuries to the "home team" were the result of friendly fire, some of which, given the date, was more enthusiastic than accurate. Gradually the terrorists' return fire dwindled and became sporadic as Abdullah was dead and Gool wounded. Deciding that he was not quite ready for the glories of any warriors' paradise, Gool, grossly underestimating the level of animosity his little venture had engendered, stood up with a white rag attached to the muzzle of his Martini-Henry. Despite Resch's call for a ceasefire, Gool was immediately shot. On Resch's orders, the bodies were taken back to the still-extant mosque at Camel Camp for disposal but the Muslim community, to their credit, said they were so disgusted by the men's action that their bodies would profane their place of worship and could not be admitted. Where the remains ended up is not known but, with the local dingoes unlikely as fastidious as the imams at the mosque, that is probably how the locals chose to recycle the rubbish. Not long after the incident, Resch married local girl Emma

Fletcher, assuming her name to shed the German roots of his family. While several members of his family were herded into the notorious Holsworthy interment camp for hostile aliens, just outside Sydney, he continued his career in the Australian Army as one of the most prolific recruiting officers in the territory. "Tiger-Eye" Nyholm also married, to produce the son who would become Sir Ronald Sydney Nyholm (1917–1971), the internationally famous chemist.

CHURCHILL HEADS FOR PORTES IN A STORM

There were, as one might expect, several attempts to assassinate Churchill during World War II – even the maverick Otto Skorzeny led an abortive attempt, on Hitler's instruction, to kill him, Stalin, *and* Roosevelt at the 1943 Tehran Conference – but none got so close to success as Helene, Countess de Portes (1902–1940), the petulant and slightly unhinged paramour of the French wartime leader Paul Reynaud (1878–1966).

Born Helene Rebuffel in Marseilles, she soon proved to be something of a headstrong handful and, when not ensconced in private Swiss clinics, she enjoyed unleashing her considerable sex-factor on any man she thought might be useful. Deciding that a title might be rather handy in the circles at which she had set her cap, she married the penniless Comte de Portes before abandoning him in search of bigger fish. More a social mountaineer than a mere climber, her course of self-advancement was unswerving until she eventually began rubbing shoulders, and other anatomical bits and pieces, with the high-profile financier and politician Reynaud in the mid 1930s. To give some indication of the cynical set of the woman's attitudes, knowing Reynaud to be married, de Portes first made it her business to meet and befriend the wife to get her measure before making her move on Reynaud himself. Having built up a psychological profile and a pretty accurate idea of what Madame Reynaud would be likely to tolerate and what she would not, de Portes closed in for the kill and Reynaud folded quicker than France itself under the forthcoming German invasion. All were amazed; Reynaud was a little chap, possessed of such boundless energy that his friends called him Mickey Mouse, and de Portes was hardly a thing of beauty; she had slightly protruding teeth, a sallow complexion, a braying laugh, and a somewhat coarse demeanor. However the lady was without doubt intelligent and focused, and possessed of her own brand of "boundless energy" in other departments. In a nutshell, de Portes harbored the ultimate ambition of ruling France, as a satellite of a victorious Germany, through the bedchamber like some latter-day Madame Pompadour. Yet again, so many lamented, the destiny of France was held firm in the grip of an ambitious woman's thighs.

De Portes made no secret of the fact that she was a fan of Hitler and thought France's best option was to sign an armistice with Germany as soon as possible, becoming a willing participant in whatever came with that; nor was Berlin unaware of her political inclination. Her immediate objective in the opening months of 1940 was to do anything she could to break Reynaud's links with Churchill and Roosevelt, both of whom were anxious to keep France onside and actively resistant to Germany for as long as possible. Her game moved up a notch on March 21, 1940 when her lover became the French Premier but, to her fury, Churchill moved into Downing Street on May 10, which, coincidentally, was the very day that Germany began the invasion of France. De Portes now became even more dominating of Reynaud, and all observers – French, British, and American – stood agog at the way she ordered him about and insisted on being involved in all meetings and policy decisions. Sometimes she even dismissed Reynaud, telling him to go take a nap while she would "see to any matters of state that might arise." The British Sir Edward Spears (1886–1974) regularly saw her chairing cabinet meetings and once, when he demanded to know the whereabouts of the latest telegrams from London, she loftily informed him that they were in her bedside cabinet and that when she had a minute she would send someone to fetch them. Roosevelt's main eyes and ears in France was diplomat William Christian Bullitt (1891–1967), who did not mince his words in telegrams to the White House that informed the president that Reynaud was "completely dominated" by de Portes and "no longer had any control over her." Whenever Reynaud and Bullitt were drafting telegrams to Washington, de Portes would rant and rave until certain words and phrases were toned down or altered completely. Bullitt would later record that he felt he had no option but to take a leaf out of the French history books and "flatter and pay court to the King's mistress" if he wanted to get anything done. On June 12 she actually went as far as visiting another American diplomat, Anthony J. D. Biddle (1896–1961), to announce (falsely) that she was there on Reynaud's explicit instructions to instruct Biddle to inform Washington that all his, Reynaud's, previous telegrams should be ignored, as the situation was now so bad that a French armistice was the only sensible option. But the lady's best party trick was yet to come.

By June 1940 the French government had decamped to Tours and, perhaps rashly, Churchill decided to pay Reynaud a visit on June 13, in the aftermath of Dunkirk. In the company of his trusted bodyguard, Walter H. Thompson (1890–1978), Churchill landed at the already badly bombed airfield at Tours to find no one on hand to meet him. (De Portes' hand was likely behind that little "oversight.") Thompson had first been Churchill's bodyguard in 1921 but retired to run a greengrocer's shop only to be recalled by Churchill himself in 1939, despite his age. Ever competent, Thompson hot-wired an abandoned car and the two drove into Tours where they pounded on a few doors, eventually tracking down Reynaud and his entourage in the prefecture. With the Germans by now in full advance, the residents of Tours must have been more than a little bemused by the sight of the British prime minister and a greengrocer stamping around their town barking questions in atrocious French.

Anyway, having done all he could with Reynaud, through threats and promises, Churchill was bidding farewell to the French government-in-exile when Thompson became aware that de Portes was making her way steadfastly across the room, her slightly scary expression setting off alarm bells in his head. Not the sort of chap to balk at gunning down his hostess, even if she was the "fleur-de-lit" of the French prime minister, Thompson covertly drew his .45 automatic and stood ready. Suddenly de Portes' intentions became clear as she lunged at Churchill's throat with the knife she had hidden. Thompson was within a gnat's whisker of firing when the others present brought her down. As she was dragged screaming from the room there followed one of those embarrassed "Good Lord, is that the time?" moments before Thompson bundled Churchill back into their stolen car and away to the airfield.

Churchill returned to the UK unscathed, while Reynaud resigned on June 16 and, with de Portes in tow, made a dash for Bordeaux in a journey cut short by a crash. De Portes died of a broken neck and Reynaud was led away from the scene in handcuffs, with minor injuries, to be handed over to the Vichy French. After a short stay in a hospital in Montpellier, Vichy-French leader Marshal Pétain (1856–1951) passed Reynaud onto his German masters for safekeeping.

As for the Winnie-killer *manqué*, to label de Portes a Nazi spy, as some have done, is going way too far, but it is also fair to say that, upon the successful conclusion of the German invasion, few would have been a more enthusiastic collaborator. But in this she would not have stood alone, as millions of French, Vichy or not, would soon demonstrate. (Even the high-profile Coco Chanel whiled away the Occupation, sharing a suite in Paris's prestigious Hotel George Cinq with her Gestapo lover and knocking up posh frocks for high-society Hitler-chicks.) That said, with Berlin being long aware of her sympathies and proximity to Reynaud, it is inconceivable that they did not have some Svengali-like character close to her, declared or not. It is, of course, only conjecture but any one of Reynaud's inner circle could well have been such a traitor, briefed to ensure de Portes kept up the pressure for the German cause. Who knows, but the heirs of both Reynaud and de Portes successfully sued prominent French writer Jean-Jacques Servan-Schreiber (1924–2006), founder of the 4.5-million-readership *L'Express*, France's first weekly news magazine, which he set up in 1953 to throw a spotlight on the French Indochina War (1946–1954). In his *Passions* (1991), Servan-

Schreiber repeated old falsehoods concerning the depth and "intimacy" of de Portes' connections to Berlin before he trotted out the other old chestnut concerning the boot of their crashed car being filled with the government's gold bars. In the year of publication the author had to stump up the equivalent of about £25,000 in today's money.

Reynaud, ever the survivor, returned to the French political arena in 1946, and despite being 71 still had enough of his "boundless energy" left to marry a much younger woman and father three children, before dying on September 21, 1966. Thompson married Churchill's secretary, May Shearburn, and retired for the second time in 1945. The next year, with Churchill out of office, he wrongly thought there would be no problem with publishing his memoirs; as Churchill's bodyguard he was paid the princely sum of £5 per week – perhaps £250 at present values – so he was likely in need of the money. Instead of there being no problem, he was threatened with loss of pension if he proceeded. That pension totaled an impressive £353 p.a., which left Thompson having to supplement his income by collecting rents for Romney Council and moonlighting in pest control. So, after much deliberation, Thompson decided he simply could not afford to proceed in the hope that Whitehall was bluffing. During the 1950s highly edited and sanitized snippets of Thompson's recollections were allowed to be published in dribs and drabs, but it was not until after his death in 1978 that his grand-niece, Linda Stoker, found the complete 350,000 word manuscript in the loft of his Somerset home, allowing *Beside the Bulldog* (2005) to finally see the light of day.

THE FOOL MONTY

In the lead up to the D-Day landings of World War II, there were countless operations designed to keep the Germans guessing where the strike would be. All of these were, naturally, designed to divert attention from the Normandy coast and was none more audacious than Operation *Copperhead*, which relied on keeping an Australian sober for five weeks.

A couple of months before the scheduled landings, Lieutenant-Colonel J. V. B. Jervis-Reid was leafing through a copy of *News Chronicle* when his eye was caught by a picture of what he first thought was Field Marshal Montgomery in the uniform of a lowly lieutenant. The tagline under the photograph read, "No! It's not!" The text explained that the man in the picture was actually Lieutenant Meyrick Edward Clifton James (1898–1963), an Australian serving in the Royal Army Pay Corps. For some that might have been the end of the matter but Jervis-Reid happened to be Second-in-Command of the Special Means Committee, which was responsible for most of the aforementioned deceptions; and James's picture had given him an idea. Still unable to believe the likeness, Jervis-Reid made a few discreet inquiries to establish that James did indeed bear such a striking resemblance to Monty and had been reprimanded on several occasions for amusing his mess mates with decidedly off-color impersonations of his more elevated double. Not only that, but when he had enlisted in 1940 his application was for the entertainments section as he had been an actor for the previous 20 or so years.

His mind made up, Jervis-Reid made a phone call to a colonel he knew in the British Army Film Unit and asked him to get James up to London on some pretext or other. That colonel, none other than actor David Niven, delegated the task to his lugubrious batman, Corporal Peter Ustinov, who told an elated James he was to present himself in London for a screen test to see if he was suitable for morale-boosting films. James was even more excited when he got to his audition to see that not only was he the sole attendee but that David Niven was there to put him through his paces. James was asked to strike all sorts of poses, walk about, read a bit of Shakespeare, or whatever, before Niven asked him to give them a laugh with his Monty gig. James was thanked and told he was to stay in London for the foreseeable future and that his unit would be informed. Niven, Ustinov, and Jervis-Reid looked over the rushes from the day's work and agreed that while the physical likeness was without doubt more than enough to fool anyone, the voice, mannerisms, and stance were all wrong and required work. Worst of all, when James reappeared in the morning he was obviously still a bit the worse for the previous night's indulgences and smoking like a chimney. Monty abhorred both vices and would not even tolerate others to drink or smoke in his presence. Knowing they had to have James ready to fly to Gibraltar on May 25, he was put in the picture, told he was on the wagon with no more cigarettes, and as he had lost most of the middle finger from his right hand during action in World War I he would soon have a prosthetic one glued to the stump.

With the involvement of yet another "deceptions" officer, Wing Commander Dennis Wheatley (1897–1977), better known today for his satanic thrillers, James was put through a grueling crash course requiring him to study hours of films

Australian actor Clifton James with his mini-me. James doubled as Montgomery throughout World War II, to deceive the enemy. (Topfoto)

and recordings of Monty so he could perfect the man's mannerisms, voice, and gestures. Finally, with time running out, James had his appearance altered so he could be attached to Montgomery's staff for a week and observe up close and personal. While James was dogging Monty's footsteps and noting all his idiosyncrasies, British agents throughout the Mediterranean were busy spreading false rumors about Monty being due any day to make a tour of inspection in preparation for a massive invasion of southern France. At 6am on May 25 James, suitably attired, strolled out of Whitehall and waved to the assembled mob of well-wishers and the tipped-off press before climbing into Monty's own staff car, which was waiting to take him to RAF Northolt. At the airfield there was another crowd, which had been infiltrated by intelligence officers spreading rumors that Monty was flying back to North Africa. This certainly fooled the British press into their famous headline of "MONTY FLIES BACK TO FRONT," which, along with "THE EIGHTH ARMY PUSH BOTTLES UP GERMANS IN NORTH AFRICA," remains a World War II classic.

With the false Monty settled on the plane, his group of minders relaxed and took their eye off the ball as, perhaps giving in to stage fright, James took himself off to the restroom. Unfortunately and unbeknown to his minders, he had managed to smuggle on board a bottle of Dutch courage and was busily guzzling Monty's treble, let alone his double. When his continued absence from the cabin caused sufficient concern for the restroom door to be booted in, James was so gassed that the initial and quite gentle cures – black coffee and such – soon gave way to more animated and desperate measures: fingers down the throat before his head was wrapped in a wet towel and shoved out of the emergency portal to give him a blast of fresh air. Unsurprisingly, by the time they landed James was sober – terrified but sober – and it was decided that from then on he would be accompanied by two minders at all times; if they appeared to observers to be acting like paranoid bodyguards, so much the better. Either way, from that point on James was not even allowed to visit the bathroom on his own.

There were more crowds to wave at on landing before James, reeking of peppermints, was whisked away to the residence of the Governor, Lieutenant General Sir Thomas Ralph Eastwood (1890–1959), who as a friend of the real Monty was at first not sure if the plan had been cancelled and he was in fact shaking hands with the full Monty; to be fair, James really was that good when sober. With showtime over for the while, James was locked in his bedroom at the residence by his "booze-cruisers," who let him out only in time for the official party that evening. Eastwood had made sure he invited a couple of prominent Spanish bankers who were wholly unaware that British intelligence knew all about their dealings with Berlin. During the evening, James and Eastwood made for a good double act with James openly musing about Plan 303 and the invasion of France, just north of the Spanish border, and Eastwood tugging at his sleeve and staring sternly at him until he said, "Yes, quite. Quite right, old boy," or some such.

The next day the *Copperhead* team, with Eastwood, returned to the airport where one last game was played out. The captain of their plane said there would be a delay due to minor engine problems so James and Eastwood, under guard, retired to the airport facilities for some tea. Positioning themselves near the bar that was known to be staffed by two pro-German Spaniards who pretended not to speak English, James and Eastwood went into a huddle and spoke at length of the imaginary Plan 303 – whether the planned landings at Les Landes might not be augmented by a secondary force hitting further up the coast at, say, La Rochelle, and so forth. With the non-existent gremlins banished from the engines, the team flew to Algiers where James had several highly visible meetings and tours with General Maitland Wilson (1881–1964), Allied Commander in the Med. After a few days of hushed meetings, appearing on the balcony with maps to wave out to sea, and other theatricals, Operation *Copperhead* was stood down, with James being "un-Monty'd" and flown to a seedy hotel in Cairo. Here he was again locked in his room until D-Day was over, but this time he was given all the booze he wanted just to keep him docile. According to Wheatley he was treated "rather shabbily" before being returned to the Pay Corps where he spent the rest of the war with everyone thinking he had been off on a six-week bender. As soon as the Ten Year Rule was exhausted, James published *I Was Monty's Double* (1954), which, four years later, was made into a film with James playing himself and Monty. By 1963 the bottle got him, and when approached by the press for a comment, Montgomery said, "He was not a friend. I only met him the once. Of course, he observed me a great deal. He did a very good job and fooled the Germans at a critical time of the war. I am sorry to hear of his death."

—◦◦◦—

FOX-ON-FOX

Until 1946 it was generally accepted that Field Marshal Erwin Rommel had died of the injuries sustained when his car was strafed off the road in France, whereas he had, as all now know, been forced to take poison on direct orders from Hitler, who wrongly believed him to have been involved in the Valkyrie bomb plot.

Late in the day of July 17, 1944 Rommel was preparing to leave the command post of 1st SS Panzer Brigade, under SS General Sepp Dietrich (1892–1966), when he paused to ask him a very dangerous question; would he, Dietrich, follow Rommel's orders under any circumstances, even if they were in direct conflict with directives issued by Hitler? Dietrich was not the first high-ranking officer that Rommel had sounded out in such manner, but perhaps he was the most dangerous to be asked such a question in that he was an old-timer who had risen through the ranks having started out as Hitler's chauffeur. After a long pause Dietrich's answer, as witnessed by Captain Helmuth Lang, was that Rommel's orders would override anyone's directives, even those issued by Hitler. Nodding his satisfaction, Rommel got back into his open-topped Horch staff car with Lang, Major Neuhaus, and an enlisted man, Feldwebel Hoike, whose job it was to keep a lookout for the Allied fighters that plagued the area after gaining superiority in the air over northern France. Rommel's driver, Daniel, was speeding along the N179, just outside Livarot, when a Canadian Spitfire popped up out of the blue and let loose a three-second burst of 20mm cannon fire, which, at 300 yards, was more than enough. Daniel, dying at the wheel, lost control and the car ploughed off the road into a ditch from which Lang and Neuhaus escaped with minor injuries; Rommel, on the other hand, had such serious head injuries that the military days of the Desert Fox were effectively over.

The attacking pilot, who had not a clue as to the identity of his target, was Canadian Charles Fox (1920–2008), who, perhaps inevitably, picked up the nickname of the Flying Fox. On landing back at Beny-sur-Mer, the Normandy base of RCAF 412 Squadron, Fox made his report, giving a pretty accurate indication as to the location of the incident, and left it at that. It was only after word got out that Rommel's car had been shot off the road that all the spurious claims came forward, notably that of American pilot Lieutenant Ralph Jenkins, who claimed to have completed said task in his P-47 Thunderbolt. Unfortunately for that particular glory-grabber, there is nothing in the logs to indicate he was even in the air that day, let alone in the vicinity of Livarot. Besides, Rommel, Lang and Neuhaus were adamant the attacking plane had been a Spitfire with Canadian markings and Fox, and his wing-man, Steve Randall, were the only two Allied planes of any make or nature known to have been in the area at the time.

Actually, Fox has another flying distinction to add to his strike on Rommel; he also flew the very last Allied air patrol of World War II. On the evening of May 4, Fox's Wing Commander, Geoff Northcott, stood up on a chair in the mess at their airfield at Wunstorf and called for silence so he could read out the message: "From 83 Group to all units. All hostilities on the Second Front will cease at 0800 hours tomorrow, the 5 May 1945." Realizing there would be some serious partying that night he further cautioned that he would be leading the routine dawn patrol, last day of the war or not, and that pilots Bill Klersey, Don Gordon, and Charles Fox would be taking off with him at 6.30am so they had best bear that in mind while at the bar. All four landed back at Wunstorf at 8am having seen neither hide nor hair of the enemy, who were in all likelihood still too drunk themselves to fly. Ironically, Fox would be the only one of that group to long survive the war. Klersey was the first to go, flying into a hill in fog on May 22, just outside Wessel, in Germany; when Gordon had been operated on in Holland to remove minor shrapnel from his back and neck they evidently missed a bit, which shifted against his spine and killed him in 1948, and third to go was Northcott, who, on returning to Canada flew a time for Air Canada before dying in a horse riding accident in 1958. Fox outlived them all, with a varied life throughout which he maintained links with his old unit and comrades. In fact, he was on his way home from one such reunion in Tillsonburg, Ontario, and was still in uniform when *his* car ploughed off the road, leaving him dead at the wheel.

As for Rommel, he was still recuperating from Fox's attack when Hitler decided he should die. Although none of the Valkyrie plotters had given any implication of Rommel's involvement before they ended up twanging on piano wire, Hitler was irked by Rommel's well-known opinion that

Germany was losing the war and simply had to come to some kind of accommodation with the Allies, including, as thought Patton, that they should team up together and go for the Russians. On October 14, 1944 generals Wilhelm Burgdorf (1895–1945) and Ernst Maisel (1896–1978) were told to sign out a car and driver and pay the field marshal a visit. Rommel must have known they were coming because at about 11.30am that day he suddenly went upstairs and changed into his Afrika Korps uniform and stood waiting, with his field marshal's baton under his arm, in the hall of his house near Ulm.

According to his son, Manfred:

At about midday a dark-green car stopped in front of our garden gate. Two generals – Burgdorf, a powerful and florid man, and Maisel, small and slender – entered the house. They were respectful and courteous and asked to speak to my father alone. A few minutes later I heard my father come upstairs and go into my mother's room; anxious to know what was going on I followed him. He was standing in the middle of the room, his face pale, and bid me follow him to my room. Here he informed me, "I have just had to tell your mother that I shall be dead in fifteen minutes. The house is surrounded and Hitler is charging me with high treason. I am to have the chance of dying by poison. The two generals have it with them. It is fatal in three seconds. If I accept then none of the 'usual steps' will be taken against my family. They will also leave my staff alone."

Hardly the most touching of fond farewells, but that was Rommel to a T; straight to the point, and no time for "ifs" or "buts." At this point Rommel's aide, Captain Hermann Aldinger, joined them, he already knowing the bare bones of the matter and aware of the futility of any resistance as the whole area was swarming with SS and Gestapo, so Rommel assured him, "It is all prepared down to the last detail. I am to be given a state funeral. I have asked that it take place at Ulm. In a quarter of an hour you, Aldinger, will receive a phone call from the Wagnerschule Hospital in Ulm to say that I have had a brain seizure on the way to a conference. I must go. They only gave me ten minutes." Pausing at the door, he told Aldinger that he had no knowledge or prior warning of the Valkyrie plot and that, effectively, a deathbed statement from a man like Rommel can be taken as unimpeachable.

Outside, the driver of the Opel, SS Sergeant Hans-Hermann Doose, leaped to attention and opened the doors for all three to get in. It was a very short ride. Just a few hundred yards from the house Doose was ordered to pull over onto a verge, where all but Rommel got out. From the woods appeared the troops that were meant to shoot Rommel and everyone in his house if he offered the slightest resistance or objection. After a few moments Doose was told to go and check inside the car, which he did, just in time to hear Rommel's last gasp. He put the field marshal's hat back onto his head and then, most likely, it was Doose who stole Rommel's baton, stuffing it inside his tunic before standing up to announce to Bergdorf and Maisel that all was as it should be.

The world was told that Rommel had died as a result of the injuries inflicted by Fox in France, and he did get his state funeral – with Hitler sending a wreath so big it would hardly fit through the church doors. The whereabouts of Rommel's baton remains a mystery; there are many replicas on display in various collections but the original is believed to remain hidden in Swabia.

THE ANNE FRANK
BLACKMAILER

In 1950 the American publishing house of Alfred A. Knopf rejected a manuscript they deemed "A very dull read ... a dreary record of typical family bickering, petty annoyances, and adolescent emotions. Even if the work had come to light five years ago, when the subject was timely, I don't see that there would have been a chance for it." Having previously thrown out *Animal Farm* (1945) on the grounds that "animal stories are just too hard to market," Knopf had to eat vast quantities of humble pie as the private musings of Anne Frank sold over 30 million copies worldwide. Although widely known as *The Diary of Anne Frank* this has never been the title of the book, which was first published in 1947 in Holland as *The (Secret) Annex: Diary-notes from 12th June 1942–1st August 1944*; the title used for the English/American edition was *Anne Frank: The Diary of a Young Girl*, and the first mentioned was in fact the title of a 1955 Broadway stage production that was responsible for so many of the present misconceptions surrounding Anne and her life in hiding. Anne was no "sliced-white" angel and the Franks were not hiding in solitary in one cramped room, but with others in a suite of rooms comprising over 500m^2; so, before looking at the bit-players in this tragedy, perhaps best to examine the realities.

As Hitler rose to power in Germany, Otto Frank (1889–1980) thought it prudent to move the family to Holland, where he seems to have seriously underestimated the Nazi threat to the Jews of that country – even after the German invasion of May 10, 1940. Julianne Duke, who had lived next door to the Franks in Amsterdam, recalled after the war that her parents saw the writing on the wall and made a hurried exit for the United States, asking the Franks to accompany them. Apparently Edith Frank (1900–1945) was all for it but husband Otto "saw no need to leave Holland. He trusted in man's basic goodness, rather than focusing on the darker, irrational side of human nature." That misplaced trust, which would claim his entire family, eventually gave way to a cold realization of what the Nazis had in mind for all Dutch Jews, thus prompting Frank to kit out the annex of his business premises for long-term hiding and enlist the help of several very brave and trustworthy people to keep his family supplied. When shipment papers arrived for Margot Frank (1926–1945), Anne's older sister, the family retreated to that suite of rooms and prepared to sit out the war.

Family friend and business associate Hermann van Pels joined the Franks in 1942, along with his wife, Auguste, and their son, Peter. On November 16 the group was informed of the dire straits of Jewish dentist Fritz Pfeffer (1889–1944) and agreed he could join them. Thus there were eight people in hiding with a support team of about half a dozen, most of whom worked for the Franks' business, so it is a miracle that the annex kept its secret for more than two years. Anne's diary was begun a few days before the family went into hiding, but because several versions have seen light of day, this alone gives license to Holocaust deniers and other loonies to hail it all a fake. Anne was well into her labors when she heard a broadcast from the Dutch government-in-exile asking all citizens under the jackboot to keep a personal record of events for postwar publication. Harboring ambitions for a career in journalism, Anne laboriously rewrote her diary, eschewing the parts she thought best not made public. The work subsequently underwent postwar bowdlerization by Otto, for reasons that will become obvious. Puberty is not an easy time for anyone, especially if you are locked up in a suite of rooms with immediate family and a bunch of strangers, and Anne had

Anne Frank, second from right, with her sister and parents, 1941.
(Topfoto)

a tendency to be extremely bitchy and unjustly critical of all except her doting father. The aforementioned play also gave the impression that the work included a sugar-sweet "Disney" glimpse of the romantic awakening of a young girl, because it censored all rudeness of the original writing, sanitizing her private world.

As was perhaps inevitable, the group was eventually betrayed and Gestapo officer Karl Silberbauer (1911–1972) led the raid on the annex on August 4, 1944. With all eight under arrest, Silberbauer grabbed the box containing Anne's papers and notebooks and tipped it out onto the floor so he had a container for the collection of his prisoners' papers and personal possessions. All except Otto would die in the camps but leading light of the support team, Miep Gies (1909–2010), a close friend of the family and supervisor of their spice and pectin business, gathered up the fallen papers, thinking to keep them safe for Anne until after the war. She would later say that they lay unread in a box until Otto's lonely return and that had she read them she would have burned them, as Anne had made pretty free with the names of all the support team and the black-market suppliers.

The fate of Anne is a sad and well-documented fact, but her real story did not begin until Otto started his campaign to make public an edited version of her musings from the annex. Sales were not that great until the 1955 play by husband-and-wife team Frances Goodrich and Albert Hackett, whose previous endeavors had been award-winning but restricted to musicals and comedies such as *Easter Parade*, *Seven Brides for Seven Brothers*, and *It's a Wonderful Life*, so it is perhaps little wonder that such a team largely ignored the reality of the original diary notes to present a sugar-coated version, complete with villains and buffoons within the group, to make the story "acceptable" to American audiences. As can easily be imagined, in doing so they managed to upset many of those still alive and the descendants of those who weren't. Needless to say, the play was a roaring success and, brushing aside any angry correspondence from relatives of those maligned and critics pointing out the fact that the play bore little or no resemblance to Anne's writings, they decided it was time to approach Hollywood. If anything, the 1959 Goodrich–Hackett screenplay took even more license with the core material and forever set in stone the toothsome-Annie image. Otto, who was constantly falling out with the writing team, wanted Audrey Hepburn to take the lead but she refused, saying she was already committed to other projects and that by then she was too old to play a teenager. She was also undoubtedly, and rightly, concerned that the very nature of the film might drag up the fact that while Hepburn herself had lived in the Netherlands throughout the German Occupation, both her parents were Fascist sympathizers. Either way, as a part of what many – Otto included – saw as a systematic de-Jewification of the whole sorry saga, the lead went to the obviously non-Jewish Millie Perkins (b. 1938).

Despite its acclaim and awards, the film was spawned by the town that gave us *Braveheart*, films showing American forces effecting the crucial capture of the Enigma machine, and other historical inaccuracies; even Anne's time in the camps and any reference to her death was eschewed after test audiences complained they didn't like unhappy endings. Instead, after the arrest, the camera pans skyward with a suitably inspirational voiceover. Between their play and the film, Goodrich and Hackett foisted upon the world the image of Anne as some terrifying meld of saint and ever-smiling martyr instead of the sexually aware and stroppy little madam she actually was – a perfectly normal teenager, in other words.

Pfeffer's widow, Charlotta Kaletta (1910–1985) complained bitterly to both the writers and to Otto over her husband being presented as "Mr Dussel" or Mr Nitwit, a drunken buffoon who knew nothing of Jewish culture and tradition whereas, according to any who knew him, Miep Gies included, he was a tall, handsome, and cultured man who was a master of Hebrew and not far short of rabbi standards when it came to matters of Jewish tradition. Goodrich–Hackett wrote back saying that she had to understand the realities of commercial theater/film and if they had stuck to the truth then their play would have folded on the first night. Her demands to have the wrongs of the play righted in the film fell on deaf ears and Charlotta was but one of many who wrote in protest to Otto Frank, who, to be fair, had by then lost all control over the production. Not content with depicting Pfeffer as a bumbling oaf, Goodrich and Hackett had Hermann van Pels creeping round the annex at night stealing food and otherwise acting to the detriment of the group, with his wife unfairly morphed into a "Hyacinth Bucket"-type character, more concerned with the condition of her fur coat than with others' needs or problems. From that point on Charlotta and quite a few others cut their ties with Otto Frank and refused to have anything to do with him or those, such as Miep Gies, who remained in his camp. But who was the hidden player; who betrayed the Franks to the Gestapo?

Over the years, suspicion has been focused on several people, some close to the Franks and others with but remote connection. Some have unkindly conjectured that, fearing exposure was inevitable anyway, someone on the support team struck an immunity deal with the Gestapo. It must be said that it is most unusual that apart from those arrested, only two other people at the address, Johannes

Kleiman and Victor Kugler, were carted off to prison. The premises at 263 Prinsengracht were hardly cramped; the hidden annex ranged over two floors and the rest of the building housed Otto Frank's pectin and spice business, Opekta, which employed several people. It is hard to believe that there was anyone at that address who remained oblivious to the presence of the owner, his family, and four others on-site − if only from the amount of food being brought in − and to suggest that only a few were aware of such presence across two years is plain stupid. The Gestapo were many things, but "stupid" did not feature on their list of qualities so it is unlikely that they would have fallen for the rolling-eyed denials of all at 263; normal procedure would have been to presume all were involved to one degree or another and put the lot up against the nearest wall as a warning to others in the city. Either way, the 1947 publication of the Dutch edition of Anne's writings rekindled interest in the case and public demands for an investigation to find the traitor.

The 1948 inquiry, conducted by the Amsterdam police, interviewed Miep, Kleiman, and Kugler, before turning their attention to the Opekta warehouse staff, especially Willem van Maaren and Lammert Hartog, as the latter freely admitted that, two weeks before the arrests, he and van Maaren had discussed the potential danger presented to all by the Jews being hidden upstairs. Hardly the most officious or probing of inquiries, the matter was let slide as inconclusive and had it not been for a bunch of neo-Nazis kicking off in a Vienna theater in 1957 that might have been the end of the matter. During a translated performance of the Goodrich−Hackett play in that city, a bunch of Holocaust deniers stood up to mouth off about the whole story being a hoax. One member of the audience stood up to confront them and was challenged to prove it all true by tracking down the arresting officer, Silberbauer. Unfortunately for the neo-Nazis, that man was Simon Wiesenthal and he willingly took up that gauntlet to embark on his career as a Nazi-hunter.

Finally, in 1963, he found Silberbauer working in the city's police, just around the corner from the theater. Silberbauer was subsequently suspended pending an inquiry, which found he was only obeying orders and, because Otto Frank himself had come before them to testify that Silberbauer had behaved impeccably throughout the arrest, he was allowed to resume his normal duties. But the whole affair was again in the spotlight and, with Frank's post-trial statement to the press that it was not the arresting officer but the traitor who should be found and punished, another inquiry was set up.

Increasingly, the 1963 focus tightened on Hartog and his wife Lena, she having been "forgetful" in 1948 about mentioning the fact that she worked as a cleaner at 263 Prinsengracht. Further digging revealed she also cleaned for Petros and Anne Genot, who worked for a company owned by Kleiman's brother. When interviewed, Anne Genot stated that in late July 1944, Lena had told her of the "stowaways" at 263 and how she felt their presence to be a grave danger to her husband and everyone else at Opekta. But yet again the inquiry was inconclusive.

But now it seems that Otto Frank's little-known collaboration with the Nazis provides the key. Although he certainly held no regard for the Nazis, Otto had no problem in doing business with them and garnering the profits. He was also careless about what he put into writing and to whom he wrote disparaging remarks about Holland's new "friends." One such anti-German letter fell into the hands of a Dutch collaborator and informer, Joseph Jansen, who lost no time in sending it into the local party headquarters where it landed on the desk of Dutch Nazi Anton "Tonny" Ahlers who hooked it out of the system and stuffed it into his pocket with plans of private gain. Although an anti-Semite with a criminal record, Ahlers himself was doing business with Frank through his own company and so popped round to see him, ostensibly to save the Franks from immediate deportation and certain death. Unfortunately, he also began to blackmail Frank. In the lead-up to the arrests of August 1944, Ahlers was supplementing his income by betraying Jews and members of the Dutch Resistance at 40 guilders per head, and by July 1944 his own company had gone bust, leaving the survival of the Franks and their friends no longer of any financial benefit to him. With the "contents" of the annex worth about 500 guilders – the Nazis built a quantity bonus into their incentive schemes – Ahlers turned them in. Although imprisoned for such activities after the war, Ahlers never owned up to the betrayal of the Franks, as it would certainly have gone seriously against him in the climate of 1945, but he would later boast of his part in their downfall as testified by his brother, Cas, and his son Anton. He also continued to blackmail Otto after the war and right up until his victim's death in 1980, this time the lever being the Opekta dealings with the Nazi occupiers. In the postwar witch-hunt for collaborators, Frank felt he might lose his firm to confiscation if the truth became known and, after the rise of the whole Anne Frank phenomenon, it would hardly do any good if he was revealed to have been dealing with those who killed his family. According to Cas and Anton Jr., Tonny lived pretty well until his gravy train crashed in 1980, when he again became morose and increasingly drunk and violent, his wife finally leaving him in 1985 after he tried to mow her down with his car; grounds for divorce if ever there were. Apart from the evidence of members of his own family, which at the end of the day is only hearsay, there is a host of circumstantial and corroborative evidence pointing to Ahlers as the betrayer of the Franks, not the least of which is the fact that one of the officers accompanying Silberbauer on the raid was Maarten Kuiper (1898–1948) who lived with Tonny and his wife. Among the catalog of crimes for which he was executed was his disgusting shooting of Dutch Resistance heroine Hannie Schaft, aka The Girl with the Red Hair.

But there was another family in hiding, in the building facing 263. On the other side of the Merwedeplein the Geiringer family had gone into hiding in a remarkably similar style to the Franks. Although the families knew one another, both were at the time ignorant of each others' situation; the Geiringers had gone into hiding a few months before the Franks and they too lasted an incredible two years until their betrayal in May 1944. Father Erich and son Heinz died in the camps but the mother, Elfiede (1905–1998) and the daughter Eva, a friend of Anne's, survived. In the confused horror and chaos of the liberated Auschwitz–Birkenau, these two bumped into Otto and accompanied him back to Amsterdam. Otto and "Fritzi" married in 1953 to settle in Basle, Switzerland and Eva (b. 1929), now Eva Schloss, lives in the UK. Her own account, *Eva's Story: A Survivor's Tale by the Step-Sister of Anne Frank* (1988), is itself extraordinary but unlikely to become as famous as Anne's.

THE GIRL WHO STOPPED A WAR?

Although few will know her name, it is a fair bet that most readers will have in their mind an image of the iconic photograph of the little Vietnamese girl running naked and burning up the road in shock. It is also a fair bet that most will also "remember" it was an American napalm drop that caused her agony and that her plight, once made public, was instrumental in the American withdrawal from Vietnam. All false.

Born in 1963 Kim Phuc lived in the innocent and insignificant village of Trang Bang, which on June 8, 1972 found itself in the middle of a minor engagement. The accepted version of events has Kim and her family taking refuge in the pagoda of the Buddhist temple when it was napalmed by American planes, killing her two brothers and maiming her in the condition so vividly recalled. The iconic photograph, that would come back to haunt her in later life, was taken by Nick Ut of Associated Press, who drove her to hospital in nearby Saigon where she endured 17 separate operations across the next 14 months, most of these conducted by American plastic surgeon Dr Mark Gorney, who had flown out from San Francisco. With treatment concluded, Kim returned to Trang Bang while the world did its best to forget all about her, but her image would not go away. Ten years later in 1982, the Vietnamese authorities dragged her out of medical school to be touted about as a symbol of the war, this being her lot in life until she and her husband, Bui Huy Toan, managed to slip off a plane during a refueling stop in Newfoundland in 1992 and successfully claim political asylum in Canada; both still live in Toronto. Unfortunately for Kim, she was then and still is "the girl in that photograph," this epithet dictating the path of her entire life.

On Veterans Day 1996 she was invited to be the star attraction at the opening of the Vietnam Veterans Memorial in Washington DC. After her introduction, which trotted out all the old inaccuracies, Kim rose to give a carefully crafted speech in which she spoke of her forgiveness of the pilot responsible, but not once taking the opportunity to correct any of the inaccuracies in the introduction. The very fact that she was standing at the monument to talk of forgiveness only reinforced the notion, held by most, that American forces had been responsible for the air strike. And then came the "miracle." Vietnam veteran and newly ordained Methodist minister the Reverend John Plummer moved toward her to confess, "I am that man." The crowds went wild as a tearful Kim and Plummer hugged and beamed, cheek-to-cheek, into the cameras so anxious and perfectly positioned to record this "spontaneous" and emotional "closure" for posterity. Naturally, the whole thing had been rehearsed well in advance and, as things turned out, Plummer was a complete fraud. Once in the spotlight, Plummer swiftly shifted ground to stress that he was not the strike pilot, merely the coordinator who called in the air support, but he did not have to worry; his fame, albeit short-lived, was assured. With his byline, "I still hear the screams of the children," Plummer became an overnight celebrity, even appearing in President Clinton's Second Inaugural Parade, wearing a cavalry Stetson, identical to that made a famous symbol by Robert "I love the smell of napalm in the morning" Duvall in *Apocalypse Now* (1979). Wearing such a hat, he waved enthusiastically at the crowds from a Vietnam-era attack helicopter that was towed through the streets on a float by other Vietnam vets; how is that for taste and sensitivity?

But this was 1997 and the truth was closing in on Plummer and his little bandwagon. The following November the Third Regional Command logs were declassified to show that the suspicions of the few in the know were well-founded. Photographer Nick Ut had always maintained that there were no American troops within 100 miles of Trang Bang, which, on the day in question, had been the focus of an exclusively North–South Vietnamese conflict: this had long been the standpoint of other journalists in the zone, such as New Zealander Peter Arnett, also of Associated Press, Fox Butterfield of the *New York Times*, and UPI Television's Christopher Wain. These men, and others, had always been adamant that the napalm drop was made by an old prop-powered Skyraider of 518 Squadron, South Vietnamese Air Force; it was not a deliberate act of enormity but, as explained below, an error typical of those forced by the kind of split-second judgment that has to be made in the heat of battle. The strike had not been directed by Plummer, who turns out to have been in a bunker 50 miles away at the time, but by the 25th Divisional Commander of the South Vietnamese Army. Kim had not been hiding in any temple but was running up the road when hit, her two brothers escaping unhurt. Ut took them, along with their aunt and uncle, to the same hospital to be with Kim. The main casualties of the disaster were other South Vietnamese troops.

The collective memory often plays tricks of suitability and convenience to make sure that certain events go into certain pigeon holes, but it is a simple matter of fact that by the time

Kim suffered her fate there were fewer than 6,000 American troops in the whole of Vietnam; the withdrawal was all but complete. Her suffering stopped nothing, certainly not American involvement and certainly not the war itself. Long before June 8, 1972 it was planned that all American troops would be gone by March 1973, which was well before the fall of Saigon on April 30, 1975, despite some harboring false memories of American troops still being there at the time. The firebombing of children is an inexcusable horror and, while the Americans are innocent of the Trang Bang incident, there were countless other children not so "lucky" as Kim.

Perhaps the last word on the incident should be left to Christopher Wain, who had a full view of the tragedy. According to his eyewitness reportage, the village was not the target at all; the South Vietnamese air force was striking at enemy positions well outside Trang Bang. At one point many of the South Vietnam troops and a few civilians, including Kim, broke from cover and began running out of the village and towards established South Vietnamese positions. The pilot of the Skyraider, noticing these running troops, thought them to be an enemy attack squad and suddenly diverted from his path to bomb them with napalm. Naturally keen to preserve his anonymity, the pilot, now apparently living in America, has confirmed this to have been his own terrible error of judgment.

A FEW WRONG TURNS

History is littered with examples of serendipitous navigational error, the most celebrated "wrong turn" being that of Douglas "Wrong-Way" Corrigan (1907–1995), the pioneering aviator who took off from New York's Floyd Bennett airfield on July 17, 1938, bound for California, only to land at Dublin 28 hours later. Corrigan's wrong turn was front-page news around the world but had no far-reaching consequences, which is more than can be said for the inability of Lieutenant Colonel Franz von Harrach (1870–1934) to tell *his* left from right.

As a member of one of the most important families of the Hapsburg territories, von Harrach had been selected to stand bodyguard for the Archduke Franz Ferdinand during his ill-fated visit to Sarajevo on June 20, 1914. Unbeknown to him, or indeed anyone else, a team of assassins had already been selected and given the details of the planned route for the entourage and were standing ready with guns and grenades. The only thing operating in the authorities' favor was the fact that the team comprised of rank amateurs whose main appeal to the Black Hand that recruited them was their avowed willingness to commit suicide after the job was done, to prevent any back-trace. But no matter, in view of what happened on that day it is a miracle that World War I ever got started.

Positioned in order along the route the precedence was as follows: First was the 27-year-old carpenter and Muslim extremist Mehmed Mehmedbasic, whom the motorcade passed at about 10.10am. He did nothing. Moving about the crowds was the unarmed "supervisor" of the operation, Danilo Ilic, to whom Mehmed muttered something about the bomb failing to activate and the gun jamming, before he disappeared into the crowd. Mehmedbasic was the only member of the team to escape. Next down the line stood 17-year-old Vaso Cubrilovic, who also failed to act, later claiming that he had come out without his glasses and did not want to risk hitting an innocent bystander; some assassin! Next up to bat was the sterner Nedjelko Cabrinovic. As the motorcade drew level with him he hit the percussion cap of his bomb against a lamp post and tossed the bomb in a high lob of remarkable inaccuracy that intervening events almost made good. Harrach, hearing the percussion cap explode, thought the car had just blown a tire and called upon the driver, Leopold Lojka, to pull up. The bomb was by now arching through the air and, as Lojka turned to query Harrach's instruction, he saw the incoming device and put his foot down. It is a fair assumption that Cabrinovic's lob would have gone wide of the open-topped limo had it remained unseen but, with Lojka's lurch forward, three things happened; first Harrach lost his grip on the side of the car and was flung off the running board and, second, the bomb was put on-target. Franz Ferdinand also spotted the flying bomb and put out a defensive and deflecting arm, which caused the device to glance off his elbow, hit the folded-down canvas canopy, and "trampoline" off that to detonate under the following vehicle, causing injuries to quite a few of the occupants and nearby members of the flag-waving crowd. Thirdly, Lojka crashed into the back of the leading car, which was carrying the mayor, Fehim Curcic, and Doctor Gerde, Sarajevo's Commissioner of Police.

Two of Archduke Franz Ferdinand's assassins, Princip and Cabrinovic, photographed with Ciganovic, who supplied the weapons for the attack of June 28, 1914. (Topfoto)

With some semblance of order hurriedly restored, the motorcade moved off again at a smarter pace as Cabrinovic swallowed his cyanide capsule and threw himself into the River Miljacka for good measure. Unfortunately for him, not only was the river at that point a matter of inches deep but the suicide capsules were duff, leaving him ankle-deep in the Miljacka and being violently sick, before the mob dragged him out for a serious going-over. Meanwhile the motorcade passed by yet more ineffectual assassins, 18-year-old Cuetko Popovic, 19-year-old Trifiko Grabez, and, finally, Gravilo Princip. Only Princip stayed the course; even though he had heard the bomb, he remained on station and ready to act but, as the cars approached and he reached inside his coat for the gun, the crown surged forward for a better view, pinning him helpless against a lamp post until the motorcade had passed. Seriously disgruntled, Princip crossed over Appel Quay, along which his quarry had passed, and wandered down Franz Joseph Street to Moritz Schiller's deli-café, where he sat at a pavement table, eating sandwiches, drinking coffee and brandy, and wondering what to do next.

By now the motorcade had reached the reception point where the Archduke gave the mayor and the commissioner a piece of his mind, before the former, at a loss for anything else to do, launched into his prepared speech: "Your Royal and Imperial Highness. Our hearts are filled with happiness..." as Franz Ferdinand sat "hurrumphing" throughout. Civic festivities were cut short by Ferdinand's insistence on visiting the hospital to check up on those injured in the blast so, with the mayor's car again taking the lead, the two-car convoy set off back down Appel Quay and into history. Not long into the journey the mayor's car turned left off the Quay instead of turning right across the Lateiner Bridge. In a fluster, Harrach kept shouting at Lojka to turn left, while he in fact meant to say, "Turn right!" Lojka, not even realizing that the mayor's car too had got it wrong, assumed Harrach's instructions irksome and unnecessary as he could plainly see where he should turn, and so with Harrach still shouting, "I said turn left, you fool!" Lojka did just that; he turned left into Franz Joseph Street. Realizing the error, the mayor's car had already stopped, right outside Schiller's deli, where Princip sat drop-jawed at his good fortune. As he approached the Archduke's car, Lojka spotted the raised pistol and tried to reverse out but his foot slipped off the accelerator and got jammed under the pedal. Princip simply strolled up and fired the shots that would start World War I.

Casting aside his pistol or, by other accounts, having it wrested from him, Princip shouted something unintelligible and swallowed his suicide capsule. He was still writhing around in his own vomit as bystanders closed in to increase his discomfort. Whatever the capsules contained, it certainly wasn't the cyanide that the assassins were led to believe. Lojka regained control of the car and sped off to seek medical aid but both the Archduke and his wife were mortally wounded and died shortly after. According to Harrach himself:

As the car quickly reversed, a thin stream of blood spurted from His Highness's mouth onto my right cheek. As I was pulling out my handkerchief to wipe the blood away from his mouth, the Duchess cried out to him, "In Heaven's name, what has happened to you?" At that she slid off the seat and lay on the floor of the car, with her face between his knees.

I had no idea that she too was hit and thought she had simply fainted with fright. Then I heard His Imperial Highness say, "Sopherl, Sopherl, don't die. Stay alive for the children!" At that, I seized the Archduke by the collar of his uniform, to stop his head dropping forward and asked him if he was in great pain. He answered me quite distinctly, "It's nothing!" His face began to twist somewhat but he went on repeating, six or seven times, ever more faintly as he gradually lost consciousness, "It's nothing!" Then, after a short pause, there was a violent choking sound caused by the bleeding.

Under the kind of hand-to-throat interrogation one might expect to occur after such an event, Princip and Cabrinovic quickly gave up their teammates, who were all arrested, except for Mehmedbasic, who had made a clean getaway to

Serbia. Despite all being found guilty, Austro-Hungarian law of the time did not permit the death sentence to be handed down to anyone under the age of 20 and it should be noted that, with most of the assassins being too young to hang and the "death capsules" guaranteed to incapacitate the taker to such a degree they were rendered helpless to capture, it does seem as if someone, somewhere, did not want the men dead and unable to talk.

Nedjelko Cabrinovic, Gavrilo Princip, and Trifko Grabez received the maximum penalty of 20 years; Vaso Cubrilovic got 16 years; and Cvijetko Popovic 13 years. Veljko Cubrilovic, Danilo Ilic, and his "lieutenant," a chap called Misko Jovanovic, were over 20 so they were executed on February 3, 1915.

HOLLYWOOD AND THE MAFIA PAIR FOR WAR

There were two unsung heroes of Operation *Husky*, the Allied invasion of Sicily in July 1943, they being the unlikely duo of Douglas Fairbanks Jr. (1909–2000) and Charles "Lucky" Luciano (1897–1962).

Although he was equally at ease swinging in the rigging of a mock-up pirate ship as he was "swinging" in the boudoirs of the rich and famous, there was a lot more to Fairbanks than his raffish charm and easy smile. Few today know he was in fact one of the most highly decorated American Navy officers of World War II, not only collecting battle-bling from home but from France, Italy, and Britain.

His most notable achievement was the setting up of the unit, then known as the Beach Jumpers, which after the war would become the US Navy SEALs. While still a reserve officer, Fairbanks was sent to England as an observer to the training methods and tactics of the new Commando units operating under Louis Mountbatten (1900–1979). Not content to sit by as an observer, Fairbanks went on several Commando raids into Occupied France and was quick to grasp the significance of the deceptive tactics whereby a relatively small group of men could operate in such a way as to convince the enemy they were under attack by a much larger force. He reported home to Admiral Ernest J. King, Chief of Navy Operations, who on March 4, 1943 issued orders for similar units to be set up and trained in the same tactics, the first batch of volunteers gathering at the Amphibious Training Base at Camp Bradford in Virginia. Here they perfected tactics designed not only to confuse the enemy but also to "scare the be-Jesus" out of him; Fairbanks's constant reference to the power of the "B-J factor" is said to have been euphemized into the unit's cover name of Beach Jumpers.

Although they did indeed conduct several successful – if minor – operations before *Husky*, that was the first time the Beach Jumpers were used to the considerable benefit of other forces landing en masse. On the night of July 11, 1943, they put up such a show off Cape San Marco, more than 100 miles to the west of the true landing sites, that the Germans were convinced a major force was standing offshore in the dark. A similar farce was enacted the following night, complete with loud flashes and bangs and loudspeakers blaring out recordings of destroyers "whooping" alarms and thousands of men shouting and carrying on. This was so successful that the confused Germans kept an entire division in reserve and well away from the real beaches dotted about the southern coast of the island.

Disbanded after the war, the Beach Jumpers were reactivated in 1951 in the face of considerable opposition from the command-strata of the navy, who felt that deceptive pranks and charades had no place in modern warfare. Just to prove their point, the newly formed Beach Jumpers found out there was to be a massive navy exercise with all the commanders kept in touch through a sealed and secure radio link in Washington. The BJs managed to infiltrate the radio room and sent messages for all commanders to report to the flagship to discuss the termination of the exercise and, when many of the objectors to their existence had fallen for the trick and turned up on the nominated ship only to realize they had been duped, it was roundly agreed that the Beach Jumpers had a role to play in any theater of war. As for Fairbanks, he retired from active service to become embroiled in countless boudoir battles, including his taking the leading role as the infamous "headless man" in the Duchess of Argyll's "family snap" of her indulging in a spot of the "love than can not speak its name" that featured front and center of her high-profile divorce case of 1963. And so to that other "hero" of Operation *Husky*.

Charles "Lucky" Luciano was born Salvatore Lucania [sic] on the country estate of Sicily's Mafia supremo, Don Calogero Vizzini. In 1907 his family moved to America, where, by the tender age of 11, he had already set up his first racket, extorting protection money from the Jewish kids on the Lower East Side. This is how he met Meyer Lansky (1902–1983), the man through whom he would forge links with military and naval intelligence and even the White House in order to "grease the way" for the American invasion of Sicily in 1943. At the time, Lansky was just a skinny kid who refused to pay up, no matter how many times Luciano kicked him up and down the sidewalk and, in the end, the two became unshakable friends. Ever watching each others' backs, the pair moved swiftly through the ranks, with Luciano emerging as one of the country's leading mobsters and "capo di tutti capi" of all the New York crime families. His famous luck finally ran out in 1936 when he was jailed for a term of 50 years with the recommendation that he serve a minimum of 30 before review. Not finding prison life to his taste, in the January of 1941 Luciano hatched a plan whereby the American authorities would be forced to deal with him for certain services he could render, in exchange for his eventual release and repatriation to Sicily. Still very much in control of New York's underworld from his cell in New York's Clinton Correctional Facility, Luciano sent word to his second-in-charge, Meyer Lansky, that he should approach military intelligence staff with the proverbial "offer they couldn't refuse" – the Mafia-controlled dock workers and longshoremen as a counter-intelligence network to combat the rash of onshore sabotage and German U-boat activity in American waters.

A Jew by birth and conviction, Lansky and other members of the "Kosher Nostra," such as the charming but decidedly psychopathic Ben "Bugsy" Siegel, had personal reasons to hate the Germans. The Kosher Nostra's indulgence in a spot of playful "Kraut-bouncing" had already come to the attention of the authorities, who tended to turn a blind eye to their breaking up neo-Nazi meetings, even when they tossed their brown-shirted victims off the roof to see how far they would bounce. It was also known that in 1938 Siegel had been at a party in Italy with American socialite Countess Dorothy diFrasso when he had to be disarmed and dragged from the room after he started to march through the joyful throng of partygoers announcing he was going to "take out the fat junkie and the shriveled gimp," this being Siegel's colorful way of declaring his intention to shoot dead, canapés in hand, Göring and the vertically and athletically challenged Goebbels. Now, that *really* would have influenced the war! But, all such well-attested anti-Nazi feelings aside, none of those approached by Lansky felt it "appropriate" to deal with him or his kind, which left Lucky no alternative but to up the ante.

The massive French liner SS *Normandie* had the misfortune to be in New York in 1940, when France fell, so she had been impounded by the Americans, who by 1941 had almost finished converting her to a troopship. Luciano got word to his chief executioner, Albert Anastasia (1903–1957), the head of Murder Inc., as it was affectionately known to those who availed themselves of its corporate services, that *Normandie* should have a terrible accident. On February 9, 1942, with the work in its final stages, a fast-moving fire broke out, which soon had the ship heeled over at her moorings on New York's Pier 88.

Although the fire had been the work of Albert's brother, Tony "Toughboy" Anastasio [sic], the press howled of German sabotage, and the collective authorities – who were of pretty much the same opinion – were forced to reconsider Luciano's offer. Between December 1941 and March 1942, 72 American ships had already been sunk off the eastern coast and the docklands were known to be heavily infiltrated by German agents. The dockland bars and brothels were the happy hunting grounds for these agents, who routinely harvested valuable information about sailing times and what-have-you from drunken and loose-lipped sailors. The most infamous of such places already identified by the authorities were the Highway Tavern and Schmidt's Bar,

"Lucky Luciano," back home in postwar Italy, enjoying his hard-earned freedom. (Topfoto)

both in New Jersey, and Manhattan's Old Hamburg Bar. With the fate of the *Normandie* the last straw, the morning of April 11 saw Lansky having breakfast in Vito's Diner on West 58th Street with Moses Polakoff, who was Luciano's lawyer, District Attorney Murray Gurfein, and Commander Charles Radcliffe Haffenden from the Office of Naval Intelligence (ONI) and the man responsible for New York dockland security. The substance of that meeting was that the Mafia would make sure that nothing like the *Normandie* ever happened again, the glut of Nazi agents would be shown the error of their ways, without the ONI having to get its hands dirty, and all harvested intelligence would be passed back to that same office. In return, Luciano would appreciate being moved to more relaxed and comfortable confinement and, for the time being, that was all he wanted.

So began Operation *Underworld*, and this highly dangerous relationship between the Mob and the authorities ramped up significantly in 1943 with the planning of Operation *Husky* – which would lead to the Allied invasion of Sicily on July 9. With President Roosevelt kept in the loop by Cardinal Francis Spellman (1889–1967), Archbishop of New York and Vicar-in-Chief to the Armed Forces of America, increasingly focused talks were opened up with Luciano, who was by now in comfortable and quite spacious prison quarters in Albany, where he routinely briefed his minions and sent them forth to do his bidding, be that for the ONI or for Luciano's own business concerns. Informed in loose detail about *Husky*, Luciano immediately smelled victory and made it clear to his uniformed visitors that he could get them into Sicily with the minimum of fuss on the understanding that, when the war was over, he would be released and sent home. And that was non-negotiable. Knowing exactly how valuable the Sicilian Mafia could be to any invading force, the Americans had no choice but to agree. Nevertheless, ever cautious, Luciano said he wanted Spellman to tell him to his face that the president was aware of the deal and gave his word too. That assurance given, Luciano established contact with Don Vizzini, Capo of Sicily, who agreed on the condition that, the war over and the Allies gone, Sicily and Naples would be Mafia enclaves. And with Vizzini assured of that, everything started to fall into place.

With the Sicilian Mafia now effectively working for American military intelligence, a veritable cataract of information was sent, through Luciano, to inform the Americans on the location and number of troops, gun emplacements, which were German and which were Italian, numbers and locations of tanks and airfields, which mayors and other officials could be counted on and which might prove hostile; in fact, with Vizzini having an interest in all the bars and brothels frequented by the Germans and Italians on the island, nothing escaped his grasp. In the lead-up to the invasion proper the Mafia stood ready and, according to local tradition, on the morning of July 9 an American fighter flew over Vizzini's mountain stronghold in Villalba in the middle of the island, and dropped a small sack containing a yellow silk handkerchief bearing Luciano's monogram, this being the pre-arranged signal for the local Mafia to move to their action stations. As Vizzini's "troops" began assassinating their allotted targets, a small column of American tanks slipped through enemy lines and headed straight for Villalba to collect Vizzini, who would spend the first two weeks of the invasion moving at the head of the advance, making it known to the population as a whole that he and his associates would take it as a personal insult if the Americans were not rendered all possible support and assistance.

As Vizzini, now appointed Mayor of Villalba and Honorary Colonel in the American Army, was addressing the locals from the top of his tank, the later-infamous Vito Genovese (1897–1969) was taken into the heart of the American Military Government of Occupied Territories as driver, interpreter, and personal adviser to Colonel Charles Poletti (1903–2002), AMGOT's Commander-in-Chief. This was very much a volte-face for the man who had previously been a close friend of Mussolini, even organizing the 1943 New York murder of Italian journalist Carlo Tresca for his persistence in writing unflattering things. "Uncle" Vito was also the main drug dealer for the fast set led by Mussolini's son-in-law, Count Ciano, Minister for Foreign Affairs, who Mussolini would soon have shot for treason, an incident immortalized in print by son Fabrizio Ciano's page-turner, *When Grandpa Had Daddy Shot* (1991). But for Genovese, business was business, and Poletti and his staff were all highly impressed with his diligent and unpaid assistance, especially when it came to reporting the countless black marketeers operating on the island. What was initially unknown was the fact that Genovese and Vizzini were themselves in partnership in the biggest black market ring and simply did not like the competition. Even when this did become apparent, along with the fact that the pair transported their ill-gotten merchandise about the island in captured Italian Army trucks stolen from American compounds, the matter was overlooked. The only person not to appreciate the level of AMGOT/Mafia involvement was the splendidly named Sergeant Orange C. Dickey of the Military Criminal Investigation Department, who, having found out that Genovese was also wanted for murder in America, tried to have him shipped home for trial. Despite the Mafia offering hefty bribes and his own Military Command leaning on him to make his life hell, Orange Dickey would not budge. By the time he succeeded, however, all the witnesses against Genovese had met with terrible accidents or wisely decided to take a long vacation.

With the war concluded and the Americans gone, the Mafia got their power bases of Sicily and Naples as promised and by 8am on February 10, 1946 Luciano was standing on those same chilly New York docks where it all began, waiting to board the SS *Laura Keene* for Sicily. In a solemn ceremony, observed by less than happy Feds, a small group of minor Capos bid their farewells with beautifully tooled leather cases; the one handed over by Lansky known to contain something in the region of $3m. Despite the fact that Lansky used the money to set up the supply lines of heroin into

Miami that was to prove the bane of American life from 1950 onwards, the authorities continued to use their Mafia connections right up until the Kennedy Administration, which recruited Sam Giancana (1908–1975) to put out a contract on Castro. This was canceled at the last minute so as not to rock the boat for the 1961 Bay of Pigs fiasco. Of course, there are plenty who believe that a CIA-backed Giancana and his chums were behind the 1963 assassination of Kennedy himself, because of that administration's anti-Mafia crusade. Jack Ruby (1910–1967), the man who shot Oswald, had Mob connections going back to his youth, when he ran errands for Al Capone, and throughout the '40s, '50s and '60s, when he was an established and routine associate of both Lansky and Giancana. Knowing he was dying anyway, or so the theory goes, he had nothing to lose by shooting Oswald for his friends on prime-time television in front of 100 million witnesses, but it is doubtful we will ever know the full story behind that particular can of worms.

KLOSE ENCOUNTERS OF THE THIRD REICH KIND

People wandering around with metal detectors can be a mixed blessing; at the time of writing there is much jubilation in the UK over the find in a Shropshire field of 1,500 gold and silver Saxon artifacts reclaimed from the past; others, like Ken Small, simply dig up the past per se. Having retired from the British police force in 1968, Small took over a small guesthouse near Slapton Sands on the south coast of Devon. Recovering from a breakdown, he would often take long walks along the local beaches and when he started to notice a very wide and varied presence of low-grade militaria – spent and unspent ammunition, buttons, bits of uniform, buckles etc – he began prospecting with a detector to eventually unearth the truth about Exercise *Tiger*.

You didn't need to be a genius in 1944, Allied or German, to know the invasion of France was nigh; the only question was where and when. Determined to be properly prepared for their big day, the American forces massed in the south of England had identified Slapton Sands (the beach is actually pebble) as a near-perfect replica of "Utah" beach, so in late 1943 the 3,000 residents of Slapton and the nearby village of Torcross were evicted from their homes and businesses, without a word of explanation, so that various exercises could be conducted in complete secrecy. On an ever-increasing scale, the Americans conducted numerous exercises; *Duck*, *Fox*, *Muskrat*, *Otter*, *Mink*, *Beaver* ... and finally, *Tiger*, the first full dress rehearsal, involving 300 ships and 30,000 men, scheduled for the night and early morning of April 27–28, 1944. Across the Channel in Cherbourg, the flotilla of German S-boats also stood ready for what was surely coming their way, and their monitoring stations became aware of a significant increase in radio traffic, indicating something was afoot. Known to the British as an E-boat – E for enemy – the S-boat (or Schnellboot), was the fastest motor torpedo boat (MTB) afloat; it was vastly superior to anything the Allies had and, with its triple propellers giving a top speed of about 40 knots, it would retain that position of maritime superiority for quite some time. As late as the mid-1950s, British intelligence was still

Allied troops in one of the more successful rehearsals at Slapton Sands conducted on May 6, 1944, shortly after the dust had settled from the Tiger fiasco. (Topfoto)

using not only the S-boats but also the crews who that night inflicted on Exercise *Tiger* fourfold the casualties that would be sustained on the real landings at Utah.

The Cherbourg flotilla was under the command of Gotz von Mirbach, the most famous and heavily decorated S-boat captain of the war, and on the night of the 27th he dispatched a group of nine S-boats under Hans-Helmut Klose (1916–2003), with Gunter "The Raven" Rabe as his "wing-man." Well aware of the Cherbourg presence, the American Rear Admiral Don P. Moon requested the British mount special patrols to issue warnings if the S-boats put to sea. In the first of many communications failures that night, either these early warning patrols never put to sea or did so only to patrol the wrong sectors, for after the war both Klose and Rabe were adamant that until they ran into the middle of *Tiger* they did not see a single ship that night. Not knowing what was taking place, they hung around the usual shipping lanes for a while, thinking a massive convoy might be inbound, but when nothing hove into view they pressed on, heading for the Lyme Bay area, where they struck lucky. According to Rabe: "We crossed the convoy route without any sign of ships and cruised easterly in the inner bay. Shortly before 0200 on the 28th we saw in the southeast the indistinct shadows of a long line of ships that we did not immediately identify as Landing Ships-Tank [LST]; we thought they were tankers or possibly destroyers." The S-boats slowed to ten knots and let loose a salvo of 18 torpedoes, but hit nothing. Rabe explained it now dawned on them that their shots had passed harmlessly beneath the ships and that they might indeed be looking at some shallow-draft vessels, such as LSTs. Making the necessary adjustments to the depth-running, Rabe fired another two torpedoes and: "At 0207 we saw that we had hit the target. Fire was spreading rapidly from bow to stern and dense smoke rose from the ship."

What Klose and Rabe had stumbled on was the tail of the *Tiger*, Convoy T-4, with all before it safely ashore. Unfortunately the eight LSTs in T-4 were loaded with troops from the United States 4th Infantry Division and the 1st Amphibian Engineer Brigade, crammed aboard beside numerous vehicles that were themselves laden with petrol and explosives. The first hit by Rabe was on LST 507, swiftly followed by LST 531, which sank in under five minutes; LST 289 was also hit and seriously damaged but managed to make port. Given the second communications failure of the night it is a miracle that the nine S-boats managed to sink only two LSTs. The escort, mainly in the shape of HMS *Azalea*, was transmitting on the emergency frequency issued in orders and was radioing frantically to the LSTs, who, through a typing error in their orders, were happily tuned to a different frequency. In short, no one knew what on earth was going on. There were even tales of the various ships of T-4 firing on each other in the confusion, this compounded by misguided "friendly" fire from the shore. In all, over 900 American personnel were either dead or missing, including ten officers who knew everything there was to know about the impending invasion of France. Commander-in-Chief Eisenhower was incandescent when he heard that the S-boats had been seen scanning the waters with searchlights for survivors of their attack. Had they picked up any of those officers?

As it turned out it was not the S-boats but American and British searchlights that survivors had seen, and no prisoners had been taken; to Eisenhower's relief, the bodies of all ten officers were recovered. Rear Admiral Moon was selected as can-carrier-in-chief for the fiasco, which does seem a bit unfair as most of the blame lay elsewhere. The Commander at Plymouth, Admiral Sir Ralph Leatham (1886–1954), offered his full and unconditional apologies to the Americans for the abortive patrols that failed to watch for the S-boats, and for other communication failures, blaming overworked staff and the late distribution of information regarding the nature and location of *Tiger* – but it was Moon who took the flak. Although he held his post to oversee the proper landings at Utah beach, he shot himself on August 5, 1944 with the official explanation being battle fatigue. Those in the know thought him to be wrongly burdened with a sense of guilt and shame that made him the last casualty of *Tiger*.

Not wishing the Germans to glean an inkling of what they had blundered into or how successful they had been, there was a complete news blackout of the affair, this leading to the recent notion that it was not until Small began digging up half the Devon coast that the "truth" was revealed. Along with thousands of bits and pieces, Small did indeed unearth old memories of some of the locals, but most of these were false recollections of the American dead being bulldozed into unmarked mass graves with no notification of their death given to their families, who would be later told their loved ones perished either on Utah or in the push through France.

Small was certainly convinced he had stumbled across some cynical cover-up of callous disregard but, despite the number of books and sites still claiming this to be the case, it simply was not so. The sea took more than were killed in the torpedo attacks; the raw troops had not been instructed in the proper use of their lifebelts and many jumped into the sea with them round their waists instead of under their arms. Also, many who jumped still had their packs and weapons; not a good move. It is reckoned that perhaps 450 still lie at the bottom of Lyme Bay. The several hundred bodies that were recovered were held in temporary graves at the United States World War I Military Cemetery at nearby Blackwood, and after the war most were transferred to the United States World War II Military Cemetery outside Cambridge; some, at the request of family, were returned to the States for individual burial at various sites. As for any cover-up, this was only temporary and for good reasons; but as early as July 1944 Eisenhower's own headquarters issued a release giving the bare bones of the tragedy, and a more detailed article appeared in *Stars and Stripes*, the American Forces' own magazine. On top of that, immediately after the war and more than 20 years before Small began his own investigations, Captain Harry C. Butcher, Eisenhower's naval aide, gave a full and detailed account of *Tiger* in his *My Three Years with Eisenhower* (1946) as did *Cross Channel Attack* (1951) by Gordon A. Harrison, *Logistical Support of the Armies, Volume 1* (1953) by Roland G. Ruppenthal, and *The Invasion of France and Germany* (1957) by Samuel Eliot Morrison, to name but a few sources that gave a candid account of the matter. The simple truth is that there was no cover-up; in the mood of jubilation at the turning of the tide of war and subsequent victory, no one really wanted to be reminded of any calamitous failure; the tragedy of Slapton Sands was simply pushed to the back of the general mind. In 1954, still 15 years before any activity by Small, the United States Army returned to Slapton Sands to erect a monument of gratitude to those who had so unceremoniously been evacuated, and during that ceremony General Alfred M. Guenther spoke at length of the *Tiger* tragedy.

MOLASSES JUNCTION

In 1725 Richard Blackburn quit his hometown of Rippon (now Ripon) in Yorkshire and headed for the New World, where he settled in North Virginia, building Rippon Lodge on a promontory overlooking the Neabsco Creek and the Potomac river. Life was good and the Blackburns prospered, with the granddaughter marrying Bushrod Washington (1762–1829), nephew of George. In time, the Blackburn family moved off their beloved Yorkshire Plantation, selling out to Wilmer McLean (1814–1882) and his family.

There are many who can attest to having been present at the commencement of major conflicts, or indeed at their close; a few can affirm to have witnessed both the beginning and the end; but only Wilmer McLean can lay rightful claim to a war having started in his kitchen and ended in his front parlor.

Wilmer had carefully harvested the proceeds from his wholesale grocery business and in 1854 had retired to Rippon Lodge, which would soon find itself slap-bang in the middle of the First Battle of Manassas Junction, aka the First Battle of Bull Run, the first proper confrontation of the American Civil War (1861–1865). The Confederate forces were under the careful hand of the magnificently named General Pierre Gustave Toutant Beauregard (1818–1893), who made the McLean house his headquarters. As the respective forces maneuvered about, looking for best advantage, Beauregard and his staff were chatting in the kitchen when one of the first shells fired in the war came straight down the chimney to hit the cauldron of stew they were waiting for. Liberally coated in Mrs McLean's culinary efforts, they all raced off to take up their positions. The war had started.

The McLeans survived this rude interruption to their meal and Wilmer returned to his grocery trade to supply comestibles, mainly sugar and molasses, to the Confederates. Business was good but he would soon be forced to the conclusion that his beloved Rippon Lodge might be jinxed after his old friends returned for a rematch with the Second Battle of Manassas/Bull Run in 1862. Feeling a retreat further south might be good for their health, the McLeans upped sticks and headed down to Appomattox, Virginia, where they bought a nice residence, right next to the courthouse. The war would again catch up with poor old Wilmer as he took his Sunday constitutional on April 9, 1865, his reverie interrupted by Colonel Charles Marshall, Robert E. Lee's military secretary. Marshall asked Wilmer if he knew of any nearby and suitable building where Lee and Grant could finalize the treaty to end the war and, perhaps feeling the fickle finger of fate pointing yet again in his direction, Wilmer took Marshall in the opposite direction to his own abode and into a deserted building. Once inside, Wilmer's resolve to distance himself from anything military was ground down by Marshall's objections to such a hovel serving so grand a purpose and, with a sigh of resignation to his place in the history books, Wilmer led Marshall back to his own home where he let him set up shop in the parlor.

By late afternoon all business was concluded and, with Grant and Lee departed, the looting began in earnest; even General Sheridan got in on the act, stealing the table on which the terms of surrender had been written. In a matter of minutes every stick of furniture had gone; anything too heavy to move was smashed up to be sold piecemeal to souvenir hunters. Even the upholstered chairs and curtains from other rooms were torn into strips to be sold on in like manner. Essentially the place was trashed by the very people Wilmer had invited in. Feeling no little aggrieved, the McLeans were on the move again, this time to one of Mrs McLean's properties in Prince William County, Virginia. Wilmer deliberately defaulted on the payments of the Appomattox house, forcing the bank to sell the place to one Nathaniel Raglan, his widow reselling in 1891 for $10,000 to a Captain Myron Dunlap, who had grand ideas of making a national exhibition of the place. He had the structure dismantled and shifted to Washington but went bust before reconstruction could begin, leaving the pile of bits and pieces again at the mercy of thieves, vandals, and the elements, which between them accounted for the lot. After World War II interest was resumed in the reconstruction of the McLean house and a replica was opened on April 9, 1949 by descendants Major-General Ulysses S. Grant III (1881–1968) and Robert E. Lee IV (b. 1925), and this time no one was allowed to steal the furniture.

FROM ROCKET-MAN TO DR STRANGELOVE

As the war wound down to its close in 1945, President Truman gave his blessing to Operation *Overcast*, the American part of the undignified rush undertaken by the various Allies to gather up as many of the Nazi specialists as they could. With the British counterpart known as T-Force, Truman's sanctioning of *Overcast* carried the overrider that anyone "established to have been a member of the Nazi party and more than a nominal participant in its activities, or an active supporter of Nazi militarism" would have to be excluded. It is doubtful in the extreme that Truman really thought that *Overcast*, to be conducted under the aegis of the Joint Intelligence Objectives Agency, would exclusively seek out Mr Nice-Nazi who had perhaps spent the war improving the lot of the physically handicapped, or whatever. He must have known, as did everybody else involved with either *Overcast* or T-Force, that the hunt was on for Werner von Braun and other weapons specialists; the experimental doctors from the death camps; specialists in chemical warfare; and those who knew the secrets of Nazi Germany's industrial processes, whether they had used slave labor or not. Truman was just covering himself in the event of it coming to light that America was profiting from the knowledge accrued by those who ran the horrors of the Nazi war effort in general and the Holocaust in particular. But come to light it did – in spades – on both sides of the Atlantic.

With the inevitable involvement of the omnipresent Allen Dulles, head of the OSS (CIA to be), *Overcast* soon changed its name to Operation *Paperclip*, as the dossiers of those chosen to be spirited back to the United States – or away to a new life in South America with a fresh identity – had their transport dockets paper-clipped to the front of their file, which thus made them stand out in the stack. Rummaging through the rubble of postwar Germany, the hunters from both *Paperclip* and T-Force found no end of "suitable" candidates who had been working on everything from jet fighters and stealth technology, to biological and psychological weapons as well as more conventional industrial processes of great financial interest to non-military America and Britain. Cautious of Truman's overrider, the respective teams set about the de-Nazification of anyone they selected, especially Werner von Braun. He was top of everybody's shopping list – so much so that the *Paperclip* hunters were told that if they could not get him for America then they should "make sure" that no one else – especially the Russians – got him. As it turned out, von Braun himself had already decided that he wanted to go to America and, fed up waiting to be found in the ski resort on the Austrian border in which he and his entourage were hiding, sent out his brother Magnus (1919–2003) on a bicycle to find some Americans to whom he could surrender. Skidding around the local lanes, Magnus eventually ran into – quite literally – Private Joe Minto of the 44th Infantry Division, who took him back to his commanding officer to put everything in motion.

Once under the *Paperclip* umbrella, von Braun presented Dulles and co. with something of a problem in that not only had he been a member of the Nazi party, and an enthusiastic one to boot, but he had also joined the SS. And this was just the tip of the iceberg, for von Braun had been no dedicated scientist forced to work for the Nazis under duress; when his first V1 hit London he cracked open the champagne and danced around the room with his team, with similar celebrations taking place after the first V2 made it to the same target zone. After that, von Braun sat down to work on the designs for the A9, which, although never constructed, was intended to take 1,000k payloads to New York, this being something that *Paperclip* was most definitely disinclined to let the American public find out about. But the fact that he had also completed his plans for his A12, capable of taking ten metric tonnes into orbit, meant it was a case of letting bygones be bygones for the sake of the coming space race. The A12, a veritable giant with a take-off weight of 3,500 tons under 10 million kgf of thrust, would soon debut at Cape Canaveral, rebranded as the Saturn V that would be pivotal to the Apollo missions.

Von Braun always claimed that he had been forced to join the Nazi party in order to continue his work, but he had in fact become a quite voluntary member way before the war in 1937, and in 1940 quite happily accepted a personal invitation from Himmler to add SS rank to his ever-lengthening list of accolades. As with his Nazi party membership, von Braun always insisted that this was a condition forced on him so he could continue his work at Peenemunde, yet the SS had had no interest or involvement in that installation in 1940. Besides, von Braun gratefully accepted further SS honors from Himmler to end up, in June 1943, with the rank of Sturmbanführer. When challenged with a photograph of him standing behind Himmler in his natty black uniform, von Braun said it was the one and only time he had worn it but countless witnesses, both SS and slaves in his program, attested that he routinely jackbooted around in full SS fig.

He also claimed to have been wholly ignorant of the horrors of the Holocaust, but as early as April 1945 American Private John Calione, on a recce near Nordhausen in the Harz Mountains of central Germany, stumbled across what he thought at first was the dumping ground of some nearby concentration camp. The clearing was piled high with skeletal cadavers: "Some of them so thin you could see their backbones through their stomachs," he would later report. Calione was half right – it was a dumping ground, but that of the underground Mittelwerk V2 factory, which ran on slave labor drafted in from the nearby Mittelbau-Dora. This concentration camp, always running short of Zyklon-B poison, was happy to offload its "excess" to be worked to death in von Braun's underground installations. Calione spotted a nearby tunnel into the mountain, and after a brief scout round the interior he reported back to his unit, which notified *Paperclip* and sent in a transport column to clear the place of anything useful or interesting. The site, which was basically a converted gypsum mine, was slated for Russian Occupation but by the time they got there in July the cupboard was bare. Von Braun had visited Mittelwerk on numerous occasions and could hardly have failed to notice the physical conditions of the labor force. Besides, in a letter dated August 15, 1944 and addressed to Albin Sawatzki, manager of V2 production, he casually mentions his own personal visits to Buchenwald to select slave labor for other rocket production installations. No one could have set foot in that hell-hole for an instant without realizing its purpose, let alone spend hours on site selecting men for death duty; more than 20,000 slaves died on the production lines of the V2, far more than were killed by it as a weapon.

Fully aware of all this and more, *Paperclip* whitewashed von Braun's file and whisked him off to America, short-circuiting passport, immigration, and customs control to keep him under wraps with an embargo on all his war files, which would remain classified until 1984, seven years after von Braun died. The release of those papers brought forward several new accusations, not only of von Braun's full knowledge and callous disregard for the Holocaust but also of his own personal brutality. Two former members of the French Resistance, Guy Morand and Robert Cazabonne, who had the privilege of toiling troglodytic for von Braun, both made statements that not only reinforced the image of him habitually parading in his SS uniform but also spoke of his nonchalant disregard for the fate of his slave labor and the inmates of the camps in general. Morand said that on one occasion there had been some real or imagined sabotage, with himself held as one of the suspects: "Without even listening to my explanations, he ordered the Meister to give me 25 lashes. Then, deciding that the strokes weren't sufficiently hard, he ordered that I be flogged more vigorously. Von Braun made me translate [to the Meister] that I deserved more, that in fact I deserved to be hanged." And, in response to von Braun's frequent assertions that he had never seen any brutality or killings, Robert Cazabonne testified that von Braun often stood and watched as slaves were punished by being hung in chains from the factory hoists, or strung up by the neck for more serious misdemeanors or simply because they were too weak to work as hard and fast as Sawatzki's production schedules required.

As Cazabonne pointed out, with a daily death toll of about 250, either from exhaustion, disease, or execution, no one who made so much as a single visit to Mittelwerk could have failed to observe routine and sadistic abuse, let alone a man who spent days on end in the place. But none of this mattered a damn at the time to those nice people who would later bring you the likes of Klaus Barbie; their job was to whitewash von Braun and any other useful "rocket-men" so they could be smuggled into America. Sawatzki, who had previously overseen Tiger tank production for Ferdinand Porsche (1875–1951) with equally lethal efficiency when it came to his death workers, was also inducted by *Paperclip* but dismissed as "non-essential," after which he died mysteriously in detention, allegedly beaten to death by other inmates, and by 1946 von Braun and his new team were all safely under wraps in Texas. By the early 1950s their presence on American soil was an open secret, with Jewish and left-wing groups causing such uproar that *Paperclip* had to mount a damage limitation PR exercise to "sell" their Nazis to the American public. Realizing that they didn't have a cat's chance in hell of marketing some of their flock, the *Paperclip* team concentrated on von Braun. The opening gambit was a series of "Carl Sagen"-style articles in *Collier's* magazine – how it was man's noble destiny to reach out into space, the final frontier, and all that – after which they teamed him up with J. Edgar Hoover's main FBI agent/informant in Hollywood, Walt Disney, a good right-winger who ratted out more "Communists" to the McCarthy Commission than anyone else. The Disney–von Braun collaboration was a winner for *Paperclip*; the two got on like a house on fire and turned out several blockbuster television movies, both fact and fiction, but always about space travel, which the American public embraced enthusiastically. Von Braun was transformed overnight from jackbooting Nazi to the man who would put America where it belonged – at the head of the space race.

Worst of the NASA "black sheep" was Dr Hubertus Strughold (1898–1986), aka the Father of Space Medicine. He was eventually the head of the NASA aerospace medicine department, and *Paperclip* had him earmarked as a good catch from the word go. After all, one of the major problems any space program would encounter was the effects of massive pressure and vacuum on the human body and Strughold knew more about that than any man alive, having had an endless supply of Jews in Dachau concentration camp to shove into compression chambers to see at what point their eardrums gave out and their eyes bled. Alternatively he would pop a couple of inmates into his fun-chamber and observe their antics of agony in a virtual vacuum. Contrary to popular opinion, as guided by science-fiction films, the human body does not burn, freeze, shrivel, or explode in the vacuum of space. As Strughold established, a person takes a few minutes to die, by which time most body fluids have vaporized, the lungs turned to mush, and the body swollen to twice its normal size before death by hypoxia. He had also conducted experiments to establish minimum and maximum temperature tolerance levels of the human body, and the attendant survival times, as well as radiation-exposure programs to likewise establish the survival rates in relation to time and strength levels of various elements.

Naturally it pays to tread carefully marketing such a man as he to the nation, but in time even Strughold was fed to the American public as an avuncular savior of their beloved astronauts, with the Daughters of the American Revolution presenting him with a medal and the Texas Senate declaring in 1985 that June 15 would thenceforth be known as Doctor Hubertus Strughold Day. The only Nazi rocket-man harvested by *Paperclip* to be outed and deported was Arthur Rudolph (1906–1996), one of von Braun's right-hand men in both Germany and America. Having helped put the first Americans into space and developed the Pershing missile, anti-Nazi elements dug up the dirt on his treatment of the slaves in Mittelwerk so, with *Paperclip* by then disbanded and no one to shield him, in November 1983 Rudolph was stripped of his American citizenship and shipped back to Germany. Anyway, while Hitler's finest were beavering away on the American space program, even more unpleasant characters were being gathered into the *Paperclip* nest, while others were variously hidden or spirited away to safety in South America. Whenever one thinks of organizations helping high-ranking Nazis to escape, the name of the shadowy Odessa leaps to mind, but before stating that no such organization existed outside the mind of Simon Wiesenthal, he having invented such a "bogeyman" to keep himself in the limelight and the donations rolling in, first a bit of background on him.

Although portrayed as some sort of secular saint in films such as *The Odessa File* (1974) and *The Boys from Brazil* (1978), there are so many inconsistencies between Wiesenthal's three main memoirs, and between those memoirs and contemporaneous documents, that it is impossible to establish a reliable narrative from them. Ben Barton, director of the prestigious Wiener Library, the oldest and largest institution dedicated to the study of the Holocaust, has acknowledged the contribution Wiesenthal made, but agreed that the man was "a showman, a braggart, and, yes, even a liar."

In short, Wiesenthal lied about many things, from having two university degrees to having been instrumental in the capture of Eichmann, this latter claim being publicly trashed in no uncertain terms by Isser Harel (1912–2003), the head of Mossad, who pointed out that Wiesenthal was still looking for that particular target in Germany and Austria while they, Mossad, had tracked him to his lair in South America. Unchallenged by Wiesenthal either in court or in any public forum, Harel went into print, calling Wiesenthal a liar for his claims to have had anything even remotely constructive to do with the apprehension of Eichmann in 1960. Rejecting the claims as "complete fabrications" Harel further declared that: "Wiesenthal's reports and statements at that period prove beyond all doubt that he had no notion as to Eichmann's whereabouts." As Harel and his men were closing in on Eichmann, Wiesenthal at the time was proclaiming him to have just quit Japan for Saudi Arabia. Dismissing Wiesenthal as a blundering amateur, a phony, and a base opportunist, Harel further stated, in writing: "All the information provided by Wiesenthal, before and in anticipation of the Eichmann operation, was utterly worthless and sometimes even misleading and of negative value."

Harel was no more complimentary when it came to Wiesenthal and the hunt for Mengele. According to Wiesenthal, he was permanently but a step or two behind the Angel of Death, forcing the evil genius that was Odessa to keep him on the move round the globe. Even after Mengele was dead, Wiesenthal, not knowing this at the time, was still spotting him in any one of a dozen countries that the Nazi had never visited. And every time the old fraud claimed to have "just missed him" again, the money rolled in. In the summer of 1960 Wiesenthal was chasing him through the Greek islands, later giving a convoluted account of his Aegean venture that was completely invalidated, and later the same year he had Mengele poisoning a Jewish woman in a hotel in Buenos Aires to prevent her from identifying him. She was supposedly an inmate of Auschwitz sterilized by Mengele and the fiend, noticing her tattooed number, thought it best she died. As it turned out, the woman in question was not Jewish, had no tattoo, had never been in any camp, didn't know

Mengele from a hole in the road, and died in a mountaineering accident. Eventually tiring of his imaginary journeys about the world, by the late 1970s Wiesenthal had Mengele in permanent residence in Paraguay, where, moving about in a fleet of bulletproof Mercedes limousines, he supposedly lived the high life with complete immunity. Unaware that Mengele had died an impoverished and dribbling drunk in Brazil in 1979, Wiesenthal was still claiming to be within a gnat's whisker of arresting him in Paraguay as late as June 1984. Harel publicly stated that Wiesenthal's file on Mengele was an utterly worthless jumble of misinformation that served no other purpose than to bolster up the lies of its compiler, whose negligence and interference in the Mengele case was "folly bordering on the criminal." Benno Varon, the Israeli Ambassador in Paraguay, was even more pointed in an article he published in *Mainstream* magazine: "Wiesenthal makes periodic statements that he is about to catch him, perhaps since Wiesenthal must raise funds for his activities and the Mengele name is always good for a plug."

On the other side of the coin is the less than amusing plight of Frank Walus (1922–1996) of Chicago, a man whose life was ruined by Wiesenthal's cavalier approach to facts and accuracy. In 1978 he was accused by Wiesenthal of being the Beast of Kielce, an enthusiastic Gestapo persecutor of Jews in Poland whose party piece was kicking pregnant women to death in the streets. By the time Walus was cleared of all charges he had been seriously assaulted eight times by Jewish mobs, including one acid attack; he had lost his job, his house, and all his money, and was never again a well man, eventually dying from a series of heart attacks. Wiesenthal certainly seems to have "fabricated the whole story," as Walus claimed; nine of the 12 witnesses, all of whom eagerly identified Walus in court as the Beast, claimed to have been born and lived their war years in Poland, but this turned out to be false. The Beast was very well documented as having been in his thirties, standing slightly over 6ft, slim, elegant, and well educated, whereas Walus was 5ft 4in, dumpy, and originally of peasant farming stock. Also, he would have been barely 17 at the time of the alleged crimes and, as a Pole, barred from the ranks of the Gestapo. Apart from all that, Walus presented a veritable cataract of witness statements that backed up his assertion that he had spent the war in slave labor on German farms.

So, that is the measure of the man who invented the specter of Odessa, and did so to the enduring gratitude of those who actually *were* shunting their "tame" Nazis round the world while everybody else was busy chasing Wiesenthal's ghost. And with the war over and Russia the new enemy, who better to keep an eye on the burgeoning "Commies" than a bunch of trigger-happy Nazis? OSS head Allen Dulles recruited Reinhard Gehlen (1902–1979), Hitler's head of Soviet intelligence, who, having proved his worth by giving Dulles a list of his own OSS officers who were members of the Communist party, or even double agents, was sent back to West Germany to set up the BND, or Federal Intelligence Service, which he and several other Nazi war criminals ran until 1968. Worst of these was Alois Brunner, responsible for the death of more than 140,000 Jews, while other characters, such as Klaus Barbie, frequently did "little jobs" for the BND. Barbie also worked directly for the CIA, which grew out of Dulles' OSS, and, according to him, one of the tasks he completed for them was the hunting down of Che Guevara in Bolivia.

Dulles' "stay behind" groups in Italy, codenamed Gladio, had links to individuals in the Vatican, specifically Bishop

Werner von Braun (right), father of the American space project, in more user-friendly attire than his German workers were used to seeing him in. (Ann Ronan Picture Library / Topfoto)

Alois Hudal (1885–1963). Holder of a golden Nazi party membership badge, and instrumental in keeping his beloved Führer's *Mein Kampf* off the Vatican's Prohibited Index, Hudal was of Austrian descent and it is still argued to this day as to how much Pope Pius XII knew of attempts by Hudal to aid the escape of Nazis from justice in Europe. The Hitler Youth past of the present Pope has again called Pius's wartime behavior into question, along with a re-examination of the Hudal group, which handled the likes of Adolf Eichmann; Franz Stangl, Commandant of Sobibor and Treblinka; Gustav Wagner, who gassed more than 200,000 Jews in Operation *Reinhard*; Josef Mengele, a man who needs no introduction; Eduard Roschmann, the Butcher of

Riga; and Klaus Barbie, the Butcher of Lyons. There were countless other lesser killers – men with the blood of only a few hundred on their hands – but Hudal saved them all. Some, with false papers, remained in Italy to join Gladio, which was run by Licio Gelli (b. 1919). This was the chap who, along with Barbie, would later broker the Exocet missile deal with Argentina so they could fire them at the British during the Falklands War of 1984. Both Hudal and Gelli had strong links to the Mafia, with the latter the prime suspect in the murder of Roberto Calvi (1920–1982), who was found swinging from London's Blackfriars Bridge. Known as God's Banker, Calvi was Chairman of the Banco Ambrosiano, effectively a subsidiary of the Vatican Bank, which was the major shareholder, and the suspicion is that Calvi was creaming off some of the Mafia funds being laundered through such outlets. Anyway, with the security of Europe safe in the hands of those who brought it to its knees in the first place, other Nazis were continuing their good work in both America and Britain, and all with the help of unwitting volunteers.

The British parallel of *Paperclip*, T-Force, was largely directed by Ian Fleming (1908–1964), later to be celebrated as the author of the James Bond novels. While this organization certainly hunted out "benign" German specialists in industrial processes for the likes of ICI and Courtaulds, they too were after the darker operators whose knowledge would be of use to establishments such as the chemical and biological weapons institute at Porton Down.

After they had tried and sentenced the Nazi doctors who were of no use to them, Britain and America had both signed up to the Nuremberg Code, outlawing the conducting of experiments on uninformed or coerced individuals, but this obviously meant nothing to Dulles, who in April 1953 gave the go-ahead for *MK-Ultra*, inspired by the Nazi-harvested intelligence from the mind-control experiments conducted in the camps. Was it really possible, he wondered, to churn out "Manchurian Candidates" by the score and manipulate the minds of foreign politicians and leaders? The man in charge of these widespread and decidedly illegal and unpleasant experiments was Dr Sidney Gottlieb (1918–1999), real name Joseph Scheider, who, with a stutter, a club foot, and a passion for Bavarian folk dancing, was the inspiration for *Dr Strangelove*. Between 1953 and 1973, when *MK-Ultra* was shut down by CIA boss Richard Helms (1913–2002), the only director of that agency ever to be successfully prosecuted for lying to Congress about CIA activities, Gottlieb and his minions experimented on thousands of prostitutes and petty criminals who were allowed to "cop a plea" in return for their help; *MK-Ultra* also preyed on prison inmates and those of countless asylums who could ill-afford to have the unskilled messing with their heads and, working on the correct assumption that students would do anything for a bit of cash, Gottlieb and his not-so-merry men made inroads into several American university campuses. Indeed, the breadth and scope of Gottlieb's LSD experiments on Californian students is seen by some as being responsible for kicking off the hippie culture in San Francisco. And some of Gottlieb's experiments with LSD were most definitely and quite unnecessarily humiliating and sadistic. Some "volunteers," who had no idea what was to happen to them, were placed in sensory deprivation units before being dosed with LSD, mescaline, or sodium pentothal, and, with no "reference point" of any kind to hang on to, suffered serious mental trauma from which some of them never recovered. Also, and for no valid reason, guinea pigs from psychiatric units would have the most revealing and humiliating parts of their counseling sessions looped on tape, which was played to them over and over again as they were pumped full of whatever psychotropic was Gottlieb's choice of the day.

Inspired by the debriefings of SS Officer Walter Schellenberg, Gottlieb and Dulles augmented *MK-Ultra* with Operation *Midnight Climax*, the nuts and bolts of which sound like the plot for a very bad conspiracy or porn movie. Instead of proper brothels, which would be too hard to control with all that coming and going, Gottlieb and Dulles decided to recruit hundreds of solo working girls and rig their homes with microphones, hidden cameras, and two-way mirrors. The girls were offered immunity from police harassment or arrest and the assurance that any pimp who tried to muscle in on their action would learn some very short, sharp lessons. On top of that, they would be paid a retainer and be allowed to keep all of the money they got from their clients. What a deal; hundreds of medium- to high-class hookers went for it with both hands. Whether the client was someone they themselves had picked up or one sent in as an unwitting dupe by the CIA, the girls had to spike their drinks with LSD and then carry on as normal with the CIA filming and recording all for posterity. Quite who these men were is now impossible to say, as all of the transcriptions and films were ordered to be destroyed by Helms, but it is known that one poor sap was kept strung out on acid for an incredible 77 days, just to see what the long-term and continual-usage implications were. When they got bored of him, he was simply driven away and dumped in downtown San Francisco, last seen running away from a ten-foot purple crocodile, no doubt.

At one point burning a staggering nine percent of the entire CIA operations budget, *MK-Ultra* was as massive and wide-ranging as it was damaging. With the bulk of its "Mind-Kontrol," hence the name, experiments based on what they had learned from their "tame" Nazi doctors who had enjoyed a free hand in the camps, the leading lights of the program, in both America and Britain, brought about the permanent impairment and deaths of about as many people as had their Nazi tutors. In short, they actually learned nothing from them. And some of their damaged chickens came home to roost; Theodore Kaczynski (b. 1942), aka the Unabomber, whose deranged terror campaign killed and maimed Americans from 1978 to 1995, had by some accounts been a perfectly normal and emotionally stable young man before he was repeatedly experimented on by *MK-Ultra* throughout the 1960s. On a lighter note, another long-term "experimentee," Kenneth *"One Flew Over the Cuckoo's Nest"* Kesey (1935–2001) came out of the LSD program to establish the hippie movement. But, not content with destroying their own, Gottlieb and Dulles extended *MK-Ultra* to Britain, where, among other infringements of the Nuremberg Code, Gottlieb oversaw those LSD experiments at Porton Down.

From 1957 to 1964, the program also bankrolled Dr Donald Ewen Cameron (1901–1967) to expand his "psychic-driving" program in Montreal, where he destroyed the minds of thousands of unwitting participants who he sustained in three-month comas with a "chemical-cosh" while he tried to erase their memories and replace them with others. As president of both the American and the Canadian Psychiatric Associations, Cameron had sat in judgment at the Nuremberg Medical Trials where he hypocritically condemned Nazi doctors for conducting exactly the same kind of experiments on the unwitting and the unwilling in the camps as he himself had been conducting since 1934, these involving electroconvulsive "therapy" at up to 50 times the recommended power levels. Yes, Cameron had been frying brains long before the Nazis got their chance to do likewise, but it was the wealth of data from those camp doctors, whose unwilling participants outnumbered Cameron's by at least 100–1, which encouraged *MK-Ultra* and Cameron to resurrect and expand his experiments.

<hr />

OH, BROTHER!

They say you can pick your enemies but not your family. This was most certainly a problem confronting both Hermann Göring and Rienhard Heydrich who, despite having Jewish influence in their family backgrounds, were dedicated Nazis, with Heydrich as convener of the Wannsee Conference, a leading architect of the Holocaust.

While Göring managed to shrug off the fact that he was actually raised by Jewish godparents, who were thus not blood relatives, the Heydrich boys had a Jewish grandfather in Jacob Seuss. During his childhood in Halle, Rienhard was mortified by the street taunts of other children, who kept calling him Izzy (Israel), and in his early days in the navy he was nicknamed the Blond Moses. His father, the minor composer Bruno Heydrich, made no secret of the family lineage as he had no problem with the matter; one of his piano pupils, Alice Rohr, herself Jewish, would later state that it was open knowledge that Bruno was part-Jewish and frequently referred to as Izzy Seuss behind his back. After Heydrich's rise to power the issue was, of course, somewhat more pertinent, with Himmler and Hitler having to discuss the matter. According to SS Brigadeführer Walter Schellenberg (1910–1952), Hitler decided that Heydrich was far too valuable to be removed over such a trifle. This is hardly surprising, as some others among the high-ranking Nazis had part or full Jewish blood (Eleke Scherwitz, one of the Nazi doctors condemned at Nuremberg for concentration camp horrors, was himself Jewish). Schellenberg was quite adamant and detailed in his postwar divulgence of Heydrich's heritage and, as his one-time aide and a confidant of Himmler, he should know.

As for Heydrich's brother, Heinz, he seems not to have been so enthusiastic a Nazi as his older brother; he certainly did whatever it took to stay with the flow and not stand out, but there is no proof that he actually joined the party. Either way, after the assassination of his brother he received a package of papers and personal effects and, whatever was revealed to him therein, he executed a rapid change to begin helping Jews and other "undesirables" escape to Sweden. As he published a forces' newspaper called *Die Panzerfaust*, Heinz had ready access to all the printing facilities he needed to produce some very realistic false papers, with his family name making sure that, initially, he was above suspicion. No one knows how many owe their lives to Heinz but eventually the Gestapo closed in on him at the Eastern Front, where he shot himself, on November 19, 1944, before they got their hands on him. But, when it came to aiding Jews, Albert Göring was even more adventurous and hands-on.

With Göring Sr. a frequently absent diplomat, his wife and children were almost permanently housed with their rich friend Ritter Hermann von Epstein, who initially doted on the young Hermann and treated him like a son. Some time in 1904 Epstein began a rather passionate affair with

Fanny Göring, the mother, and, in 1905 young Albert arrived, growing up to look embarrassingly like Epstein. After the advent of Albert, Hermann was marginalized in favor of the newest arrival. When he grew up, Albert worked on the fringes of the Austrian film industry and watched the rise of the Nazis with horror. As they jackbooted into his country, with him denouncing them in public at every opportunity, his life was saved only by his brother's position and prominence within the party he refused point-blank to join. Whenever he saw Jews being forced to scrub the pavements, Albert would get down on his knees and join them, thereby leaving the officiating troops no choice but to abandon the ritual humiliation in case anyone noticed that Göring's brother was busy with a scrubbing brush. Throughout the war Albert saved hundreds; some were high profile, such as the Austrian composer Franz Lehar and his wife, not to mention German actress Henny Porten, but most were ordinary families and individuals who managed to flee the Nazis with papers ostensibly signed by Hermann Göring, Albert having perfected his brother's writing style. With the German military attitude and abject awe of rank, as soon as officials saw a docket proclaiming the bearer authorization to travel under the protection of Reichmarshal Hermann Göring, everybody leaped about saluting the Jews whom their orders would have them shoot – standing to attention while they held open the doors of escape. Albert is known to have got a big kick out of that.

Finally realizing he could do more damage from inside the tent, Albert feigned a softening of attitude and accepted a job in the upper management of the Skoda munitions factory in Occupied Czechoslovakia as was. Here he established links to the local Resistance and asked them to recommend an assistant he could rely on. Once they had got over the shock of dealing with a member of the Göring family, the local network furnished Karel Sobota as a safe go-between, after which the pair started to free Jews in greater numbers. Having responsibilities for both production and export, Albert used his name to get all the slave labor he wanted from local concentration camps; some of these lucky few were sent on through the Resistance lines in the very trucks sent to collect them, while those in better shape were found cushy jobs in the factory and kept safe and well fed. After the war Albert was arrested, simply because of his name, and interrogated at Nuremberg, but so many Jews and other members of persecuted minorities came forward in his defense that he was released. When he returned to Czechoslovakia the same thing happened; arrest but immediate release when the authorities were confronted by howls of protest from those he had saved. In time he returned to Germany but found himself shunned for his name. Undeterred, he established himself in a flat and kept busy working as a jobbing writer and translator until 1966, when his health declined. By then on a state pension, he knew that if he married it would transfer to his wife. So, in a final act of kindness, he married his Jewish housekeeper on his deathbed so she could stop working and make that trip to Israel of which she spoke so often. Several of those saved by Albert Göring have repeatedly tried to have his name entered on the list of Righteous Gentiles, but the custodians of that list are yet to get over his name, which, so far, has denied him that posthumous recognition.

Poor old Hermann Göring: his older brother, Karl, had moved to America to settle in Salt Lake City, where he married and had a son, Werner, in 1924. Raised a devout Mormon, when America joined in World War II, young Werner enlisted in the United States Air Force and as a pilot in the 303rd Bombardment Group, aka Hell's Angels, flew dozens of missions over the country that his uncle had so publicly boasted would never see a single bomb. Flying out of an airbase near Molesworth in England, Werner Göring's identity was kept secret from the rest of his crew, to which First Lieutenant Jack P. Rencher was attached as co-pilot with instructions to shoot Göring if ever they were brought down over Germany. Rencher would later reveal that the two got on extremely well and that he rated Göring very highly as a man and as a pilot; the only time Rencher ever saw Göring waver, and then only for a second or two, was over Cologne, his grandmother's city.

In more recent times Hermann's descendant, Matthias Göring, embraced Judaism in 2006 and divides his time between Basle and Jerusalem, while Katrin Himmler is married to an Israeli whose father survived the Warsaw Ghetto and, in the last interview with her that this author read, their only quandary is how they explain to their young son exactly what her great-uncle did during the war. Every family, it seems, has its skeletons in the cupboard: but some more than most.

KRIEG-HUND SUPREME

Come the fall of 1918, the close of World War I was but a matter of weeks away and, with the German forces in disarray, the Americans were advancing through Lorraine. On September 15 Corporal Lee Duncan (1893–1960) of the 136th Aero Division was ordered to take his men and check out a shelled German airfield to see if there was enough left standing to make a temporary HQ. As Duncan and his men carefully checked the site for booby traps and snipers he came across a dugout with five terrified occupants – a near-to-death German shepherd army messenger-dog and her

Lee Duncan with his boss. (Topfoto)

four puppies. One of the pups still had enough life left in him to try to hold Lee at bay in defense of its mother, so he rescued that male and a bitch, naming them Tin-Tin and Nenette. These were the names of the small woolen dolls that had started as a craze among children in Paris, who saw them as good-luck charms against the long-distance German shelling of that city with Big Bertha, a fearsome piece of ordnance with a range of about 80 miles. (The name of that gun, now an epithet for any woman of generous figure, was bestowed in the mistaken notion it had been made in the munitions workshops run by Bertha Krupp, whereas it was in fact turned out by Skoda.) The Paris papers took up the fad and ran cartoons of the loving couple, who always managed to survive whatever the war threw at them, and French children took to giving the dolls out to Allied servicemen as gestures of thanks.

Duncan survived the last throes of the war and, with Nenette dead, he and her brother, now called Rin-Tin-Tin, headed home to California. As the dog grew to full maturity, he astounded all with his ability to get over 12 foot-high fences and learn tricks at one sitting. Duncan quickly realized he had a movie star on his hands and in 1923 Rinty got his first lead in *Where the North Begins*, which his skills allowed to be finished in record time, saving the already cash-strapped studio from bankruptcy. Even today the Warner media giant freely admits they would not be here now were it not for that German army dog, which was always referred to by Jack Warner as the Mortgage Lifter. Rinty made countless films before dying aged 14 in 1932, according to Hollywood tradition, in the arms of Jean Harlow at Duncan's house on Clubview Drive.

TWO OUT AND ONE FILLING

Before *Overlord* there were, of course, several raids into Occupied France but not all of them "official"; on two notable occasions "private" expeditions were organized by British servicemen. The first was mounted in June 1941 when the much under-sung Leonard Hector Grant-Taylor nipped across the Channel to join a Luftwaffe dinner.

When it comes to fighting methods and close-quarter combat the names of Sykes and Fairbairn leap readily to the mind, but the still-shadowy Grant-Taylor was at least their equal. Born in 1891, such was his reputation in certain circles that his age presented no barrier to his being invited to become an instructor in 1940, despite some thinking his "no more Mr Nice Guy" methods decidedly unsporting. Grant-Taylor had realized during World War I that the days of chivalry in war were gone, and if victory was to be a realistic goal then the name of the new game was to kill as many of the enemy as possible by whatever means available.

In August 1941 he was shipped out to the Middle East to set up a training school and here he impressed on all his pupils the need for what Mossad still practices as "instinctive shooting." His main lesson for close-quarter killing in confined spaces was for the attacker to shoot those present in the order they reacted, not to start killing in order of proximity. And, just to keep his hand in before being sent East, Grant-Taylor took it upon himself to prove the worth of his methods. By the end of January 1941, and still in the south of England, he became aware of intelligence concerning six Luftwaffe squadron leaders from airfields in northern France who were in the habit of meeting up on the last Friday of the month in a villa outside Caen for a bit of a knees-up and to swap tall tales of their various missions over England. He decided to join the next soirée. In the guise of a French fisherman, he organized a high-speed launch to take him across to France, where, armed with two automatics and a knife, he took out the three guards, entered the dining room to kill all six revelers, and was back home for breakfast before he was even missed.

But the private jaunt of Messrs King and Cuthbertson was even more bizarre. Sergeant Peter King and Private Leslie Cuthbertson of the Royal Army Dental Corps were stationed in Portsmouth in 1942 and felt the war was passing them by. Determined to see some action before it was all over they hatched a plan to mount their own raid into northern France, Operation *Wild-Dog*, and began gathering weapons, grenades, and explosives. By June they were ready and, before going AWOL and heading for southern Cornwall where they planned to steal a boat, they sent their pay books to Winston Churchill at Downing Street with a covering letter stressing that they were not deserters and would be returning after doing a bit of damage to the Germans. Despite not knowing their stern from their elbow when it came to boats, they actually made it across one of the most patrolled, hostile, and mined stretches of water and landed safely in France. Both in full uniform, the pair started strolling around the coastal reaches of northern France looking for the enemy as if on some Sunday picnic. Highly trained and specialist personnel with civilian clothes, forged papers, and back-up from the Resistance were frequently captured within hours of landing but the gods take care of heroes and lunatics, so King and Cuthbertson, with a foot in each of those closely knit camps, were well protected.

Halfway through their first day they heard the voices of two English women discussing the cooking of wholesome meals with restricted rations and, just for a moment, thought they had sailed in a circle to end back on English soil. Peering over a wall, they saw a German radio van monitoring British broadcasts and, after blowing it up with a couple of their grenades, they went on their merry way, cutting every communication line they encountered. Unsure of exactly where they were (about 10 miles outside Cherbourg, as things turned out), when they came across some railway tracks the pair decided to follow them to the next station to get a reference point. Instead of a station, the next installation they encountered was a German army signal box, the single operator being dragged out and finished off. Standing in the box wondering how best to disable it, King and Cuthbertson's triumph was dampened a tad as a fully loaded troop-train trundled along. Telling Cuthbertson to hit the floor, King picked a lever at random, pulled it down, and stood to attention in the dimly lit box, saluting to the passing troops he was sending God knows where. Before moving on they blew the track along which they had sent the train to prevent its return to any proper course.

It was dark by the time the undaunted pair came to a German radar station, which they decided would make an ideal target. Cutting through the perimeter wire, they advanced on a blockhouse they presumed to be the control room but, having set their charges, the pair were spotted in their retreat and fired on. The charges went off and, confused by what now sounded like an inordinate amount of gunfire for such a small installation, the intrepid pair stole a German motorcycle to make good their escape, as all hell seemed to be breaking loose behind them. Returning to their boat, King and Cuthbertson struck out for home but, out of fuel and drifting, they were picked up by a Royal Navy patrol and arrested as German spies. With their true identities at last established but their tales of derring-do dismissed out of hand, they were instead arrested as deserters and scheduled for court martial. In the meantime, someone at Downing Street had rescued their letter from the mountain of correspondence within which it languished and put it before Churchill, thinking it might amuse him – which it did – he ordering that inquires be made as to the fate of the two lunatics. With the court martial in full swing, the officiating officers were more than a little surprised to be confronted unannounced by Major Desmond Morton, the Military Intelligence Officer on permanent attachment to Downing Street, asking if he might be permitted to speak on behalf of the two accused. Everything they had said in their statements was, he assured the court, perfectly true. Producing their letter and pay books, Morton further stated that he was in possession of a debriefing report from a Commando unit sent to France to capture equipment from an experimental German radar station and that the success of the mission, with zero casualties, was largely down to King and Cuthbertson blowing up the cookhouse to attract the enemy away from the control room, which was thus raided with impunity by the "official" force. Informed of Churchill's personal wish that the court go easy on the two, charges of desertion were dropped in favor of 28 days in the cooler but with full pay.

The exploits of King and Cuthbertson were explored in the little-known British film *Two Men Went to War* (2002), which, as one might imagine, incorporates a few factual errors in that King, played by Kenneth Cranham, is presented as a 55-year-old veteran of World War I, brow-beating the youthful Cuthbertson with tales of past glories. In reality both men were in their 20s and never met up again after their spell in the glasshouse; King went on to win the Military Cross in 1944 for his actions in Holland before joining the New Zealand Army to fight in the war in Korea, where, as a captain, he was awarded the Distinguished Conduct Medal for his defense of Hill 335 in late November 1951. He retired from service in 1960 to take up the post of chief ranger of New Zealand's Westmorland Park, where he died in a car accident two years later. As for Cuthbertson, he quit the army in 1946 and returned to his native Tyneside, in England's industrial northeast, where he proved a canny businessman and something of a local "character" who held various civic posts, including Deputy Lord Mayor of Gateshead and Lord Mayor of Newcastle before dying in 1996.

PAS CALAIS!

While it cannot be said that the success of the D-Day landings was attributable to deception alone, it is fair to say that the charades played out by Operation *Fortitude South* were a deciding factor; even after the beachheads in Normandy had been secured and the Allied troops were moving through France, the Germans remained convinced that the invasion was a diversion, or perhaps secondary to the main strike that would come at the Pas-de-Calais. As late as September 10, 1944, with the Allied spearhead approaching the German border, the German High Command was still sending out radio alerts warning of the imminent arrival of the First United States Army Group (FUSAG), which, massed about Southampton, would begin with the landing of more than 100,000 men on the Pas-de-Calais. But FUSAG did not exist; it was an elaborate hoax comprising inflatable tanks, gliders, and planes, and endless hours of meaningless radio traffic broadcast by trucks that kept driving up and down the south coast of England. The icing on the cake was the presence of the sort of man the Germans would *expect* to be in charge of such an important force, a less than pleased General Patton playing his part as commander of non-existent army. But the real hero of D-Day was a quiet and unassuming Spaniard called Juan Pujol Garcia (1912–1988).

A native of Barcelona, Pujol had emerged from the Spanish Civil War with an intense hatred for all political extremists, be they Communist or Fascist, and in February 1941 he visited the British Embassy in Madrid to offer his services as a spy. Rejected, he reasoned that the British might find him a more attractive proposition if he was already acting as a German spy, so he popped into the German Embassy, where, better received, he managed to persuade the embassy staff that, as he already had his visa for England, he might be of use to Berlin once there. Failing to recognize a forged visa when he saw one, the resident intelligence officer issued Pujol with a basic "Boys' Own" spy kit – invisible ink and so forth – and £600. Told to report in with the codename of Arabel, a week later Pujol sent word to his appointed handler, Karl Kuehlanthal, that he was settled in London and would soon start traveling the country to see what he could discover. In fact he was in Lisbon, where he had taken a small flat and begun to research Britain in the city's main library. Making imaginary trips around the UK, Pujol, gleaning what he could from books and newspaper articles, began to send Kuehlanthal some very impressive reports, which included such startlingly accurate deductions from what he read that his handler was suitably impressed and soon rated him a prime source. In fact so accurate were some of his predictions regarding convoy sailings, and the like, that MI6, who were intercepting many of his reports, launched a hunt for him in London. The first major clue that the British got to indicate that all was not what it seemed with Arabel was his expenses claims. Whoever and whatever Arabel was, he obviously did not know that there were 12 old pennies to the pre-decimal shilling and not ten. He also made little slips such as one report, supposedly from Glasgow, stating that the denizens of that city drank too much wine and were thus loose-lipped. Whisky and beer perhaps, but not wine — at least not in the 1940s.

With his feet firmly under the table in Berlin, Pujol again tried to present himself as an asset to the Allies in early 1942 and this time he was more successful. Lieutenant Patrick Demorest of the United States Navy, attached to the British Embassy in Lisbon, immediately recognized his potential and handed the volunteer to Kim Philby — a man who knew first-hand the value of a double agent — and a chap called Desmond Bristow, who ran the Iberian Section of MI5. By this time MI5 had figured out that Arabel was a phony but they had no idea that Berlin's new ace agent was a diminutive and bespectacled freelancer with a pile of newspapers and a vivid imagination. Once Philby and another of his agents, Klop Ustinov (1892–1962), Peter Ustinov's father, were satisfied that Pujol was indeed Arabel, he was whisked off to London where he was to operate under the direct control of the Head of MI5, Cyril Bertram Mills. (It was Mills's family background that was responsible for that department long being known as The Circus.) Under Mills's tutelage Pujol, now codenamed "Garbo" by MI5, slowly "expanded" his imaginary network to 24 operatives so, with those running costs funded by Berlin, and Pujol on the British payroll to boot, he was absolutely coining it. Just to keep things real, from time to time one of his agents would be reported dead in an air raid or some freak accident, with the appropriate notices published in the press to give credence to such claims. Mills was very hands-on when it came to crafting Garbo's reports, most of which had the one main objective – to keep the Germans convinced that they were spot on with their erroneous belief that the invasion of Europe, when it came, would strike on the Pas-de-Calais. This was already the known conviction of Hitler and his High Command, and Mills's family background had taught him one thing about the human psyche – always tell people what they want to hear and let them see what they want to see. It keeps them happy.

As part of *Fortitude North*, a parallel to *South* and one designed to keep German forces tied up anywhere other than northern France, Garbo also sent reports of a planned invasion of Norway and such was his reputation in Berlin that, in May 1944, the nine German divisions already in that country were augmented by a further three. As D-Day itself drew near, Garbo was sending increasingly pointed information to suggest that the German forces in northern France were soon to be subjected to a show-invasion to force them to move resources from other areas – specifically the Pas-de-Calais, which was where the main force would land. On June 4, the Mills–Garbo team told the Germans to stand by for an important message and on the 6th, when it was already too late for the Germans to rush any last-minute reinforcements to the real beaches, Garbo sent a frantic message detailing the actual landing points but with the overrider that Hitler should not be sucker-punched into shifting resources from where they sat. Garbo was taken at

The urbane and smiling Philby who knew a lot about double agents.
(Topfoto)

his word and Hitler ordered that the panzers and troops on
the Pas-de-Calais should stay put. Remarkably this was still
the case as late as July 29, when Garbo received a radio
message informing him of Hitler's express wish that his
invaluable work be recognized with the Iron Cross First

Class. As Pujol was also given an MBE by the British, this makes him one of the few to be decorated by both sides.

Fearing reprisals after the war, he faked his own death and disappeared to Venezuela to live the quiet life on his amassed wealth. He made such a convincing job of his disappearance that even Mills thought him dead. In 1982, with the need for any secrecy long passed, Mills and Pujol would meet up again when the latter paid a visit to the UK to receive his MBE from the Queen. After that, he returned to Venezuela, where he died six years later in Caracas.

—◦◦◦◦—

MUSSOLINI'S BARBER

The main problem faced by any averagely hairy ruler, be they king or dictator, is whether they end up looking like Bigfoot or run the risk of letting someone get up close and personal with a sharp blade. English kings frequently entrusted the task of the royal shave to their jester or whoever served as their whipping-boys – yes; there really was such a post. (Inspired by the Divine Right of Kings, a doctrine that made it blasphemy to lay hands on the ruling monarch or the heir apparent, English princes each had a friend selected from a noble family for frustrated tutors to beat in his stead.) In the case of Mussolini, the hand that held a razor to his throat was Luigi Galbani (1918–2004).

It seems that famous pate had to be kept shaven because its owner did not want his adoring public to know he was going bald – better the Telly Savalas look than a comb-over. Until the opening of World War II, Mussolini had always favored the tactic of having a barber picked up at random and brought to him immediately to shave his face and head, this precluding any established pattern through which a regular barber could be "got at" by Mussolini's enemies. For reasons uncertain, all this kidnapping of barbers ceased in 1939 and Il Duce settled for new-man-in-town, Luigi Galbani, a member of the family that was already making a reputation for itself in the cheese business – Gruppo Galbani is now Italy's leading producer and exporter of dairy products. Galbani was a mere 21 when he first put a razor to Mussolini's throat, but despite his youth he had already established something of a reputation in Rome, not only as a barber and a gentlemen's hairdresser, but also as a man-about-town who was never seen without a pretty face in tow. Very much a showman, Galbani also knew the value of a "trademark," his being a white linen suit, white shirt, bright red tie, and a black Malacca cane with a silver top. According to his niece, Silvi Fattorini, he never wore a hat in case it messed up his immaculate coiffure and in later life continued this look to become an aging dapper gent.

Before he was ushered into Mussolini's presence for the first time, it was explained to him in words of one syllable that any betrayal of any confidence he may overhear, any attempt to inflict harm on his new client, or any transgression of any kind would result in wholesale retaliation on his family and friends, who would not survive the experience. Galbani nodded his understanding of such conditions and was led into a side room where his new client was waiting. According to Ms Fattorini, her uncle recalled that, after getting Mussolini "sheeted up" and frothy-faced, he nervously picked up his razor only to feel the muzzle of a gun being rammed into his spine by one of the bodyguards. Halfway through that first shave he downed tools and told

Mussolini in no uncertain terms that he simply could not function under such conditions and that perhaps he, Mussolini, had better find another barber with sterner nerves. Shaving a dictator while on the brink of a bad case of the shakes was not, he opined, to be recommended. Mussolini agreed and told the bodyguard to holster his weapon and stand back; it was only when Galbani had finished and removed the white cloth from his client that he saw that Mussolini too held a cocked pistol in his lap. Galbani laughed nervously and said that he had several other high-profile clients who, when visiting his barber shop, always kept a pistol at the ready when reclined and vulnerable in the chair. Although the two never became close, they did come to an understanding of trust, with Galbani on occasions even required to shave the legs of Mussolini's mistress, Clara Petacci (1912–1945).

After the war Galbani moved his shop into the ground floor of Rome's Excelsior Hotel on the Via Veneto, and no matter how many incentives he was offered by journalists or inquisitive customers, anxious to get him to reveal some hitherto unknown snippet, he always replied that his lips were sealed. According to Silvi, this was not out of any misplaced loyalty to the dead dictator but a fervent desire by Galbani for it to be common knowledge throughout the city that he was saying nothing; Rome still teemed with disgruntled Fascists who might pay him and/or his loved ones a visit. Only in the mid-1960s did he feel safe to talk, and told family members of something that only became guessed at in the early years of the new millennium. It was common knowledge that Mussolini was an adulterer but no one outside the Fattorini family knew that he was also a bigamist who had murdered his first wife and son when they became politically "inconvenient."

In 1909, Mussolini was an up-and-coming political thug with a rough charm that attracted Ida Dalser (1880–1937), who ran a beauty parlor in Milan. They married in 1914 and, with Benito Albino born the next year, Ida sold her business to fund her husband's political ambitions. But Mussolini soon tired of her and, abandoning her and Benito Albino, returned to his previous mistress, Rachele Guidi (1890–1979) with whom he entered into a bigamous marriage on December 17, 1915 in Treviglio, Lombardy. Ida knew nothing of her errant husband and his new domestic arrangements until his rise to prominence, when, not a lady to take it lying down, she made a nuisance of herself, claiming to be the first and rightful Mrs Mussolini with a son to prove it. Mussolini responded by sending out agents to track down and destroy any paper trail that linked him to Ida and, just for good measure, in 1922 he had her committed to Pergine Valsugana lunatic asylum. From here she was transferred to the hospital island of San Clemente, Venice where she would die of a "brain hemorrhage." Benito Albino (1915–1942) was also abducted in 1922 and, told his mother was already dead, was adopted as an orphan by the Fascist controller of Sopramonte in Sardinia. But, like his mother, he too would not keep quiet, constantly announcing himself to be Mussolini's son. As a result he was whisked away to the Mombello Asylum in Milan Province to die of "consumption."

Apparently, while waiting one day to do Mussolini's head and Petacci's legs in the one sitting, Galbani overheard the latter on the phone in the adjoining room discussing the fate of Dalser and son, both of whom were, it seems, dispatched with lethal injection. Realizing that this would be his fate too, if anyone thought he had overheard, he swiftly lay down in the prepared chair and, drawing a towel over his face, pretended to be taking a nap while waiting. It was a full 15 minutes before Petacci came into the room, by which time Galbani had indeed fallen asleep and was thus quite convincing in his awakening act.

Although Petacci was the latest acquisition, Rachele never complained and remained loyal to her husband to his death and beyond. One of their children, Romano (1927–2006) became quite a famous jazz pianist who married Sophia Loren's sister, and their daughter, Alessandra (b.1962), Loren's niece, managed the unusual shift from soft-porn to politics to sit in the Italian Chamber of Deputies as an outspoken defender of her grandfather and a volatile neo-Fascist. As for Galbani, in the 1980s he was consulted by the makers of George C. Scott's *Mussolini: The Untold Story* (1985), the stars and producers all being anxious to get the right look, so who better than Galbani? But by this time he had hung up the razors and retired, his business one of the many casualties of modern electric shavers. Few today have the time or the money to indulge the luxury of an old-fashioned wet shave and a phone call to that hotel, now the Westin Excelsior, reveals that no one on the desk even remembers a time when the foyer boasted the city's most famous barber.

─◦◦◦─

O COME ALL YE FAITHFUL

Historically speaking, Scotland's worst enemy was its own divisive geography, which produced the localized attitudes of its lairds and chieftains who, swapping allegiance at the drop of a groat, and couldn't see past the next cattle raid on their neighbor. Each laird was monarch of his own glen and, spending most of his time stuck up some obscure valley, never saw the larger picture; any temporary show of clan unity was simply a matter of profit or expediency, to be abandoned at the first inconvenience. Few Scottish "heroes" matched up to their Hollywood image. Rob Roy McGregor was a murderous criminal who sold intelligence to the English during the First Jacobite Rebellion of 1715, the original Agent Orange, no less; William "Braveheart" Wallace was a decidedly shifty piece of work and his one-time ally, Robert the Bruce, betrayed Scotland to join the English. As for the so-called Bonnie Prince Charlie, he wasn't bonnie, he wasn't a prince – he wasn't even Scottish – so all the guff about his having been a windswept Highland romantic bent on leading Scotland to its destiny is best left on the lids of tartan shortbread tins sold to the tourists. The final nail in his well-deserved coffin was hammered in by an Irish adventurer called Dudley Bradstreet (1711–1763).

The First Jacobite Rebellion of 1715 (its name is a good linguistic clue to the fact that "Jack" is the by-form of "James" and not "John") was an abortive effort to oust the Protestant William of Orange from the throne in London and replace him with the Catholic James "The Old Pretender" Stuart (1688–1766). Naturally it all ended in tears, with James heading for the protection of Rome where he married the Polish Maria Sobieski (1702–1735), who sounds as if she could have done with a few oranges herself as she died of scurvy when only 33. But she had by that time produced two sons, Henry Benedict Stuart (1725–1807), Charlie's brother who became a cardinal in the Vatican, and Charles himself (1720–1788). Something of a petulant fop, Charles took it into his head in 1743 that he could rally the Scottish and, with military help from France, put his father on the

English-Scottish throne. Courtesy of a French frigate, BPC – as we shall refer to him from now on – was put ashore, seriously drunk, at Eriskay in the Outer Hebrides on July 23, 1745 where the locals couldn't understand a word he said. It was no better when he tried English and so his mission did not get off to the most auspicious of beginnings, with the locals shrugging and sniggering, and eventually shuffling off to leave the arm-waving loony and his seven companions on the beach. As BPC was pondering his next move, he was approached by someone indicating they should follow him to the house of Angus MacDonald, principle landowner of the area. Here they were given food and shelter, with their host cautioning BPC that he should pass himself off for the meantime as a visiting Italian priest, such visits to the isles being so routine as to arouse neither interest nor suspicion.

Despite the majority of Scots being Protestant and regarding BPC as a drunken waste of space, he did manage to rally a small army that was soon swelled by those aforementioned lairds and warlords who saw the potential for profit through looting. After they took Edinburgh, the Highlanders were all in favor of calling it a day; they had no interest in marching south of the border until BPC lied through his teeth about an army of English Jacobites just waiting for the call. Thinking only of the loot, the army leaders agreed to enter England and, as is well known, by December 4, 1745 they had made it as far south as Derby, a scant 120 miles from London. Here they sat arguing and, unaware that the road ahead was open and London largely deserted in panic, the lairds were again in favor of throwing in the towel; there was no help from France; there was no sign of any English Jacobite force; their pockets were full; and they just wanted to go home. And, while BPC reeled around in drunken petulance, the Duke of Cumberland's ace card wandered into their meeting room, in the city's Exeter House, on December 6.

Born in Tipperary, where his family had profited under land grants from Oliver Cromwell, Dudley Bradstreet had led an interesting if erratic life; by 1745 he had variously attempted and failed as a linen merchant, a brewer, a soldier, a playwright, and a professional gambler. But he was a plausible rogue and had wormed his way into the confidences of

Prince Charles Edward (1907), also known as Bonnie Prince Charlie, the last serious Stuart claimant to the British throne and leader of the unsuccessful Jacobite rebellion of 1745–1746. (The Print Collector / Topfoto)

the Duke of Cumberland, son of George II and the man delegated to deal with BPC and his motley crew. Since the first whisper of BPC's arrival, Bradstreet had conducted some pretty comprehensive spying missions, mainly among the Jacobite supporters in London, who were very easy to find. Although Catholic worship was illegal in the city, the embassies of Catholic nations, such as Spain, Portugal, and, of course, Italy, were allowed to have places of worship in which they could observe their own practices. To the ire of the English authorities, these nations bent the rules by building massive churches capable of accommodating hundreds and threw the door open to any who cared to join them. The rallying song of these supporters of a Catholic monarch was "Adeste Fideles," as penned by rabid Jacobite John Francis Wade and sung lustily in all such Catholic enclaves. Better known today as "O Come all ye Faithful" and mistaken for a Christmas carol, the printed songsheets for this seditious little ditty were adorned with Jacobite symbols and the lyrics riddled with sly reference to what was going on at the time − "Star-led Chieftains" and so forth. Anyway, these were the groups infiltrated by Bradstreet who kept Cumberland up to date as to who was in which Church and who they associated with when not enjoying the diplomatic protection of other nations. It was from these Church infiltrations that Dudley had learned so much about Jacobite thinking, rituals, and coded signs that he could easily pretend to be one of them. Cumberland, as a result, decided to send him north to spread false rumor in BPC's camp.

When he arrived in Derby on December 6, BPC and his commanders, Lord Murray in particular, were virtually at each others' throats; no one apart from BPC wanted to go deeper into England and even the Scottish were becoming concerned about how much booze he was packing away. The stage was thus set for Bradstreet to deliver the death blow to the Jacobite cause. Presenting himself as Captain Oliver Williams, he told the assembly that he had ridden to warn them that Cumberland was already at Lichfield in Staffordshire, barely 25 miles away, with an army numbering 9,000. Bradstreet obviously had a sense of humor; the false name he adopted was the real name of Oliver Cromwell, whose family abandoned the surname to hide their Welsh origins. But no matter the name, he won the game; Murray and the others took him at his word and told BPC they were all heading north whether he liked it or not. Although he was nowhere near at the time, Cumberland did indeed catch up with the retreating rabble, at Culloden in the following April, where he wiped them out in less than an hour. Murray and the others wanted to make their stand on the far side of the river and force the enemy to come to them, but BPC would have none of it and ordered the force to array on open ground. Not having a clue how to run a battle, he left his men standing under Cumberland's artillery for more than 20 minutes, while he was safely out of sight and range with his bottle. Berated by the clan chieftains he eventually ordered a charge, by which time the sadly depleted force succumbed to grapeshot and disciplined musketry. It was BPC who butchered these men, as much as Cumberland. A good indicator as to the level of affection and regard that the Scots in general felt for their drunken messiah is the fact that there were more of them in Cumberland's force than fighting with BPC.

Leaving his men to the English bayonet, BPC fled north to Skye where, dressed as a maid and aided by the legendary Flora McDonald, he managed to escape on a French frigate that took him home to Italy. There he degenerated into a fat letch who was always so full of booze and self-pity that few gave him the time of day. Flora and her husband, Allen, moved to North Carolina where they both played prominent parts in the Loyalist ranks during the American War of Independence (1775–1783). Allen was captured at the patriot victory at Moore's Creek, resulting in the pair of them being expelled to Nova Scotia in 1776. As for Dudley Bradstreet, he hurried back to the safety of London to wait for Cumberland to return from his ruthless suppression of the Highlands and then made representation for the handsome payment he had been promised for his various missions. When Cumberland fobbed him off Bradstreet decided it was time for one last con and then back to Ireland. Having booked the Haymarket Theatre, Bradstreet started a whirlwind of publicity about a one night performance of a wonderful magician who would demonstrate his ability to play every musical instrument known, six at a time, and then fit himself into a large wine bottle. On the appointed night the audience sat patiently but the curtain never rose and by the time the mood turned ugly Bradstreet was already on his way with the takings, leaving his frustrated punters to trash the theater. He settled in Westmeath and wrote a book of his life's adventures before dying there in 1763. The more "respectable" side of the family, headed by his brother, Simon, established the Irish Baronetcy of Bradstreet.

—⟨ᴗ⟩—

LUCKY YAMAGUCHI

Born on March 16, 1916, it is difficult to say whether Tsutomu Yamaguchi is the luckiest man alive or the unluckiest, as he is the only person known to have survived both the Hiroshima and the Nagasaki atomic bombings. His friends and co-workers, Akira Iwanaga and Kuniyoshi Sato, come a pretty close second.

In May 1945 these three technical draftsmen of Nagasaki had been sent by their supervisor to the Mitsubishi shipyards at Hiroshima to check and sign off some designs and blueprints and were due to finish on August 6 – the day *Enola Gay* came calling. Early that morning, all three quit the company lodgings and were heading for the bus to the shipyard when Yamaguchi realized he had forgotten the personalized stamp he needed to monogram the last few remaining documents at the shipyard. He told Iwanaga and Sato to carry on and he would catch the next bus. The terminus was perhaps 2 miles from the shipyard, and by the time Yamaguchi was making this walk his friends were already in the offices saying their goodbyes and assuring everyone that he, Yamaguchi, would be there any minute. At the mid-point in his journey, Yamaguchi recalls:

It was a flat and open spot with potato fields of either side. It was a very clear and fine day, nothing unusual and I was in good spirits. As I was walking along I heard the noise of a plane, just one. I was looking up in the sky and saw the B-29; it dropped two parachutes. I was still looking at them when suddenly it was like a flash of magnesium in the sky; a great flash and I was blown over. I didn't know what had happened. I think I fainted for a while. When I opened my eyes everything was dark, and I couldn't see much. It was like the start of a film at the cinema, before the picture has begun when the blank frames are just flashing up without any sound. I saw my baby son, and I saw my wife and brothers – they all came to my eyes in a flash. I thought I might have died, but eventually the darkness cleared and I realized I was alive. When the noise and the blast had subsided I saw a huge mushroom-shaped pillar of fire rising up high into the sky. It was like a tornado, although it didn't move, but it rose and spread out horizontally at the top. There was prismatic light, which was changing in a complicated rhythm, like the patterns of a kaleidoscope. The first thing I did was to check that I still had my legs and whether I could move them. I thought, "If I stay here, I'll die." Two hundred yards ahead there was a dugout bomb shelter, and when I climbed in there were two young students already sitting there. They said,

219

"You've been badly cut; you're seriously injured." And it was then I realized I had a bad burn on half my face, and that my arms were burned.

After resting in the shelter a while, Yamaguchi made his way to the shattered shipyard offices to find that Iwanaga and Sato too had survived: "We had no idea what kind of bomb it was, of course. All we knew was that it had been just a single bomb, but it had done all this." Perhaps not thinking too clearly, the three men commandeered a power launch to make their way back to Hiroshima, where the full impact was played out in front of them; apart from the constructional damage there were naked, burned, and blinded "zombies" everywhere:

> They didn't cry. I saw no tears at all. Their hair was burned, and they were completely naked. I saw so many of these children. Behind them big fires burned. Miyuki Bridge, next to our dormitory, was still standing, but all over it there were burned people, children as well as adults, some of them dead, some of them on the verge of death. They were the ones who couldn't walk any more, who had just lain down. None of them spoke; none of them had the strength to say a word. It's funny that during that time, I didn't hear human speech, or shouts, just the sound of the city burning. Under the bridge there were many more bodies, bobbing in the water like blocks of wood.

With nothing on their minds but getting home to their respective families, the three made their way through the confusion and at some point Sato got separated from Yamaguchi and Iwanaga. Once home, Yamaguchi sought treatment for his extensive burns and recalled that he was so bandaged up that his own family failed to recognize him until he spoke. After all that, the most diligent worker might have pulled a sickie, but not Yamaguchi, who thought he ought to report directly to his supervisor the next day – August 9.

> I reported to the director who had sent me to Hiroshima and he asked me what was going on there. I said that I didn't know what kind of bomb it was but that a single one had destroyed the entire city. I told him that I had come back with Iwanaga, but that I failed to come back with Sato, although I knew he was alive. Well, the director was angry. He reproached me for losing Sato. He said, "A single bomb can't destroy a whole city! You've obviously been badly injured, and I think you've gone a little mad." At that moment, outside the window, I saw another flash and the whole office, everything in it, was blown over. We were both on the ground. The director was shouting, "Help me! Help me!" I realized at once what had happened, that it was the same thing as in Hiroshima. But I was so angry with the director. I climbed out of the window and got away because I had to help myself.

As Yamaguchi was wisely abandoning the truculent supervisor to his own devices, Iwanaga was several kilometers outside the city on an inbound train and quite uninjured. Sato too had made it back to Nagasaki in time for his second brush with the atomic age and was in the city's dockyards, trying to convince scoffing colleagues of the fate of Hiroshima, when he saw the flash and instinctively flung himself into the dock and stayed under until his lungs drove him to the surface again.

Burned and injured again, Yamaguchi made it home and collapsed in the shelter he had built behind his now destroyed house. Tended by his wife, he came round on the 15th, just in time to hear Hirohito's capitulation speech, at which he says he felt neither pleasure nor sadness; just numbness.

Iwanaga and Sato took postwar jobs in local government and are still living in the Nagasaki area.

Yamaguchi, the oldest of the three, continued in the Mitsubishi Corporation after the war. Katsutoshi, the newborn son he had to leave behind in May 1945 to go to Hiroshima, died of cancer in 2004, aged 59. Yamaguchi was, as one might imagine, a very active opponent of nuclear weapons in general right up until his death on January 4, 2010.

THERE'S SOMETHING WRONG HERE

Few below the age of 50 would today recognize the name of My Lai, an unremarkable Vietnamese village soon to be dragged back into the limelight by Oliver Stone's fourth cinematic take on that war, *Pinkville* (2011). Those already familiar with the horrors visited upon My Lai will no doubt remember Lieutenant William Calley as the prime mover, but who gave him the orders he claimed he was following; who were the only true heroes of the hour; which now-famous military figure first tried to bury the truth; and who finally dragged that truth from beneath its stone?

In the lead-up to the 1968 massacre of more than 500 unarmed civilians – the youngest less than a year old and the oldest in their eighties – at the cluster of villages known as My Lai, tacit "kill targets" had been set by certain commanders, and Charlie Company of the 1st Battalion, 20th Infantry Regiment, 11th Brigade, 23rd Infantry Division were not doing so well in the league tables. It was suspected, rightly or wrongly, that some of the villagers, willingly or not, were giving supplies to Vietcong insurgents in the area and orders were given by Colonel Oran K. Henderson that "Pinkville," as he called it, was to be "closed down." Charlie Company was under the unsteady hand of Second Lieutenant William Calley, he in turn receiving his orders from Captain Ernest Medina, who came straight from Henderson's briefing. Calley, and others present, were told by Medina that all bona fide civilians would have left the villages for market by 7am, so anyone remaining should be considered Vietcong or Vietcong sympathizers. Asked directly whether these orders covered the killing of women and children, some of those present at that briefing would later testify that Medina was quite specific and affirmative that Vietcong combatants and "suspects," including women and children, were to be shot before the livestock was slaughtered, the wells polluted or blown up, and the village razed to the ground. He was quoted in the subsequent inquiries and trials as having wound up the briefing by saying, "They're all V.C. now; go and get them. Who is my enemy? Anyone running away from us; anyone hiding from us and anyone who even *appears* to be the enemy. If a man is running, shoot him and if a woman is running, shoot her."

The next morning, March 16, Medina and Calley moved into the village and what happened next matches any nightmare you can conjure up. There were no Vietcong, there was no enemy, no booby traps, no arms cache; just villagers. But none the less it started. Over the next three hours every atrocity imaginable was inflicted; it is extremely doubtful that Oliver Stone could come anywhere close to depicting what happened in My Lai that March. But a little-known hero of the day did arrive – Warrant Officer Hugh Thompson (1943–2006), a helicopter pilot who flew over My Lai and could not believe his eyes. His recorded transmission to the other pilots in his group was: "It looks to me like there's an awful lot of unnecessary killing going on down there. Something ain't right about this. There's bodies everywhere. There's a ditch-full of bodies that we saw. There's something wrong here."

Having witnessed Captain Medina kicking an unarmed woman about the ground like a football before shooting her in the head, Thompson landed near the ditch and, realizing that some were still alive, he asked one Sergeant David Mitchell to help get them out and away to safety; Mitchell's response was to spray the ditch with automatic fire. Thompson next tried to get sense out of Calley, who said he was simply following orders, that he was in charge on the ground and that Thompson should get back in his helicopter and "mind his own fucking business." Spotting a group of women and children running from giggling troops, Thompson took off and landed between the civilians and the troops before giving the bravest order of his life; he got out, telling his door gunners that if the troops opened up on him or the civilians as he brought them out to safety then they, the door gunners, were to open up with their .50 cals and shoot to kill. His two door men, Glen Andreotta and Lawrence Colburn, gave Thompson their word that they would, without hesitation, follow his order to the letter and the murderers backed down. Thompson and the crew then ferried out 16 survivors while the mayhem continued; by the time they returned the only living thing in My Lai was a completely traumatized four-year-old boy, so they flew him out too. Thompson and the other pilots reported what they had witnessed to their company commander, Major Frederic W. Watke, but the cover-up was already in progress.

Despite Thompson talking directly to Colonel Oran Henderson, My Lai hit the front pages of every newspaper in America as a stunning victory in which 128 Vietjetcong had been killed during a day-long and bloody firefight. General Westmoreland, Commander-in-Chief of American forces in Vietnam, was wheeled out to congratulate Calley and his men publicly for the wonderful job they had done. The only "good" thing to come out of the horror was the fact that all the punitive exercises planned for other villages were immediately put on indefinite hold or canceled altogether. Thompson was hurriedly awarded the Distinguished Flying Cross and praised for his having rescued a child from the middle of an "intense crossfire" and for his "sound judgment, which greatly enhanced Vietnamese-American relations in the operational area." Almost sick with laughter, Thompson threw it in the bin. But the truth that the High Command was so desperate to keep captive was already worming its way free of their grasp.

Nothing stops gossip and, with rumors spreading fast through the rank and file, within six months, Tom Glen, a 21 year old in the 11th Light Infantry, wrote a letter to General Creighton Abrams, Westmoreland's replacement. Stating that he deplored the general brutality of American troops to the civilian population in general, Glen also hinted at the horrors of My Lai without actually mentioning the village by name. Fearing this to be the first crack in the can of worms they dreaded being opened, the "investigation" of these allegations was put into the carefully selected and "safe" hands of a 31-year-old major who could be trusted not to fumble the ball. Then holding the position of Assistant Chief of Staff for Operations G-3 at the divisional headquarters in Chu Lai, this major was careful to conduct his so-called investigation without talking to Glen, and swiftly concluded the matter with a risible report that dismissed all Glen's allegations. Using a distorted kind of "Catch 22" logic, the report stated that Glen's allegations of atrocious relationships between American troops and Vietnamese civilians, caused by the brutality of the former, must be false because, as everybody knows, relationships between American troops and the Vietnamese were just peachy. As it turned out, Colin Powell, author of the the report, was wasting his time because another, far more damaging letter was already in the post.

Ronald Ridenhour (1946–1998), a helicopter gunner who had been a member of Charlie Company before the massacre, had built up a full and damning file of evidence and statements on the incident and in March 1969 sent a letter to President Nixon, the State Department, the Joint Chiefs of Staff, and several members of Congress. The following is a precis of what he had to say:

All the men from whom I heard reports of the "Pinkville" incident were reassigned to C Company, lst Battalion, 20th Infantry, 11th Light Infantry Brigade. In late April 1968 I was awaiting orders for a transfer from HHC, 11th Brigade to Company E, 51st Inf., (LRP), when I happened to run into Pfc "Butch" Gruver, who told me how Charlie Company 1/20 had been assigned to Task Force Barker in late February 1968 to help conduct "search and destroy" operations on the Batangan Peninsula. Gruver said that Charlie Company had sustained casualties, primarily from mines and booby traps, almost every day from the first day they arrived on the peninsula. One village was particularly troublesome and seemed to be infested with booby traps and enemy soldiers. It was located about 6 miles northeast of Quang Nhai city and nicknamed Pinkville. One morning in the latter part of March, Task Force Barker moved out from its firebase to destroy Pinkville and all its inhabitants.

The other two companies that made up the task force cordoned off the village so that Charlie Company could move through, destroying the structures and killing the inhabitants. Any villagers who ran from Charlie Company were stopped by the encircling companies. I asked Butch if all the people were killed and he said he thought so. He recalled seeing a small boy, about three or four years old, standing by the trail with a gunshot wound in one arm. The boy was clutching his wounded arm with his other hand and then the captain's RTO [radio operator] put a burst of 16 [M-16 rifle] into him. It was so bad, Gruver said, that one of the men in his squad shot himself in the foot in order to be medivaced out of the area and away from the slaughter. Although he had not seen it, Gruver had been told by people he considered trustworthy that one of the company's officers, 2nd Lieutenant Kally [this spelling may be incorrect] had rounded up several groups of villagers (each group consisting of a minimum of 20 persons of both sexes and all ages). According to the story, Kally then machine-gunned each group. Gruver estimated that the population of the village had been 300 to 400 people and that very few, if any, escaped.

When I arrived at "Echo" Company, 51st Infantry (LRP), the first men I looked for were Pfcs Michael Terry and William Doherty. Both were veterans of Charlie Company, 1/20 and Pinkville. They corroborated Gruver's story, adding some information of their own. Terry and Doherty had been in the same squad and their platoon was the third platoon of

C Company to pass through the village. Most of the people they came to were already dead. Those that weren't were sought out and shot. The platoon left nothing alive, neither livestock nor people. Around noon the two soldiers' squad stopped to eat. "Billy and I started to get out our chow," Terry said, "but close to us was a bunch of Vietnamese in a heap, and some of them were moaning. Kally had been through before us and all of them had been shot, but many weren't dead. It was obvious that they weren't going to get any medical attention so Billy and I got up and went over to where they were. I guess we sort of finished them off.

Terry went on to say that he and Doherty went back to their meal. Doherty thought that the population of Pinkville had been 400 people.

In late June 1968 I ran into Sergeant Larry La Croix, who had been with Kally at Pinkville. He verified the others' stories, further stating that he had been witness to Kally's gunning down at least three separate groups of villagers. Kally had his men drag men, women, and children of all ages out of bunkers and hootches and put them together in a group. As soon as he felt that the group was big enough – maybe 30 or 40 people – Kally ordered an M-60 set up and the people killed. La Croix said that he bore witness to this procedure at least three times. When the first group was put together Kally ordered Pfc Torres to man the machine gun but after a few bursts he refused to fire again, no matter how many times Kally told him to resume fire, so Kally took over the M-60 and finished off the first groups himself. La Croix told me that Kally didn't bother to order anyone to take the machine gun when the other two groups of villagers were formed. He simply manned it himself and shot down all [the] villagers.

In the middle of November 1968 I talked to Pfc Michael Bernhardt, who told me that because he refused to take part in the slaughter he was approached that evening by Captain Medina, who warned him not to do anything silly, like writing to his Congressman, or anyone else, about what had happened. Something black happened in Pinkville in March 1968; I have considered sending this to newspapers, magazines, and broadcasting companies, but I somehow feel that investigation and action by the Congress of the United States is the appropriate procedure. I have no desire to further besmirch the image of the American serviceman in the eyes of the world.

Unbelievably, all recipients bar one buried their heads in the sand; only Arizona Congressman, Morris "Mo" Udall (1922–1998) stepped up to the plate to make sure that Ridenhour would not be ignored. But the military and the Nixon administration had already set in place a damage limitation plan to make sure the trials that started in September 1969 would go the "right" way. To cut short a long and seedy story, of the 26 officers and men indicted for either participating in the atrocity itself or in the subsequent cover-up, everybody walked except Calley, who was sentenced to life in Leavenworth. The trial itself was a whitewash of such magnitude. As it turned out, with Nixon's intervention, Calley was instead placed under house arrest in his own quarters in Fort Benning and paroled in November 1974.

Thompson and Ridenhour suffered vilification from many quarters, with L. Mendel Rivers (1905–1970), Chairman of the House Armed Services Committee, opining that the only person who should be prosecuted was not that nice young Bill Calley but Thompson for ordering his men to fire on American troops. Rising above the endless death threats, hate mail, and physical abuse, Thompson completed his military career to retire a major in 1983 and, in 1998 he, Colburn, and Andriotta (posthumously) were awarded the Soldier's Medal, America's highest award for bravery that does not involve contact with the enemy.

—⟨✕⟩—

THE WHORE WHO SAVED GIBRALTAR

By 1939 Kitty Schmidt was 57 and, as one of Berlin's premier Madams, had amassed a considerable fortune, which she had for years been salting away in London. As things grew darker in prewar Berlin, little was to Kitty's taste; the bulk of her old-time clientele, especially the rich Jewish bankers and businessmen, had been muscled out by prominent Nazis and it just wasn't the same game anymore. Also, all the normal police harassment and demands for bribes had mysteriously come to an abrupt halt so she suspected that there must be some kind of major raid and closure coming her way some time soon. Unaware that she was already under constant surveillance by the Gestapo, Kitty packed her bags on June 26 and headed for the Dutch border, intending to sail from Amsterdam and perhaps begin again in London. When she reached the border she was whisked out of line and back to Gestapo headquarters at 8 Prinz Albrecht Strasse, where she was ushered into a room to be confronted by Obersturmführer Walter Schellenberg.

The more polite and conciliatory Schellenberg got, the more worried Kitty became, until he laid all his cards on the table. He explained that he was fully aware of all her transgressions: the illegal transfers of money to London through some of her old Jewish clients and aiding and abetting some of those same Jewish bankers to escape the country with forged papers and passports that she had obtained for them. This was more than enough to have her hanged – but she could rehabilitate herself in the eyes of the Reich if she would agree to continue in business, with a few significant alterations. Schellenberg knew well the lip-loosening power of booze and sex combined, as they had already bugged a few of the top-class brothels and found the results to be most rewarding. How better the harvest would be, they reasoned, if they actually ran the best brothel in the city with all the rooms bugged, proper recording facilities in a secure basement next door, and all the girls trained in low-key, surreptitious interrogation techniques. Until the war began it would be interesting to hear what diplomats and other prominent non-Germans had to say and, after the outbreak of hostilities, it would be a neat way of keeping tabs on the true opinions and "trustability" of the Nazi elite, military and non-military, who would be channeled through Kitty's doors. Given the Hobson's choice of die or comply, Kitty had no option but to agree.

As her premises at 11 Giesebrechtstrasse were gutted, extended into the adjoining properties, and refurbished to the highest standards, Schellenberg was busy putting together the "pride of loins" that would be the powerhouse of this overblown honey trap. Having interviewed and assessed over a thousand possibles – the poor chap must have been exhausted – he eventually had his coterie of 30 girls to send for training. All selected for their beauty and social skills, some of these were genuine working girls and some were volunteers from the ranks of the SS and Gestapo. All were told never to discuss, even among themselves, the true nature of the operation or whatever they heard from the clients and, since none of the girls knew which of them was Gestapo and which not, their collective secrecy was assured through fear of immediate death. While the surveillance experts wired the brothel from top to bottom, the girls were taken off for five weeks' intensive training in the Ordensburg at Sonthofen in the Bavarian Alps, this being a sort of indoctrination center for prospective members of the SS or the Nazi party per se. Having taken over a wing and segregated themselves from all the others, the girls were lectured and put through role play to train them how to elicit information from subjects without asking direct questions. Those with language skills were given crash courses in the regimental insignia and rank indicators of the relevant army, and all had to learn by heart the gamut of German military paraphernalia. As their training drew to a close the brothel was standing ready with every bedroom, corridor, restroom, and lounge wired for sound; no one could utter a word within those walls without it being picked up and recorded on the bank of machines in the underground operations center.

With the girls back in Berlin it was time to give the whole shebang a dummy run, so a group of unsuspecting junior SS officers were given some soft-soap story of them all having come to the attention of their seniors due to their diligence and devotion to duty, which was to be rewarded with a special pass for an all-expenses-paid night on the town, the highlight of which would be a visit to Madam Kitty's. To the jubilation of the listeners the girls performed admirably, coaxing, cajoling, and flattering their clients into the most outrageous indiscretions about their units' locations, strengths, and likely postings. Schellenberg wanted to arrest the lot but knew he could do nothing without blowing the operation; it is safe to say, however, that those men had their cards marked to be "glass-ceilinged" for the rest of the war. But no matter, Operation *Kitty* was up and running to test the loyalty and discretion-rating of all the Germans who made use of Kitty's hospitality and to pick the brains of any visiting dignitaries who popped in for a bit of "diplomatic service."

Not only did the girls become extremely good at the "pillow talk" side of their jobs but the bugging of the softly lit lounges proved invaluable, as the clients tended to use these to relax afterwards, over the ever-flowing drink, and those unguarded conversations also proved to be most revealing. As with any intelligence gathering mission, most of the recordings made – more than 10,000 in 1940 alone – were mundane and of little value, but several high-ranking officers revealed decidedly kinky predilections that might prove useful blackmail material for the future, while others let slip that they were not exactly great fans of Hitler and thus not to be trusted. Count Ciano, the Italian foreign minister and Mussolini's son-in-law, amused the monitors with an anti-Hitler polemic in which he revealed that both he and Mussolini regarded the Führer as a ridiculous little man whose grasp of military strategy was laughable. This was just one of the several recordings that Heydrich kept for a rainy day. Another impressive visitor was SS Major-General Sepp Dietrich, a man who had come far from the early days of the party when he had been Hitler's chauffeur and the man from whose headquarters in northern France Rommel had been traveling when strafed off the road. He demanded a dozen girls for a private party on his own and the only thing he revealed to the monitors was an indefatigable stamina; not one of the 12 managed to get anything out of him. But Operation *Kitty* now had a mole.

In the June of 1940 the man masquerading as Ljubo Kolchev, press secretary of the Romanian Embassy, was observing the brothel, as rumors of the true nature of the place had already started in diplomatic circles. From his pavement table at a cafe across the street he started watching a group of the most unlikely looking workmen who were busy routing a new cable into the newly expanded listening post; a bit like plain-clothes police officers trying to look "cool" at a rock concert, these SD intelligence officers, in their brand-new overalls, stood out like sore thumbs. Kolchev, who was in reality MI5 officer Roger Wilson, decided it was time he tasted the forbidden fruits of Miss Kitty's Uber-Sensorium. The pleasures afforded therein were not for the penny-conscious and Wilson had a devil of a job convincing his controllers that his visits to Kitty's would, while personally onerous, be well worth the outlay; eventually granted permission and a suitable budget, Wilson became a regular. After a while he established some sort of relationship with Kitty herself and, through handwritten notes and off-site meetings, he managed, with her connivance, to infiltrate the brothel with other "clients" who were themselves surveillance experts sent in to tap some of the lines.

Apart from listening to the rambling indiscretions and "Achtungs" of ecstasy of the other clients, this was how the British learned of Spain's attitude to the German proposal of their invasion of Gibraltar. In mid-September the Spanish foreign minister, Ramón Serrano Súñer (1901–2003), who was also Franco's brother-in-law, was in Berlin for a series of meetings with Hitler and the Nazi hierarchy, to whom he confided that there was more chance of Spain joining the Axis if he were at the helm instead of Franco. While relaxing in one of the private lounges at Kitty's with Ribbentrop, the conversation turned again to such subjects, with Súñer

Walter Schellenberg, whose "anthology of pros" made secret love for the Führer. (Topfoto)

revealing that Franco too had plans to invade and annex Gibraltar, while the British were otherwise occupied, but he would definitely not take Spain out of its declared neutrality and into the Axis camp until there was a successful German invasion of the UK. Ribbentrop disclosed to Súñer that the Germans were working on their Operation *Felix* for the taking of Gibraltar to secure their supply routes into North Africa, so it might be a good idea if Franco was made aware of that and lied to about Gibraltar being handed over to him at some later date. Essentially the idea was to convince Franco that, if he sat back and did nothing, he would end up with Gibraltar in his lap without having to take overt and irrevocable steps against the British to get it.

This plan seemed to have suited all involved; the last thing the Nazis wanted was for Franco to be in possession of Gibraltar, which would then be in the unassailable position of being part of a neutral country. Fortunately for the British, this conversation took place in one of the rooms that Kitty had allowed Wilson to tap, so immediate steps were taken to "up" the defenses and naval presence around Gibraltar, which left Operation *Felix* on the drawing board for the rest of the war. That Súñer was to be found chatting in such a place as Kitty's is little wonder as he was for most of his adult life a devoted carnal gymnast with a string of illegitimate offspring scattered across Europe. This came back to haunt him in the late 1960s, when he found out that his son, also Ramón, was engaged to a young lady called Carmen Diez de Rivera (1942–1999). He had to explain to the loving couple and their respective families that the engagement had to be broken on account of Carmen being his daughter through a wartime dalliance with her mother. It is perhaps a great tribute to his political skills that he managed to survive this scandal to live to the ripe old age of 101, which meant he outlived every Nazi and Fascist he ever dealt with.

As for Kitty, German intelligence handed her back her brothel in 1943, as the increased bombing raids over Berlin had scared off most of her clients, who didn't fancy feeling the earth move in quite such a literal way. The original coterie of beauties was also diminished as all the "volunteers" returned to less strenuous duties, leaving the others with little to do but lie around drinking the ample liquor stock.

Kitty survived the war to run a string of girls for the American and British – officers only – and died a relatively wealthy women in 1954. As for her Svengali, Walter Schellenberg, he managed to salt away some of the more "interesting" of the nigh-on 30,000 recordings, which revealed, among other things, that Goebbels was a frequent visitor and liked a few of the girls to put on a lesbian display for him, while the less said about Hess the better.

───⟨✿⟩───

TUNNEL VISION

On the afternoon of August 17, 1943, Colonel Henry Cartwright, Military Attaché at the British Embassy in Bern, was enjoying his customary tiffin of Earl Grey tea and bourbon biscuits when this ritual was interrupted by a short and very flustered German being ushered into his office. As Cartwright continued to calmly sip his tea – no milk, of course – the interloper explained that, although an employee of the German Foreign Office, he was and always had been anti-Nazi and that he had with him a batch of decoded telegrams, along with the original coded versions for comparison. The German then went on to suggest that he and Cartwright set up lines of communication so more documents could be forwarded without the risk of further meetings. Replacing his teacup in its saucer with exaggerated care, Cartwright stood up, calmly strolled to the German's side of the desk, and, taking him by the ear, as an old-fashioned headmaster might chastise a wayward pupil, hauled him to his feet, explaining the while that he, Cartwright, was nobody's fool and far too wise to be played for a patsy by some grubby little jackanapes of a Nazi. Continuing to remonstrate in a similar vein, Cartwright dragged the protesting chap to the main door of the residence and, with no little panache, threw him into the street and the telegrams after him.

Unfortunately for British intelligence, Cartwright was indeed a fool, a very nice fool but a fool none the less; his only claim to fame being his escape record of World War I. Best described as Basil Fawlty on Mogadon, he was captured in his first week and spent the rest of the war building tunnels out of POW camps. Having picked a line to the wire and beyond, nothing could change his mind. Disregarding any and all advice to re-route because of obvious obstacles and problems with his chosen path, he then began burrowing like some laser-guided mole until the job was done. And, to be fair, he did escape an amazing 12 times, although due to his habit of marching smartly up to locals and prodding them with his swagger stick, barking questions about local transport, or whatever, either in English or his own brand of pantomime German, he was also recaptured 12 times. Even his captors had a soft spot for him; it was very much a case of slap the lederhosen and, "Oi, zat krazy Cartwright; vot a wag," before they sent transport out to bring him back to camp. Everybody liked Cartwright but no one could take him seriously, which is why he was sidelined to Bern, where, it was thought, wrongly as things turned out, that he could do little or no damage.

As for the German, he hurriedly picked himself up from the pavement outside the British Embassy, gathered up the scattered paperwork, and scurried away, fearful that such a place would be under constant observation by some of his less appealing compatriots, who might recognize him. And he had taken one hell of a risk going there in the first place, for this was none other than Fritz Kolbe (1900–1971), Special Secretary to German Foreign Minister Joachim von Ribbentrop, and the man whose job it was to read and re-route as he thought appropriate all the top-secret coded and decoded telex traffic of the Third Reich. There were only two people in Nazi Germany who saw *all* top-secret missives; one was Hitler and the other Kolbe. As with Cartwright in the British Embassy staff, no one in the German Foreign Office took Kolbe seriously, despite his brief. Short and stocky, with pointed ears, it is perhaps unkind to say but he would not have been long in the make-up department if an extra in *Lord of the Rings* or *Star Trek*, and that seems to have been his salvation. His physical appearance, compounded by the fact that even his name meant club or club-shaped, meant that everyone spent time making jokes about him instead of considering what a danger he might present and monitoring him accordingly.

He managed to wangle his trip to Bern by weaving some yarn about having to finalize his divorce to his wife, a Swiss national, which meant that all the paperwork had to be raised and signed in that country. His trip sanctioned, Kolbe contacted Dr Ernst Kocherthaler, a German Jew of Spanish citizenship who had settled in Bern, this being the chap who set up the meeting for Kolbe with Cartwright that descended into such farce. Returning to Kocherthaler's practice in a state of some agitation, Kolbe was eventually persuaded to give it another try with the Americans. Kocherthaler said he had a contact called Gerald Mayer and that, while he went to see him at 24 Duforstrasse, Kolbe should turn up for work at the German Embassy as normal. While Kolbe sweated it out at his desk, Kocherthaler showed Mayer 16 of the 20 documents that Kolbe had smuggled out of Berlin, taped to his leg. Mayer, giving nothing away, asked Kocherthaler to wait, and took the documents upstairs to the waiting Allen Dulles, head of the fledgling OSS (the CIA to be) that occupied the building. One of the cables gave details of the double agents in the Czech Resistance; another contained the contact details for many of the German agents in North Africa; and another revealed just how much the Germans knew about the deployment of British agents in the Balkans. Dulles could not believe his eyes; was this all genuine? If so, was it a "hook" to establish Kolbe as a bona fide source who would later feed him a sucker punch? The possibilities were endless but, whichever, Dulles was certainly not going to ignore Kolbe as Cartwright had. A further meeting was arranged for the following evening at Mayer's apartment, which Dulles would also attend as Mayer's assistant, "Mr Douglas."

This time Kolbe handed over all 186 of the "flimsy" copies he had with him and "Mr Douglas" abandoned his false persona, especially when he saw the layouts for Hitler's secret HQ on the Eastern Front at Rastenberg. Kolbe remained unshakeable under Dulles' questioning. He told him exactly who he was, where he worked, and why he wanted a Germany free of the Nazis – and no, he did not want one red cent for his trouble. Things eased a bit and, over a drink, Kolbe told Dulles that he had already approached the British and been thrown out. Dulles feigned disbelief, but he had the previous night been in the company of Cartwright, who warned him of "some gawky little oik doing the rounds with bogus info" and boasted of tossing out said oik on "his pointy little ear." Kolbe then said he had loads more such intelligence and, with the flow never-ending, how could he get it through to Dulles. It was decided that Sweden might be a good venue for the next meeting and, on September 16 Kolbe handed Dulles over 500 top-secret copies he had smuggled out in the diplomatic bag, these dealing with everything from the future plans for the Wolf Packs in the North Atlantic to the news that Pierre Laval of the Vichy French government was about to institute the shooting of relatives of anyone fighting for the Gaullist forces. To cut a long story short, Kolbe managed to transfer to Dulles, by various means, more than 3,000 top-secret documents, which made him the most important spy of World War II – and the lowest paid to boot.

One of Kolbe's most alarming revelations was that Berlin had a high-grade source in Istanbul who, among other things, had passed on mention of an Operation *Overlord*, which would involve June landings, but no details of any location. This German "feed," codenamed Cicero, turned out to be Eleysa Banza (1904–1971), valet to the British Ambassador in Istanbul, Sir Hugh Knatchbull-Hugessen, who had been too cavalier with the keys to the diplomatic safe. By the time this information was passed on to the British, Cicero had made a run for South America, only to find out that the Germans had been paying him with their famous forged five-pound notes. And the filter of Kolbe's information from Dulles to British intelligence hides yet another minor player who would later loom large.

Even when they were given a second bite at the cherry that was Kolbe, the British still failed to identify the value of the bounty that was beating them over the head. When Dulles first decided to share the harvested intelligence, the Head of MI6, Lieutenant-Colonel Sir Claude Dansey (1876–1974), the man who effectively set up the department in its viable form, made the same mistake that Berlin had made with Cicero – he dismissed Kolbe out of hand as a plant because the grade of intelligence, if true, was too good to be true. Although nobody's fool, Dansey's misguided dismissal of Kolbe as a German ploy was to have some very far-reaching implications for the British during the Cold War that was yet to come. One of the MI6 juniors who sat in Dansey's office as he made that rash decision was not of the same opinion, and as soon as he was back in his own office he issued a memo to the receiving office to say that Dansey was not to be bothered anymore with the Kolbe copies, which should instead be routed through the sender and nobody else. From that point on, this agent made a name for himself at Bletchley, where decoded text and the corresponding coded originals were a massive help. He also scattered a few nuggets hither and yon to make himself something of a star who was always most careful never to let slip that his "king's clothes" were OSS hand-me-downs from Dulles. And his subterfuge paid off to the great detriment of Britain when that operative, Kim Philby (1876–1947), secretly on the Moscow payroll since 1933, was rewarded for his performance with an appointment as the postwar head of the newly formed Anti-Soviet Counter-Intelligence Section. And the rest, as they say, is history.

WALLPAPER

René Duchez (1903–1948) moved to Caen in 1942 and soon established himself as a touch of "local color," with the Caenites and Germans alike thinking him a harmless buffoon known to all as René Le Con, a soubriquet best not translated here. As a member of the newly formed Centurie resistance movement, this was exactly the cover Duchez intended to build. Just to make sure, he would routinely make bizarre reports to the Germans, leaving them hooting with laughter at his having just seen Churchill and De

Gaulle arguing over their coffee in some local bar, or whatever. He was, on the other hand, an extremely good painter and decorator, who worked at stupidly low prices and thus moved routinely and freely around some of the most sensitive buildings in the area. His local controller was a chap called Marcel Girard, who, as a cement salesman, had heard of orders from the Germans so large that it could mean only one thing; the Atlantic Wall was soon to be extended through northern France.

This was the most impressive construction of the war; a defense complex running from Norway down the Franco-Spanish border with six-foot-thick concrete walls, 13,000 fortified strongholds, and 3,300 heavy gun emplacements, all backed up by 1,400 tanks and 1.8 million troops. With 500,000 beach obstacles, thousands of miles of barbed wire, and 6.5 million mines, this was no half-hearted affair and British intelligence were desperate to get any information on the layout and positioning of any guns and tanks in the Normandy sections, for obvious reasons. The local network did its best but the Germans had declared a forbidden zone along the coast and frequently demonstrated their willingness to shoot anyone who wandered therein. In May 1943 Duchez heard that the Caen offices of the Todt organization needed brightening up, so he left one of his ridiculously low quotes and was told to visit with wallpaper samples and have a chat with the Bauleiter of Caen, a sort of military works-manager, who in this case was Colonel Otto Schnedderer. It would be Schnedderer's office that would oversee and direct the efforts of the Todt workers, basically slave labor, sent to build that section of the Atlantic Wall so it was perhaps no surprise that there were blueprints all over the desk on which he leafed through the sample books while Duchez stood humming and talking to himself. At one point the colonel was called away and obviously felt no qualms about leaving René Le Con unsupervised in his office. Rooting swiftly through the pile of blueprints, Duchez was stunned to see one marked "Atlantikwall" and, knowing he had no chance of getting it out that day, shoved it up behind the heavy mirror into which he was still pulling faces at himself when the colonel returned, shaking his head at the antics of Le Con.

Schnedderer made his selections and told Duchez to start the following Monday, after the electrician had finished chasing some new wiring into the walls. As he left the building Duchez stood grinning with his arms aloft, telling the guards he should be searched but, reluctant to touch him, they told him to be on his way. In the interim, the blueprint was noted missing and Schnedderer had the electrician shot, unaware that he was one of the Gestapo's best informants in Caen. Duchez turned up at the Todt offices to be told that Schnedderer's office was first on the list and that it stood vacant and ready for him to start. Left alone, he retrieved the blueprint from behind the mirror and hid it inside a roll of wallpaper to spirit it out of the building. That evening Duchez went as usual to the Café Les Touristes, which is still there on the Boulevard du Marechal-Leclerc, and passed the plans to Girard, who sent them on to London where the British could not believe their eyes. The plan showed every detail of the 130-mile section of the wall that would run the length of the Channel – bunkers, guns, command posts, fortifications, the lot.

Duchez's cover was eventually blown, and in May 1944 some out-of-town Gestapo agents called at his house, where his audacity saved his skin yet again. Pretending to be an irate customer complaining about some wallpaper being hung upside down in his lounge, he was standing in the kitchen shouting at his wife when the Gestapo barged in and threw him out so he could make his way to safety in Spain.

INVENTIONS AND DISCOVERIES

THE BIRTH OF ROUTE 66

The camel was 40 million years in coming home to North America whence it originated, spreading south to evolve into the llama and the alpaca, and east, across the Alaska-Siberia ice bridge, to plod ever further until it became the creature of Arabian nights. The plot to bring the animal home to serve in the US Army was hatched in 1836 by an otherwise obscure individual called Major George H. Grossman (or Crossman), who, having spent some time in the East, was fully aware of the animal's ability to carry heavy loads through the most inhospitable terrain, as well as its unnerving effects on conventional cavalry; horses hate the sight and smell of camels and are often thrown into panic when so confronted. Seeing a role for camels as uber-mule trains, and ideally suited to taking the fight to the Indians in areas such as Arizona and other western states, Grossman lobbied his Mississippi state Senator, Jefferson Davis (1808–1889), the later president, who also became swiftly enamored with the idea. Both were, however, dismissed as lunatics. But in 1853 Davis became Secretary of War and again brought Grossman's Camel Corps to the fore, finally getting an allocation of funds for the trip east to source stock. On March 3, 1855, Davis managed to convince Senator James Shield of Illinois to include in his Shield Amendment to the Appropriation Bill a submission for $30,000 to be expended "under the direction of the War Department in the purchase of camels and the importation of dromedaries, to be employed for military purposes." Route 66 was soon to begin.

Grossman's fellow camel-buff, Major Henry C. Wayne (1810–1883), and Lieutenant David Dixon Porter (1813–1891), later a celebrated admiral of the Civil War, were given the job of research and appropriation, this taking them from the zoos of Europe, to observations of the camel in military transport in the Crimean War, and thence to Malta and the East, where they were handsomely ripped off by used-camel salesmen to the tune of $12,000 for 32 camels and a motley crew of trainers and handlers. (Some of these Arabs would leave their own footprints on the pages of American history, but more of them later.) Having bought their camels, Wayne and Porter now had to get their truculent stock up the gangway and aboard the waiting US Navy ship *Supply*, this task providing no end of amusement for the locals who lined the docks in their hundreds to see the fun. Once at sea, there were some heated exchanges between Wayne and Porter, with the latter saying he would be damned if he would allow traps to be cut in the decks to allow the camels to pop their heads up for a breath of fresh air. Stormy weather put a stop to all such debate as the handlers said the "passengers," during such turbulence, had to be tied in their kneeling position to prevent injury, but after this had passed Porter conceded to additional "port-holes" being cut in the sides so the camels could stick their heads out to appreciate the sea view.

Supply made American port at Indianola, Texas, to unload its cargo on May 14, 1856, this being the first time Americans got an up-close and personal glimpse of the true nature of the beast. The local band struck up some stirring ditty as the gentlemen of the press moved in for a closer look. Tired and doubtless a trifle emotional from the arduous journey, the camels, unappreciative of the brass band, cut loose with a stunning demonstration of their prodigious capacity and accuracy in the Great Expectorations game, giving all present a liberal coating of foul-smelling goop. The camel wranglers then added to the confusion by screaming at the camels in Arabic and beating them with big sticks, which improved matters no end. The confused beasts broke free of their harnessing to charge the crowd, bellowing and kicking until the spectators fled, leaving Wayne and co. to restore order. With his entourage now shunned by the locals, Wayne, who had originally planned a month's rest in Indianola to let the camels re-find their land-legs, cut short this respite and was underway with his caravan by June 4, shunning all civilization until they made Victoria, Texas. Despite this being a relatively short trip, it was more than enough to convince Wayne that, although they smiled a lot and nodded enthusiastically at everything he said, his "highly experienced" Arabs knew naff all about camels. But no matter; the trek had at least established some sort of working relationship between man and beast and their reception in Victoria was well ordered and pleasing. Here the camels were clipped and one Mary Ann Shirkey used the harvest to spin some camel wool and knit a pair of socks, which she sent to President Pierce, who apparently said something along the lines of, "Oh, goody; itchy socks!" (expletives deleted) before chucking them in the bin.

Moving on, the United States Camel Corps, as it was now formally recognized, established its HQ at Camp Verde, deep in the Arizona Badlands, with the intention of setting up drills and exercises for a long-haul pursuit unit of "camelry" to hound the Apache north. Sure, the Indian ponies would outrun the camels, but over the day, the camels would, however ungainly, cover three times their distance. What was more, they did not need regular watering and could forage where horses would starve; the camels readily took to cactus and thornbush that would tear any other animal's mouth to pieces. With the Camel Corps now seen in some quarters as the Indians' nemesis, in the spring of 1857 Secretary of War, John B. Floyd, sent forth another bit player, Edward Fitzgerald Beale (1822–1893), a one-time sidekick of the likes of Kit Carson and "Buffalo Bill" Cody,

David Dixon Porter, Union Admiral of the American Civil War and camel researcher. (Topfoto)

with instructions to use a detachment of the corps to plot and survey a wagon trail. It was to run from Fort Defiance, along the 35th parallel, across the Colorado River, on to San Bernardino, California, and through to LA – just as the song says. Although not yet called Route 66, this is how the roadway was plotted and opened up; by camels. The speed and ease with which the Beale caravan completed its task sufficiently impressed the Senate for them to earmark funds for the importation of another 3,000 camels. These, when not striding from one side of the nation to the other, would form brigades of camelry in the Indian Territories to drive the locals relentlessly north in "tortoise and hare" campaigns designed to leave the Indian and his pony too tired, thirsty, and hungry to fight back en route. But it was not to be.

Having demonstrated his camels' prowess, Beale donated all 28 of them to the city of San Francisco, where they would carry the mail and baggage from the docks for years to come. But it was now 1860 and with the American Civil War (1861–1865) just around the corner the powers-that-were had other things on their minds than camels and a bunch of troublesome Indians. On top of that there was tremendous opposition from the horse- and mule-dealing lobby, which could easily see itself being driven out of business by camels that could carry with ease four times that of any mule and for much greater distances. Plus there was the "camels look silly" lobby, members of which simply sat back and guffawed at any plans or studies put forward. Comparisons may well be odious but the United States Camel Corps fell victim to the same mentality that put paid to Benjamin Franklin's suggestion of using massed archery against the British during the American War of Independence (1775–1783). On February 4, 1776 Franklin wrote to General Charles Lee:

We have a large quantity of saltpeter, 120 tons ... but I still wish, with you, that pikes could be introduced, and I would add bows and arrows. They were good weapons, not wisely laid aside; 1st, because a man may shoot as truly with a bow as with a common musket. 2nd, he can discharge four arrows in the time of charging and discharging one bullet. 3rd, his object is not taken from view by smoke on his side. 4th, a flight of arrows, seen coming upon them, terrifies and disturbs the enemies' attention. 5th, an arrow striking any part of a man puts him *hors de combat* till it is extracted. 6th, bows and arrows are more easily provided everywhere than muskets. Polydore Virgil, in speaking of one of our [British, not American] battles against the French in Edward III's reign, mentions the great confusion the enemy was thrown into, *sagittarium nube...*

Franklin forgot to mention that the longbow outranged their musketry by more than 100 yards; they could not misfire as did muskets about 20 percent of the time; and that accuracy was not an issue, only volume of fire. It would have been the closest thing to a machine gun and just as devastating, yet, as with the later camels, the idea only failed to gain acceptance because people were afraid of looking silly.

Oddly enough, Camp Verde was an early Union loss, leaving the victorious Confederates puzzled as to how best to put the camels to use. Throughout the conflict camels made cameo appearances for both sides at various battles but their day was done. After the war, all remaining stock was slaughtered, sold off as curios, or simply turned out into the deserts to fend for themselves. And fend they did for quite some time; the last of the wild camel sightings were reported in the 1950s and their nigh-on century's presence in the American West accounts for otherwise inexplicable legislation in states such as Arizona and Nevada that prohibit the riding of camels on the highways and fishing from their backs in rivers and lakes. One of the last face-to-face encounters with a feral camel came in 1886, when one such beast wandered into New Mexico's Fort Seldon to scare the living daylights out of the post commander's six-year-old son, he growing up to be General Douglas MacArthur (1880–1964). As for the camel wranglers, after the corps was disbanded, some remained with the army to fight in the Civil War, while Elias Calles, one of the wranglers, drifted down to Sonora to drink himself to death, but not before, some say, he fathered the lad who would become Elias Calles (1877–1945), the prominent general who became president of Mexico in 1924. Another, Hadji Ali (1828–1902), known to all as Hi Jolly, became something of a "character" of Arizona, which still boasts a few monuments and statues of him. He kept a couple of the prized yellow camels for himself and was oft seen careering round in his camel cart at frightening speed. The cart too was painted the same color as the "engines," in honor of the ancient Persian prophet Zarathustra, whose name translates as yellow-camel.

BRAS AND "BUNNIES"

While it would be going too far to hail the bra an invention of war, it is certainly fair to say that this invention of Mary Phelps Jacob's (1891–1970) was brought to the prominence it now enjoys due only to the metal shortage experienced by America during World War I. As for the more intimate items of feminine hygiene and disposable hankies, these evolved from field dressings and gas-mask liners produced in America for the same conflict.

Although there had been other attempts to produce something supportive for women who did not relish being winched into the sort of bone-crunching corsets that were all the rage in prewar America and the UK, it is generally accepted that it was the particular desire of Mary Jacob to be so unrestrained that put the bra on the map in 1913. Having experimented at home with two silk hankies and some ribbon, she eventually came up with something designed to cup the breast rather then force it into unnatural shapes and positions, just to suit the morals and fashion of the day. She did register a patent and toyed with commercial production but soon bored of the idea and sold out to a young and struggling company called Warners for $1,500 and the rest, as they say, is history – but Warners would have gone bust, no pun intended, had it not been for World War I.

Despite the obvious advantages of comfort and freedom of movement, the bra failed to knock the corset off its pedestal because, especially in America, a woman who was not corporeally confined and restrained in what amounted to anti-passion body armor was not considered "decent"; those who did cavort about in their bras, playing tennis, and what have you, were dismissed as "Flappers" because all their bits and pieces could be seen bouncing up and down. But all that changed in 1917 when America launched a patriotic appeal to its womenfolk, beseeching them to cease buying corsets as the metal used to form the numerous stays could be put to better use. There was also a collection organized for all the stays already installed in the corsets that lay in ladies' closets across the country, which in 1917 alone harvested in a staggering 28,000 tons of metal for the war effort. With it now being un-American to wear a corset, Warners were hard-pressed to keep up with the ever-increasing pace of demand and during the rest of the war raked in an impressive $30 million.

Sporting their Warners, British and American women also got involved in the war, either in war production at home or at the front in the field hospitals where they proved invaluable as nurses and medical attendants. Another war shortage that plagued the field hospitals was that of the cotton they needed for dressings so the then-modest paper manufacturer Kimberly-Clark came up with cellucotton, made from wood-pulp, which was half the cost and five times more absorbent than regular cotton. To their credit, Kimberly-Clark sold vast quantities of this to the American military but always at cost plus a small percentage to cover transport and administration, as they did not want to profiteer from the war. It did not take the nurses long to figure out another use for these highly absorbent cellucotton pads, which at first they simply popped straight into their panties at "that time of the month" before starting to roll the pads into a suitable shape around a retrieval cord and wearing them internally. Previously, small squares of toweling were used, washed, and reused, so this idea from the American and British army nurses was the birth of the disposable product industry, and when news filtered back to Kimberly-Clark the sales people could see a whole new market opening up; but how to advertise such a product in such times? Any thought of the internal version would have to wait for more enlightened times but Kimberly-Clark did set up a subdivision called Kotex, as inspired by "cotton textile," and, after overcoming the initial reticence of magazines to carry the adverts, shops to stock them, and the women to buy them, they really cornered a market of which they still hold over a third.

Eventually the internal version made it onto the market, but reflected its military origins in the various brand names. Since the early 1600s "tampon" had been used to describe the wooden bung put into the barrel of a cannon to keep it free of dust or seawater when not in use. In the field hospitals of World War I the term was used for the kind of dressing used to plug a serious wound, and anecdotal evidence filtering back from the troops in current war zones suggest that the life of the tampon has come full cycle. It seems that many of the more experienced soldiers routinely carry a few tampons for emergency medical use, in that the compact versions are ideal for inserting into a bullet wound, where they immediately swell up, as they are designed to do, and staunch the flow. Not only that but there is also the cord to facilitate easy removal when the injured party is medivaced. As for any use of "tampons," in the military sense, it seems that the troops in Iraq and other dusty climes prefer to use condoms over the barrels of their 50 cals, and the like, as they do an admirable job yet do not have to be removed before firing.

Getting back to Kimberly-Clark and World War I. When the conflict ceased that company, which had been producing flat-out, found itself with warehouses packed to the rafters with the thin synthetic cotton sheeting they used to produce the linings and filters for gas masks. These had been used by those same nurses as disposable wipes to remove their make-up or as throwaway hankies and, as the Kimberly-Clark marketing department could think of no better usage, they launched Kleenex.

FUN-TIME FÜHRER

The image of Hitler dressed up as a camp comedian, judging a knobbly-knees competition in Skegness, or wherever, is not one that readily leaps to mind, but it was none other than the Fun-time-Führer who invented the concept of mass leisure cruising, package holidays, and purpose-built holiday camps to provide cheap, albeit crowded, holidays away for his workers, troops, and their families.

This unlikely story starts with Hitler's institution of *Kraft durch Freude*, or Strength through Joy, that last word, rather paradoxically, being the origin of the notoriously morose psychoanalyst's surname. By the 1930s KdF was the world's largest tourist operator, handling numbers as yet unequalled by any modern company. But, as one might expect with Hitler at the helm, there was a sinister and hidden agenda to all this fun and frolicking; the idea was to stamp unthinking uniformity on the German people; they would all drive the same kind of car, they would all work in uniformly undistinguishable factories and offices, and take their holidays in "secure" environments – afloat, abroad, or at home – but always under the ever-vigilant gaze of "Gross Bruder."

First the car. Hitler personally hired the undeniably brilliant Ferdinand Porsche (1875–1951) to come up with a cheap, reliable, resilient, and utilitarian vehicle for less than 1,000RM. It should also be utterly uniform; no variant models. Hitler's thinking was inspired by the Model T production restrictions of Henry Ford. Porsche was indeed brilliant – despite all the present eco-trumpeting about "innovative" hybrid cars today, he was producing his hybrid Mixte in 1901. So why did he need to lift ideas from a Czechoslovak designer called Hans Ledwinka (1878–1967)? But Hitler loved the design of the Kraft-durch-Freude-Wagen, as it was known, when first produced in 1934. Incensed, Hans Ledwinka couldn't fail to recognize his own Tatra T97 when he saw it and sued, but the case was still being argued when Hitler invaded Czechoslovakia in 1938 so, to help out his protégé, he had the Tatra plant blown up. (Porsche was by then working on his designs for the Tiger tanks and Hitler didn't want him bothered with legal haggles.) The case was successfully resumed after the war with Volkswagen (the people's car) stumping up three million DM in compensation. Of course, none of this mattered at the time; Hitler had what he wanted: stage one completed.

Aerial shot of Hitler's nightmare holiday camp, Prora. (Topfoto)

The hands-on overseer of KdF was a prize piece of work called Robert Ley (1890–1945); not only was he arrogant, incompetent, and roaring drunk half of the time, he was also subject to mood swings and bouts of explosive violence as a result of the brain damage he had incurred when shot down over France in July 1917. All of this might have raised a question or three in the mind of any prospective employer, but in the Nazi party he slotted right in. It was Ley who laid the foundation of Hitler's package-holiday wing of KdF through the purchase or building of self-contained Aryan-only complexes and compounds in Nazi-friendly countries abroad – Spain, Italy, Switzerland, and the Nordic countries – with all the staff, from the top down, Gestapo lackeys ever on hand to catch the odd unguarded comment from holidaymakers who relaxed a bit too much. Ley also set up the first pleasure cruise line; sure, people had always used ships to get from A to B but no one had ever before used ships as a floating holiday venue with all aboard returning to the departure point. It was a roaring success and one to be copied by others after the war; between 1936 and 1938 the KdF Line carried more than five million Germans, including a young Eva Braun (1912–1945) whose film records of such holidays are still in archives.

Flagships of the KdF Line were the *Wilhelm Gustav* and the *Robert Ley*, the former named to honor the memory of the leader of the Swiss Nazi party who had been murdered in 1936 by Jewish assassin David Frankfurter (1909–1982). Frankfurter, proving that political radicals are best advised to have unlisted numbers, simply looked up his quarry in the local phonebook before nipping round to shoot him five times in the head.

The main purpose of the KdF liners was to ensure the passengers were a captive audience for much of the time, allowing Hitler's hidden agenda to be played to full advantage. The ships were rigged for sound throughout and there was no escape from the never-ending stream of Wagnerian music interwoven with soundbites of Hitler's speeches and other indoctrinating garbage. Even the backs of the brochures, menus, and any other literature carried political messages and snippets from the page-turning Nuremberg Race Laws (1935), reminding passengers not, for example, to stoop to sex with members of the inferior races they might encounter on their travels. Having deemed these floating clinics a success, Hitler and Ley moved onto their most ambitious project – Prora.

On Rugen, Germany's largest island in the Baltic, a site was selected for building on a massive scale; indeed, "massive" hardly does Prora credit. Conceived in 1934, with construction commenced in early 1936, this was a complex of 100 six-floor apartment blocks, all joined by corridor wings and designed to accommodate 20,000 people at any one time. Under the supervision of Albert Speer, the Cologne architect Clemens Klotz (1886–1969), drew up plans that won awards at the 1937 Paris World Exhibition. But, stretching 3.5 miles along the coast, this concentration camp style building was not designed for people to come and doss about; using the cruise-ship cabin as a blueprint, the rooms were a scant two meters by four meters with two single beds apiece. Hitler did not want his guinea pigs hidden away in their rooms but out and about so they could be ear-bashed; not only would the entire complex be wired for sound but the grounds too would be peppered with loudspeakers to keep the "holidaymakers" informed of the next events on the carefully planned schedule of "enjoyment." There was even a massive auditorium laid out to hold all 20,000 guests at once so they could be bombarded with stirring lectures and speeches. Fortunately for the Germans, the advent of war called a halt to the nearly finished construction, leaving this Baltic Butlins standing empty and presenting the nightmare vista of a neverending run of the kind of charmless apartment blocks the Soviets used to throw up during the Cold War era.

Betrayed after the war by other Nazis already in Allied custody, Ley was brought to Nuremberg but strung himself up in his cell before American executioner, Master Sergeant Woods, could get a noose on him. His eponymous ship was bombed to a smoking shell in Hamburg on March 9, 1945 while the *Wilhelm Gustav* made maritime history with the greatest ever loss of life in one sinking. Bound out of Gotenhaven for Stettin, she was torpedoed in the Baltic by the Russian S-13 under the mis-command of Alexander Marinesko (1913–1963), who had not long returned to duty after a week-long drunken AWOL with a Swedish barmaid. Although it was clearly marked as a hospital ship, Marinesko dropped the *Wilhelm Gustav*, along with 10,000 women, children, and non-combatants.

Volkswagen, like the rest of postwar Germany, was on its knees and thus offered to the British motor industry as part of the war reparations. The representatives from Rootes and Morris turned this offer down flat, opining that "the vehicle does not meet even the most fundamental technical requirement of a motor car … it is quite unattractive to the average buyer… To build the car commercially would be a completely uneconomic enterprise." They also went on to say that there was absolutely no future for a car with a rear-mounted and air-cooled engine, this placing them shoulder-to-shoulder with the executive of Decca who threw the Beatles out on their ears, saying the time for guitar groups had past.

As for Prora, that monstrosity still stands, with, at the time of writing, plans being put forward to resurrect sections for their original purpose.

FANTASTICHE

It is often stated that Fanta was either invented by Hitler or that he ordered its concoction as a suitable alternative for "good" Germans who should shun Coca-Cola. But Hitler had no beef with Coca-Cola, and although Fanta was indeed a wartime German "invention" it was one born of war shortages, not political preference.

Coca-Cola's German wing, largely under the guidance of its CEO, Max Keith (pronounced "Kite"), trod a dangerous line through the war. Coca-Cola (Germany) was a main sponsor for Hitler's showcase Olympics of 1936, and Keith and his fellow executives had no problem attending trade fairs and the like. But in 1936 the rival Afri-Cola, run by a raving Nazi called Karl Flach, got his hands on some Coca-Cola bottle tops from America that had Hebrew writing on them. Although this was only a company effort to assure the Jewish buyer that all ingredients were kosher, Flach published flyers denouncing Coca-Cola as a Jewish concern. Although instructed by the HQ in Atlanta not to respond, Keith, rather foolishly, issued vehement denials that there was anything "Jewish" about Coca-Cola and, uber-foolishly, placed such denials in *Der Stuermer*, the official Nazi party rag, famed for its hate-fuelled and anti-Semitic rants.

Keith had only just gotten over that hurdle when Göring announced a four-year plan under which all German-based companies would have to become self-sufficient, sourcing all components and elements from within Germany or her avowed allies. With the "secret-recipe" syrups available only from America, this sounded like a death knell for Coca-Cola (Germany) until Keith managed to secure, by means of a hefty backhander to Göring himself, a special import permit. When Hitler invaded Czechoslovakia, Coca-Cola (Germany) appeared to make a pro-Nazi gesture; in the October 1938 edition of *Die Wehrmacht*, the German forces' own magazine, there appeared a full-page ad showing a hand holding a bottle of Coca-Cola over a map of the world with the caption, "*Ja! Coca-Cola hat Weltruf!*," or "Yes! Coca-Cola enjoys international reputation." Hot on the heels of the invading Germans, Coca-Cola (Germany) moved into the Sudetenland to build a massive new plant that would make use of forced labor. Back in Atlanta, the back-wash of profits seems to have attracted notice. It must be said in defense of the present Coca-Cola Company that they have always given generously to funds compensating those who endured such slave labor.

By 1941, with America having entered the fray of World War II, Keith's supplies from Atlanta came to an abrupt end and, having given all his remaining stock to the German Army and the Luftwaffe, he gathered his executives for a survival meeting, telling them they had to put their heads together and come up with a new product that could be sustained by domestically available ingredients. It should also be said that, by this point, HQ Atlanta had lost all contact with Keith and would not really know the full story until after the war; Keith was flying solo! On the subject of Coke and flying, some of those last-stock freebies that went to the Luftwaffe promoted considerable consternation amongst the RAF pilots in North Africa. With no ice available, the Germans took to strapping a few bottles of Coke in wet towels under the wings of their fighters to super-chill them during flight, and British pilots, seeing these strange additions to their adversaries' planes, kept reporting modifications of unknown nature to enemy fighter planes, which had everybody scratching their heads for a while. Anyway, Keith and his team eventually came up with Fanta, which they made from the unappetizing basics of apple fiber from cider-pressings, whey, and flavoring. Surprisingly, it tasted pretty good and sold in its millions.

After the war Keith was arrested as a collaborator and finally cleared, before handing over the interim profits and the recipe to Atlanta HQ, which brought him back into the fold. So while it is certainly true that Fanta was a wartime invention drummed up in Germany, it is well wide of the mark to say that the product was Hitler's "snub" to "enemy" cola or that he had anything to do with its inception. Nor in fact did Coca-Cola, for that matter, with Atlanta being ignorant of what Keith was up to until 1945.

Fanta is still going strong, and is sold in more than 180 countries, with Brazil the largest consumer. Shortly after the war, the French company Perrier, inspired by the Keith saga, decided to follow suit by inventing their own flavored fizzy drink. France's first such product to be home produced, this was marketed under a name inspired by the sound of the bottle being opened but it failed spectacularly to break into English-speaking markets. On the other hand, the still-extant product provided no end of amusement for English and American tourists, who left French waiters puzzled as to why they all broke out in peals of laughter when politely asked if they would like to try a bottle of Pschitt – orange or lemon-flavored.

SOLDIER'S LITTLE HELPER

Life is rife with paradox; consider the irony of the poppy being the symbol of remembrance for British troops when, in Afghanistan, they are trying to stem the flow of opium that funds the activities of the Islamic terrorists who are, for the time being, the generic enemy of the West. Odd then that the Victorian forebears of these soldiers were actually responsible for the very existence of most of those Afghan poppy farms, whence they shipped the deadly harvest by the hundreds of tons to anyone who would buy it. China got fed up of the addiction levels in its population but each time they tried to ban imports of opium from the British, those upright Victorians attacked China to force them to open their doors to Victoria's drug dealers. The First Opium War (1839–1842) resulted in Hong Kong being taken by the British in "restitution" but not everybody was in favor of a war in such cause; new MP William Gladstone denounced the action in Parliament, saying that he doubted there had ever been "a war more unjust in its origin, a war more calculated to cover this country with permanent disgrace." The Second Opium War ran from 1856 to 1860 and was an equally misguided affair. Of course, later British writers tried to rebrand the drugs trade by presenting it to the public as the dreaded "Yellow Peril." Sherlock Holmes stories abound with reference to fiendish Chinese people shuffling from one illegal opium den to another in London's Limehouse district, but it is a sad matter of fact that the possession of opium without a prescription was not illegal in the UK until 1920 and the Chinese population of Victorian London never exceeded but a few hundred; opium addiction was a very white middle-class affair, with prim Victorian "matrons" guzzling over-the-counter opiates, such as laudanum, like there was no tomorrow. Everyone, from Ol' Abe's wife, Mary Todd Lincoln, to Charles Dickens and Florence Nightingale, was hooked on the stuff. But the history of drugs and the military goes much deeper and darker than this.

The first major conflict in which drugs played a major role was the American Civil War, during which more than ten million opium pills and some three million ounces of opium were dished out to the Union troops alone; presumably this was not dissimilar to Confederate usage. One interesting thing about men on opium is that they tend to lose all fear and sense of vulnerability, so it seems that even those unwounded were granted open access to opiates to get them through the day; many an engagement was conducted with otherwise fit and healthy men charging into the fray as high as kites and, when the war was over, nearly 500,000 drug addicts returned home to find they could order their supplies for home delivery, care of Sears catalog. But when it came to war fueled by drugs no one can beat the Nazis, who virtually ran their *Blitzkrieg* on crystal methamphetamine.

Although ephedrine, the core constituent, had been isolated and documented in Japan in the late-19th century, it was the German pharmaceutical company of Temmler who came up with a stable tablet form in 1938 and, although the drug was intended for use in psychiatric care, its potential for use in war was immediately grasped by the Nazi military, who realized that in stronger doses it would keep the troops going for days on end without sleep. And we are not talking about the odd tablet or two when needed; between August and December 1939 a staggering ten million "speed" tablets were dished out to the troops invading Poland with no shortage of Panzerschokolade for the armored columns or Fliegerschokolade for the Luftwaffe. The story was that the pills and the chocolate were laced with multivitamins to keep everyone in the best of health, but the success and pace of the Blitzkrieg was all down to speed. As hostilities increased so too did the need for more drugs, and between April and July 1940 Hitler's finest popped a mind-boggling 35 million pills and scoffed their way through several hundred tons of "Schnellchokkie." Such excessive use of methamphetamine would not only have carried serious health implications but would also have had quite pronounced psychological effects in that "speed-freaks" have a noted lack of emotion and ability to empathize; this is in no way being put forward as even half an excuse for the brutal excesses of the Germans in Poland, or any other country through which they rampaged, it is simply a matter of fact.

While his troops thrived on their Soldier's Little Helpers, the man himself was becoming increasingly addicted to the same drug. His personal "quack," a term used quite deliberately, was a charlatan called Theo Morrell (1886–1948), some of whose "alternative treatments" bordered on the homicidal. Nicknamed Der Reichsspritzenmeister, the Reich's Injection-Master, by Göring, Morrell was injecting Hitler up to six times a day with a mixture of amphetamines and vitamins, which likely accounts for his Parkinson-like symptoms and his habit of calling midnight conferences that invariably boiled down to his shouting at everyone for hours in typical amphetamine-fueled paranoia. As the war progressed even Pervitin, the most popular "medication" was no longer enough to keep the jackboots stomping and Vice-Admiral Helmuth Heye (1895–1970) put out the call in March 1944 for something better/worse, depending on one's standpoint.

Responding to that call Gerhard Orzechowski, a pharmacist of Kiel, came forward with D-IX, a lethal cocktail of cocaine, Pervitin, and morphine in a mind-blowing 15mg pill. The trials for this horror were conducted on the inmates of Sachsenhausen concentration camp and the tribulations of those on "pill patrol" were recorded by Odd Nansen (1901–1973), son of the Polar explorer, who had been interned for helping Scandinavian Jews evade the Nazis. According to Nansen, the guinea pigs could march non-stop for about 60 kilometers with 20-kilo packs, but after that they were jabbering wrecks who didn't know what day of the week it was. Mercifully for all concerned, apart from limited trials on a few of Heye's unfortunate submariners, D-IX was never put into distribution. One of the more interesting things about Heye is that he was the man responsible for the awarding of the first Victoria Cross of World War II, and the first ever such award on the recommendation of the enemy. On April 8, 1940, in Norwegian waters off Trondheim, Heye was at the helm of the heavy cruiser *Admiral Hipper* (14,000 tons) when he was engaged by Captain Gerald Roope of HMS *Glowworm* (1,340 tons). Although the outcome was never in doubt, in a final attempt to inflict damage Roope, with his ship in tatters, rammed *Hipper* to inflict sufficient damage to force her to retire from action for repairs. As *Glowworm* went down the survivors were rescued but, as Roope was not among them, Heye sent a letter to the British Admiralty recommending he be awarded the Victoria Cross for his outstanding bravery and determination.

THE MUMMY'S CURSE

The criminal profiler, or "cracker," is today the elite of television detective-types, sitting in their offices making all sorts of tangential deductions from trifling facts, but as a science, if science it be, this development in criminology arose from the determination of the American secret services to get a psychological profile of Hitler. Some say that criminal profiling began with the British Dr Thomas Bond (1835–1901), who, an ex-officer in the Prussian Army, was asked to go over all the known facts of the Jack the Ripper murders in 1888, but most of his report dealt with the forensic nuts and bolts of the murders. He did venture the conjecture that the culprit might be a bit of a loner leading an otherwise respectable life (hardly an earth-shattering deduction) and even less intuitive and useful was Bond's opinion that the Ripper was a man subject to "periodical attacks of homicidal and erotic mania." Well, you don't say! Bond never again ventured into the murky waters of criminal psychoanalysis before flinging himself to his death from a high window because he was fed up with his insomnia. The first proper profiling of a human being was undertaken in 1943 by Walter Charles Langer (1899–1981) at the behest of William "Wild Bill" Donovan (1883–1959) of the OSS, who wanted to get inside the head of Adolf. This was to be remote profiling, as the subject, like the unidentified criminal today, was not available for questioning. This at first troubled the psychoanalyst, himself of German extraction, as did the alloted time frame of a few months, but he soon got into his stride after realizing that there was in fact a wealth of information to be gleaned from Hitler's writings and speeches. These, together with statements and accounts from those who had previously been close to Hitler but since sought refuge in other countries, helped Langer and his team get to the bottom of what made Hitler tick.

It might be going a bit far to say that Hitler invaded Poland only because his mother messed up his potty training, but the main outcome of the Langer profile focused on the Freudian make-up of the man, which stemmed from his mother's obsession with cleanliness and how this impacted on the mind and sexual development of the young Hitler. If Klara Hitler had had access to an ample supply of diapers, there might not have been any project for Langer to conduct. Repeatedly beaten by his drunken and sexually violent father, the young Adolf developed a pronounced Oedipus complex, which was only intensified by his mother's obsessional dominance of him when it came to toilet training, and the fact that she was his father's niece who constantly referred to her husband as "Uncle."

This incestuous pattern would be repeated by Hitler with his own niece, Geli Raubal (1908–1931), with distasteful overtones, and on May 13, 1943, Langer flew to Montreal to interview Otto Strasser (1897–1974), who had fled Germany after the Night of the Long Knives in 1934. A one-time close associate of Hitler and member of the "inner-circle," Strasser, also a friend and confidante of Geli, told Langer that Geli was disgusted at what she had to do for her uncle to "pacify" him. "She would have to undress with him lying on the floor. Then she would have to squat over his face where he could examine her at close range and this made him very excited. When the excitement reached its peak, he demanded that she urinate on him and that gave him great sexual pleasure. Geli said the whole performance was extremely disgusting to her and gave her no gratification." Although Stresser was certainly no friend of Hitler, who by then had put a price on his head, he was not in any way led to make such a statement, despite Langer having already arrived at the conclusion that Hitler was a masochistic psychopath with a pronounced anal fetish.

Langer's report was also sufficiently detailed to say that, while homosexually inclined, Hitler was not homosexual in the accepted sense and went on to state that: "His perversion has a quite different nature, which few have guessed at. It is an extreme form of masochism in which the individual derives sexual gratification from the act of having a woman urinate or defecate on him." Geli eventually "committed suicide", as did actress Renate Mueller (1906–1937) after she was similarly obliged to give Hitler a good kicking before using his mouth as a toilet. She ended up "falling out of a window" and, as Langer came to realize, most women who became the focus of Hitler's unpleasant attentions either committed suicide or had that choice made for them. Langer also interviewed women who had worked on the domestic staff at the Berghof, they confirming that at no time had they ever seen evidence of normal sexual activity in the Führer's bed – a good chambermaid can tell at a glance what has taken place in a bed the night before.

The entire report can be read at www.ess.uwe.ac.uk/documents/osstitle.htm and its depth and scope made it a blueprint for emerging criminal profilers of a non-military nature. The first of these was Dr James Brussel, a New York psychiatrist who was hired in desperation in 1956 by the police to see if he could apply Langer's principles to give them any lead as to the identity of the so-called "Mad Bomber" who had been plaguing the city. Using the same

Dr James Brussel, photographed May 16, 1955 with Dr Harold Berman. (Getty Images)

Freudian parameters that Langer applied to the Hitler project, Brussel quickly came up with a profile of a man who would be white, middle-aged, single, sexually inexperienced, and without any female attachment due to strong family ties that likely had him still living either at home with parents or with siblings. There were indications that he would, like Hitler, have reason to hate the father who had, as a child, driven him unnaturally close to the mother, who was likely a staunch Roman Catholic. The style of the capital letters in the goading notes sent to the press and the police indicated European education, most likely Eastern European and, on the practical side, he would be mechanically skilled and likely living in Connecticut, as that area had a high concentration of Slavs. The constant reference to the Edison power company almost certainly meant he was a disgruntled employee or ex-employee, and although blue collar he would have pretensions to white-collar status; he would be fastidiously neat and clean and wear suits whenever possible, probably double-breasted "business-style" ones.

Having nothing else to go on the police focused on the Slavic enclave of Connecticut and soon arrested George Metesky, who matched the profile to a T. When the police arrived one early morning to arrest Metesky he was still in his dressing gown and he asked if he might be allowed to dress, re-emerging from his bedroom in a smart double-breasted suit. But Brussel was no one-trick pony; between the Metesky case and 1972, the year in which Langer's work on Hitler was published as *The Mind of Adolf Hitler*, he worked on several cases, and when he produced the profile that led to the apprehension of the Boston Strangler everyone realized that for all its Freudian mumbo-jumbo the building of psychological profiles, along the principles devised by Langer and employed Brussel, now had a place in modern detection.

THE MAN-MADE WOMAN

Hitler had a pathological fear of syphilis, a disease he is widely yet falsely believed to have had himself, and perhaps it was this phobia that led to his instigating one of the weirdest research programs of World War II – the Borghild Project, which aimed to make available to troops an army of synthetic "comforters" to keep them out of the fleshpots of the various countries they jackbooted through. The first details of this tale emerged in 2005 with a statement allegedly from the last surviving member of the "production team," a sculptor called Arthur Rink, and since then further details have emerged and graced the pages of newspapers from Israel to America. Of late, there has been the odd cry of, "Hoax!" but, nevertheless, here is the story so far.

As with any conflict, many more men are withdrawn from the field by sickness and disease than by enemy fire and, in the case of the Führer's finest, they never missed an opportunity to head straight for the nearest brothels; apparently, the French prostitutes "laid low" more German troops than any single division of the Allied Forces. On November 20, 1940 Himmler wrote of his distress at these "unnecessary losses," stating: "The greatest danger in Paris is the widespread and uncontrolled presence of whores, picking up clients in bars, dance halls, and other places. It is our duty to prevent soldiers from risking their health just for the sake of a quick adventure." Hitler and Himmler decided it was time to put an end to all such "pollution" with the institution of the Borghild Project whereby plastic "gynoids" could be made available to troops most at risk of temptation. First to be recruited into the madcap scheme was Franz Tschakert, a sort of biological sculptor who was already famous for his *Woman of Glass* (1936). This was in fact made of clear plastic and had wowed the crowds in the Dresden Museum and Institute of Hygiene although some, it should be said, felt the revelation of all the internal organs in realistic color to be a trifle OTT. Initially, the day-to-day running of the project was overseen by SS Dr Joachim Mrugowsky (1905–1948), who would later be executed after the Nuremberg Medical Trials of 1947 for other, and decidedly unfunny, experiments he was involved with. Charged with producing the "master" for the mould, Tschakert toyed with various ideas, even asking the pouting actress Käthe von Nagy (1904–1973) if her entire form and facial features could serve the Führer in such capacity. Finding the idea of being squidged-in-effigy by unknown thousands to be less than appealing, the lady tactfully declined. It was at about this stage in the proceedings that Mrugowsky left the project to turn his attentions to darker matters, he being replaced by a Danish SS doctor called Olen Hannussen, who insisted that the doll resemble no living person but to have bland and generic features to allow the "user" to apply their own fantasy.

And so it was; Tschakert and Rink produced a mold of a woman of no distinguishing features in readiness for the prototypes to be formed using the highly tensile and elastic polymers already produced by IG Farben. There had been some last-minute debate as to whether the doll should have a Schneckenfrisur, snail-hair, that being the somewhat unattractive name for the equally unattractive style in which the central part of the hair is pulled back tight in a "Glasgow face-lift" while the side plaits are spiraled into those funny Tyrolean headphones; fortunately for the doll, a boyish bob won the day. Also on the team by now was psychiatrist Dr Rudlof Chargeheimer, who, seeking a remote and secluded test bed, sent the first Borghilds out to the barracks in St Helier on Jersey in the Occupied Channel Islands to see if the dolls would stand up to heavy action at the front, so to speak. Whatever the feedback, we shall never know, as, along with any trace of the Borghild Project, the Institute and Museum of Hygiene was completely destroyed in the Dresden bombings. So with the only details of the project residing in the alleged statements of Arthur Rink, best now to let him speak.

Born in 1909, trained under Reich's-Sculptor Arno Breker (1900–1991) and employed in the still-extant Käthe Kruse doll factory until 1940, Rink says that the task was daunting in that it demanded the synthetic flesh feel real while the body should be as mobile as the real thing; also, the "focal-point" should be as realistic as possible. The material was not easy to find. Tschakert, an expert on plastics, had tried several materials based on rubber or butyl-rubber; all came from IG Farben or Rheinische Gummi und Celluloid Fabrik. (The latter company, still operating under various trademarks, made scarily realistic dolls for children.) One material was called Ipolex, which was extremely resilient but developed yellow spots when cleaned with certain detergents. Borghild's presentation in Berlin was a great success; Himmler and Dr Chargeheimer were there. While they examined "her," Franz Tschakert was very nervous but Himmler was so enthusiastic that he ordered 50 Borghilds on the spot. It was considered to move the production to a special facility because Tschakert's studio was too small to cope with that level of production but, in the face of increasingly unpleasant news from the East, Himmler dropped his plans a week later and cut the budget. In the beginning of 1942, some weeks after Stalingrad, the whole project was canceled. All documents had to be returned to the SS-Hygiene Institute. "The bronze model for Type B was never completed. I have no idea as to the whereabouts of the doll but I presume that she, like all my plasters and studies, was sent to Berlin. If she was kept in Dresden it is most likely she was destroyed in the Allied bombing of that city."

While it is perhaps easy to dismiss the whole yarn as preposterous, it must be remembered that we are talking of the regime that sent a scientific expedition to Rugen Island to test out the "hollow earth" theory. The idea was to aim the radar up at the sky to see if it was possible to spy on the British fleet at Scapa Flow. This was also the regime that sent a massive expedition out to Tibet to find the "Vril" of immortality and the birthplace of the non-existent Aryan race, so the possibility of them knocking up a few sex dolls for their porn-troopers is far from inconceivable. And the story of German sex dolls does not finish with the war.

In the June of 1952 German cartoonist Reinhard Beuthien began his highly successful Bild Lilli cartoon in Berlin newspapers, she based on troops' favorite, Lilli Marlene, and having similar sexy adventures. The next year, fully featured 30cm-high Lilli dolls hit the market, sold only in bars and clubs as they were not for children! In 1956 Ruth and Elliot Handler were in Germany on holiday where Ruth, not realizing the market Lilli was aimed at, thought the dolls would make nice presents for the kids back home. Soon realizing their mistake, the Handlers ended up using the dolls as the foundation for a somewhat bowdlerized version and, naming their creation after their daughter, Barbie first saw light of day at the New York Toy Fair of 1959. Not wishing to be confronted by their inspiration in the open market, the Handlers' company, Mattel, quietly bought up all rights to Bild Lilli and, whisking her swiftly out of the lamplight, locked her away in a vault where she languishes to this day.

THE WAVES ARE ALIVE WITH
THE SOUND OF MUSAK

The bizarre collection of people involved in the invention and development of the modern torpedo are a cast to behold; everyone from Georg von Trapp (1880–1947), he of *Sound of Music* fame, the screen vamp Hedy Lamarr (1914–2000), the first woman to appear in the buff in mainstream movies, and her first husband, the morally confused Friedrich Mandl (1900–1977), an Austrian-Jewish armaments dealer who routinely entertained Hitler and Mussolini.

The story begins with the British engineer Robert Whitehead (1823–1905), whose work in Milan came to the notice of the Foundari Metali of Rijeka in Croatia (then known as Fiume and under Italian control), which is where he met fellow torpedo-buff Giovanni Luppis (1813–1875). Luppis – or Lupis, as it is sometimes spelled – had only developed torpedoes that could be launched from land and guided left and right by ropes, but it was enough to form the basis of a friendship that would lead to the German Wolf Packs of World War II and, with Lamarr's input, un-jammable guided torpedoes and the modern cellphone.

The collaboration of these two did not escape the attention of the Austro-Hungarian Emperor Franz Joseph, whose sponsorship and backing led to the rapid development of the first free-running and guided torpedoes that would make Rijeka a mecca for torpedo-buffs, and the town that forced all other nations to appreciate the value of the submarine as a serious marine weapon. By 1866, Whitehead had perfected a self-powered and guided model that ran at 7 knots and was accurate up to about 800 yards, with the running depth controlled by a hydrostatic plate governed by a spring and a pendulum. The Austrian Navy immediately placed orders while the British Navy, which had previously dismissed Whitehead as a loony, sat sulking until they too had to go to him, cap in hand.

With Luppis now pretty well marginalized, the Whitehead family fortunes went from strength to strength through the revenue from torpedo sales that were in turn boosted by some rather astute marriages. Daughter Alice married Count George Hoyos in 1869, he a member of the still-influential Hapsburgs, and in 1892 their daughter Marguerite married Herbert, Prince von Bismarck (1849–1904), son of the Iron Chancellor of Germany. With the two wives being essentially British, there must have been some interesting family chats; Hoyos was by then running the family business and selling vast numbers of torpedoes to those who would fire them at the Allies in World War I, while the British would later use Whitehead torpedoes in the 1941 sinking of the famous battleship named in honor of Bismarck Sr.

Moving forward to the troubled years before World War I, a young Italian officer in the Austrian Navy had been working his socks off to convince his superiors that the only sensible thing to do was to increase the submarine fleet and stock up on Whitehead's brain-children, which by then were far more sophisticated and running on gyroscope guidance. This young officer was none other than Georg von Trapp and, having won his case, he was sent to Rijeka in 1910 to attend the launch ceremony of three of the new submarines the Italian had fought so hard to make reality. Although ten years her senior, von Trapp fell head over heels for the young lady doing the champagne bit, this being

Whitehead's great-granddaughter, Agathe (1890–1922), and they were married on January 10, 1911. Within three years Agathe's husband would be hailed a national hero for the number of her countrymen he killed at sea with her forebear's invention. Austria's most audacious submariner, von Trapp sank more than 48,000 tons of enemy shipping including the French warship *Leon Gambetta* with a loss of 718 lives.

But wars pass and the von Trapps settled down to their domestic bliss, which was curtailed by Agathe dying of scarlet fever in 1922, this being the point at which Georg hired a tutor for his daughter Maria, who had also contracted the disease but survived. Hired only as a tutor to that one child and never as governess for the entire family of seven, Maria Kutschera (1905–1987) was hardly nun material; she could be foul-mouthed and equally foul-tempered, and was much given to throwing heavy objects at those who incurred her wrath; nor was she the musical muse who turned a dour von Trapp into a mawkish Tyrolean crooner. He and his kids were all very musical before Maria turned up to spot the family as a highly desirable alternative to the cloistered life to which she was so ill-suited. By her own admission she never loved von Trapp, before or after their marriage of November 26, 1927, when he was knocking on 50 and she just 22, but with their first child, Rosemarie, born on 8 February 1928, she would have made a funky nun.

With Austria annexed and the storm clouds gathering for World War II, von Trapp was indeed offered command of a submarine base by Berlin but felt the family's best option was to quit while still ahead of the game. Needless to say, they did not make a dramatic bid for freedom on foot, over the hills to Switzerland, as in the film. They had nothing to fear – von Trapp was an Italian citizen not an Austrian – so they bid their farewells and, making no secret of their travel plans, boarded a train for Italy from where they sailed to America in 1938, a full 11 years after their marriage, not just after the honeymoon as suggested by *The Sound of Music* (1965).

Anyway, although von Trapp no longer felt like cutting loose with a few torpedoes, their potential in war now greatly increased. The arms dealer Friedrich Mandl had, like the British Navy, secured a patent from the original Whitehead plant to manufacture under license. Hitler and Mussolini were visitors to his lavish home, which by 1933 was graced by his stunning young wife, Hedwig Eve Maria Kiesler (1914–2000). Although Jewish, she seems to have tolerated her husband's dealings, and in the first year of their marriage had caused a storm by appearing, under her professional name of Hedy Lamarr, in *Ecstasy*. This was a Czech film in which she scored two cinematic "firsts" by not only cavorting naked in the woods but also featuring in highly suggestive close-ups of her face in orgasm, such expressions of "rapture" induced, she always maintained, by nothing more romantic than the producer stabbing her in the backside with a pin. Knowing the capacity of his young wife's off-screen appetites, on both sides of the gender fence, Mandl kept her on a tight leash but was obviously not beyond exploiting her charms when it came to furthering his business.

As Lamarr would later confide to Marlon Brando, she was the only woman in the world to have endured intimacy with both Hitler and Mussolini to "cement" Mandl's considerable torpedo contracts and other munitions deals with Germany and Italy. Always dangerously candid about her dalliances with men and women, when Brando asked her at a party if

Hedy Lamarr, devoted wife and famous film star, photographed in 1940. (Topfoto)

it was really true she told him: "I was married to Fritz Mandl. In case you are the only unenlightened person in the world, he was the famous Austrian munitions magnate. If he ordered me to sleep with one of those dictators, I did the bidding of my husband. That way he could get fatter contracts. Hitler was all posturing; out of uniform he was not a man. Mussolini was the most pompous ass I have ever known. Imagine stopping every minute to ask – in Italian, of course – how he was doing. A man secure in his sexuality would never do that." When pressed for details about her encounter with Hitler she became unusually vague and evasive, which is understandable given the now-known details of his predilections; let's just say she must have drunk a great deal of water to make sure the little chap enjoyed himself.

But there was more to Hedy Lamarr than serene beauty and sexual prowess; in spite of her youth – 19 at the time of the marriage – she was an extremely sharp cookie and always paid great attention while her husband was discussing the pros and cons of torpedoes with his Axis customers. And she still had much of that information in her head when, tiring of being pimped by her husband, she drugged him and fled their mansion, disguised as a maid, to make her way to America where she had quite a few interesting chats about torpedoes with Georg von Trapp. (When the time came for *The Sound of Music* to be foisted on an unsuspecting world, Lamarr allowed her house in Austria to serve as stand-in for the real Villa von Trapp, which, although still standing, had been taken over by Himmler as his Austrian HQ and thus deemed a "tainted" location.)

By then, all the torpedoes turned out by Whitehead's were guided by a radio signal, which was good in that they were far more accurate, but also bad as any radio signal can be quickly detected and jammed. In 1941 Lamarr was lounging around her neighbor's house listening to him bemoaning the problems he was having synchronizing several pianolas for a fantasy scene in his *Ballet mécanique*. It was only when she turned her mind to this problem with said neighbor, avant-garde composer George Antheil (1900–1959), that everything slipped into place regarding her chats with von Trapp. What if, she mused, the torpedoes ran on 88 (the number of keys on a piano) ever-changing frequencies? No target ship would have a cat's chance in hell of locking onto any incoming torpedo and jamming its guidance signal. Experimenting with pianola rolls, she and Antheil came up with a system whereby the torpedo and the firing point both had identical rolls of perforated paper by which the guidance system could constantly frequency-hop in tandem, thereby denying anyone else the chance of locking on and jamming.

On August 11, 1942 their perfected system was granted US Patent 2,292,387 and Lamarr approached the US Navy to explain how even a plane could drop such a torpedo in the vicinity of the target and then sit back and steer it home. For the first time in her life, Lamarr's beauty worked against her; the navy thought she was far too pretty to be taken seriously, and after making facetious comments about piano-playing torpedoes suggested she should stick to selling war bonds and kisses and leave the big boys to sort their toys. Despite her explaining how the device could be made small enough to fit inside a wristwatch, and how torpedoes could be fired from a surface vessel that could then speed away to safety and leave the guidance to a high-altitude plane, she was patted on the head and sent packing. Which is a pity as she was years ahead of her time; after the war someone in the American War Department remembered her idea and, swapping ticker-tape-style roll for electronic circuitry, put her ideas to use in the 1962 blockade of Cuba and, with Lamarr's patent by then expired, the American military simply stole her idea and repatented it as spread-spectrum communications.

Lamarr's concept remained the province of the American military but when it was declassified in 1982 civil communications companies leaped on the bandwagon to produce that bane of modern life, the cellphone. Lamarr, who died in modest circumstances in Florida in 2000, never saw a penny nor so much as a "thank you" from anyone.

BIBLIOGRAPHY

Aarons, Mark and Loftus, John, *Unholy Trinity: The Vatican, The Nazis, and the Swiss Banks* (St Martin's Griffin, 1998)

Breuer, William B., *The Spy Who Spent the War in Bed and other Bizarre Tales from World War II* (John Wiley and Sons, Inc., 2003)

Breuer, William B., *Unexplained Mysteries of World War II* (John Wiley and Sons, Inc., 1997)

Donovan, James, *A Terrible Glory: Custer and the Little Bighorn* (Back Bay Books, 2009)

Fonseca, Sonny, *Custer: The Truth Behind the Legend* (Publish America, 2006)

Goni, Uki, *The Real Odessa* (Granta, 2003)

Hibbert, Christopher, *The Rise and Fall of Il Duce* (Palgrave Macmillan, 2008)

Hunt, Linda, *Secret Agenda: The US Government, Nazi Scientists and Project Paperclip, 1945–1990* (St Martin's Press, 1991)

Langer, Walter C., *The Mind of Adolf Hitler: The Secret Wartime Report* (Basic Books, 1972)

Lee, Carol Ann, *The Hidden Life of Otto Frank* (Harper Perennial, 2003)

Lehmann, *Joseph, Sex, War and Fancies*
(Regency Press, 1984)

Llewellyn, Sam, *Small Parts in History*
(Barnes & Noble, 1986)

Marks, John D., *The Search for the "Manchurian Candidate":
The CIA and Mind Control: The Secret History of the
Behavioral Sciences* (W.W. Norton & Co., 1991)

Newark, Tim, *Mafia Allies: The True Story of America's
Secret Alliance with The Mob in World War II*
(Zenith Press, 2007)

Sedova Trotsky, Natalia, *The Life and Death of Trotsky*
(Basic Books, 1975)

Srodes, James, *Allen Dulles: Master of Spies*
(Regnery Publishing, 2000)